SAN ANTONIO
ON FOOT

SAN ANTONIO ON FOOT

Second edition

Diane Capito and Mark Willis

Texas Tech University Press

This book was set in Palatino and Casual Script and printed on recycled acid-free paper that meets the guidelines for permanence and durability of the committee on Production Guidelines for Book Longevity of the Council on Library Resources. (∞)

Photographs by Diane Capito

Cover design by Rob Neatherlin

Printed in the United States of America

Library of Congress Cataloging-in-Publication Data
Capito, Diane.
    San Antonio on foot/ Diane Capito and Mark Willis.—Rev.
    p. cm.
    ISBN 0–89672–382–8 (alk. paper)
    1. San Antonio (Tex.)—Tours. 2. Walking—Texas—San
Antonio—Guidebooks. I. Willis, Mark. II. Title.
F394.S23C36   1998
917.64'3510463—dc21   98-22289
                                                        CIP

98 99 00 01 02 03 04 05 06 / 9 8 7 6 5 4 3 2 1

Texas Tech University Press
Box 41037
Lubbock, Texas 79409-1037 USA
1-800-832-4042
ttup@ttu.edu

ACKNOWLEDGMENTS

Thank you to all the marvelous people who, for both the first and the second editions, kindly took the time to answer seemingly endless questions and who checked the manuscript for accuracy.

For the first edition we give special thanks to travel writer and photographer Celia Wakefield for her photographs and to Mark's father, Roy Willis, for his maps. Also for the first edition special thanks go to: Benjamin Fairbank for his editorial suggestions; David Toth and the Randolph Roadrunners Volksmarch group for checking each walk; Boy Scout Troop 285 for the markers on the McAllister Park cross-country trail; Don Inman, Park Planning; the San Antonio Chapter of the American Institute of Architects for permission to use descriptions from their 1986 edition of *Guide to San Antonio Architecture*; and to Juan Hernandez, Eric Lautzenheiser, Elton Moy, Rudy Tiehes, and Ellen Maverick Dickson for interviews and special input.

Librarians are invaluable when preparing a book that involves history. Especially helpful on the first edition were Special Collection librarians Basil Aivialiotis, Incarnate Word College; Jacqueline Davis and John Manguso, Fort Sam Houston Museum; Dora Guerra, The University of Texas at San Antonio; Nelle Lee Weinek, San Antonio Conservation Society; and the librarians at the San Antonio Public Library, the Daughters of the Republic of Texas Library at the Alamo, and the Institute of Texan Cultures. For the second edition, with the addition of more neighborhood walks, it was the patient, helpful volunteers at the Conservation Society library who got bothered the most, although the Alamo Library and the Central Public Library contributed their share too.

The addition of new walks meant new maps. These were compiled by Diane with the help of Rob Neatherlin of Texas Tech University Press who also did the cover design. Thanks to Paul Barwick, Parks and Recreation Department, for providing maps and updated information on the parks.

Thank you also to those persons who helped walk through the revisions: San Antonians Zan Brown, Joe and Jill Pyle, Xonia Kargl, Hannah Margolis, and Dara Holwitt; out-of-towners Charlotte Golden, Kris de Quieros, and Diane's sister, Retha, all of whom were told, "Yes, you can come visit—if you're willing to walk."

Special thanks to Theresa Gold for her input on the cemetery walks. She not only pointed out some errors in the first edition, but graciously walked the cemeteries and provided new material. For additional input thanks go also to Mary Kargl and Charlotte Kahl.

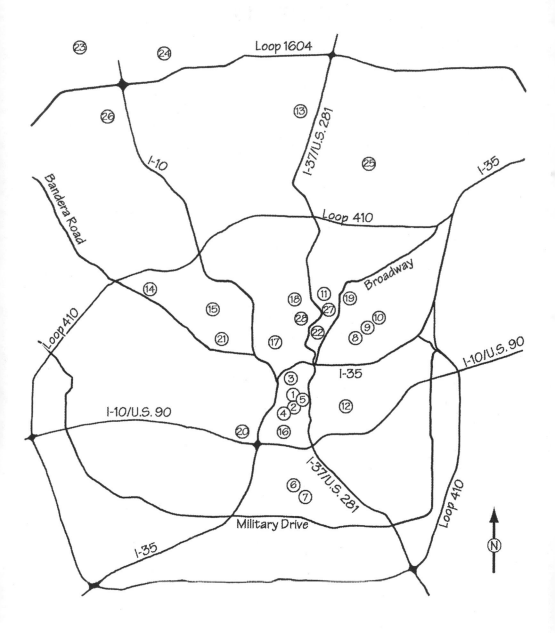

CONTENTS

COLLEGE CAMPUSES

OTHER OPTIONS

APPENDICES

INTRODUCTION

Tourists . . . [who] go sightseeing in automobiles . . . lose the warm, friendly touch that comes only with a leisurely tour on foot . . . .

Albert Curtis, *Fabulous San Antonio*

In the introduction to the first edition of *San Antonio On Foot* I related the time Mark and I stood on the windy observation deck of the Tower of the Americas, 750 feet above the twinkling lights of nighttime San Antonio. "Look around," Mark told me. "See how the streets zigzag as they radiate out from the center of town? That's because they were built along the old stagecoach and cattle trails that often followed the *acequias*, the Spanish irrigation ditches."

Wherever we went in San Antonio, Mark always had something interesting to point out or a bit of history to impart making the city come alive for me. Mark is a native San Antonian, a historian by hobby, and at that time, a tour guide by profession. We met soon after I moved to San Antonio. He stopped to chat at my outdoor craft booth in Market Square while his tour group roamed the market. We became friends and got together occasionally to explore restaurants and chat. When I had out-of-town guests I'd send them on Mark's tours. They always had a good time.

When I started walking to lose weight, Mark joined me. One night a week soon became two or three. We looked for new places we felt would be safe at night and discovered Fort Sam Houston, college campuses, and residential neighborhoods. As we walked, Mark related interesting facts or stories about what we saw. To his surprise he discovered new things too, details he had missed driving past in his tour van.

From these excursions grew the idea for *San Antonio On Foot*. We wanted it to be for both San Antonians and tourists, whether walking for pleasure or exercise. This book is not a history book, although it is impossible to walk in San Antonio without bumping into history. We have included most of San Antonio's historic sites and all the designated historic neighborhoods. Nor is this a guidebook per se, although it includes all the tourist attractions that can reasonably be reached on foot. The purpose we saw for our book was to get people out walking, to add some interest to their walks, to give the tourist a closer look at San Antonio, and to entice local people to explore their city.

Walking really is marvelous: it is good for your health; it is an enjoyable way to lose weight; it is an excellent tranquilizer; it is inexpensive; it can be done almost anywhere, at almost any time; it can be a means to get off by yourself, or it can be a social event.

Because of the tremendous amount of response to the book, the many suggestions received, and the number of changes in the city, the time has come to put out a revised edition. A comment I heard frequently from people who said they enjoyed our book was, "But the walks are too long." In this revised edition I have tried to modify the walk routes so they can be taken in one trip or divided into two or three. In a few cases, notably the mission walks, this is not possible. For these I pass on a suggestion from some friends: go in two cars, leaving one at the farthest point you plan to walk.

It is amazing how many changes have occurred in the five years since we first did these walks. Some are adventageous, such as improved access to St. Paul's Square from HemisFair Park via the Alamodome. Whether the loss of Hemis-Fair Arena for expansion of the Convention Center is good or bad is debatable (and was it ever debated!). The mural that adorned it is definitely a loss though. The oldest Woolworth's west of the Mississippi, located on Alamo Plaza, is closed. A pleasant surprise, however, is that the Cross-Country Trail at McAllister Park has not suffered any more cuts as we thought it would. It is now the featured walk for that park as originally intended.

New material has been added: Barney Smith's "gallery" on the Alamo Heights walk, new grave sites and historical information at the Eastside cemeteries, even new views—and fewer steep hills—on the Inspiration Hills walk.

New walks have been added: The Jefferson/Monticello neighborhood with its eclectic architecture, Terrell Hills with its impressive mansions, and Baja King William, the lesser-known side of the historic King William District. King William has also been separated from the downtown walk and listed with neighborhood walks. A soon-to-be new city park, the Leon Creek Greenway, is included, although all details are not yet available.

I hope that both you who are exploring *San Antonio On Foot* for the first time, and you who have already walked your way through the first edition, find these walks enjoyable and interesting.

In *San Antonio On Foot* Mark and I try to answer all the questions likely to come up about the walks: where to park, how to get there by public transit, the length of the walk and how long it takes, whether we felt comfortable walking there at night, and whether the walk is wheelchair accessible. We give the location of restrooms, drinking fountains, and phones, and mention nearby restaurants. The restaurants mentioned are inexpensive to moderate in price.

The walks are divided into sections: The first section, *Downtown*, covers the major tourist attractions and the river. The second section, *Missions*, takes you along the mission hike/bike trail with tours through three missions. The third section, *Fort Sam Houston*, covers the historic as well as the working side of this old post. The fourth section, *Neighborhoods*, incudes some of the more scenic and historic residential sections of San Antonio. The fifth section, *Parks*, covers the many attractions in Brackenridge Park, as well as San Antonio's wilderness parks. The sixth section, *College Campuses*, completes the tours. The seventh section, *Other Options*, includes an overview of mall walks and some fitness trails.

The appendices offer useful, cross-referenced lists: an alphabetical list of tourist attractions referenced by walk number, night walks, a chart of useful data on walk conditions, and a list of local organizations that have scheduled walks.

Mark and I invite you now to come along with us and see *San Antonio On Foot*.

WHY WALK?

Besides wanting to keep generally fit, we walk to relax and to lose weight. Diane lost twenty pounds, without dieting, while working on the book. (Mark lost too but didn't keep track.) Walking is easy to squeeze into almost any routine. It doesn't matter how long you walk either; any energy you expend burns calories.

In his book *Walking!*, John T. Davis (Andrews and McMeel, 1979) included a helpful chart that showed the number of days it takes to walk off a pound, with and without cutting your caloric intake. For instance, if you walk thirty minutes a day without any cut in calories it takes twenty-three days to loose one pound. If you cut just 200 calories from your diet (easy to do by eating smaller portions), you lose that pound in ten days. If you cut back 400 calories a day, you lose the pound in six days. By walking sixty minutes a day you lose a pound in twelve days without cutting calories, in seven days with a 200-calorie cut, and in five days by cutting 400 calories. See how easy it is!

One pound every ten days is three pounds a month or thirty-six pounds a year. That may not sound like much, but you didn't put it all on at once and doctors say it is healthier to take weight off gradually. Most importantly, studies show that people who lose in this way are most apt to keep the weight off!

Remember, it is not important exactly how many calories you burn. Just keep walking, and you'll keep losing. If you want to take the weight off more quickly, walk longer, eat less, or do both.

HOW TO USE THE BOOK

To provide useful information at a glance, we have set up a format that we have followed with each walk. This format is explained below.

Walk Number and Title

Features:

Distance:

Time:

Nights:

Wheelchair Accessible:

Restrooms, Water, Phone:

Restaurants:

Getting There: Car: Bus:

Comments:

Overview:

Features lists the major attractions en route.

Distance is given in miles and kilometers. Side trips are listed separately.

Time is based on walking at a moderate speed of 3 MPH. It includes reasonable time to read the text and to look around, but does not include extra browsing time. For example, Mission Trail North, Walk 6, takes you through Mission San José. Time is allowed to walk through and read our comments, but if you linger at the exhibits or watch the slide show, that time is not included.

Nights conveys whether we felt comfortable walking there at night. When we say "No" for night, it means just that. Don't do it. Sometimes we felt we'd be more comfortable walking at night in a small group (four or more people) rather than just walking by ourselves; where this is the case, we note it under Comments.

Wheelchair Accessible tells if it is possible to negotiate the walk in a wheelchair. There usually is an explanation under Comments.

Restrooms, Water, and Phone are listed for your convenience. Whenever possible we start the walk where these are available. Numbers refer to those on the map.

Restaurants are listed if there are any along the way or near the start of the walk that we especially like. We rate them cheap or reasonable ($6 or under), moderate ($7–$10), and expensive (over $10).

Getting There gives the nearest intersection and some suggested parking places near the beginning of the walk or the bus name and number that will take you there. (Bus directions are from downtown.)

Comments lists any additional information we think would be helpful such as hours of museums or other attractions and if there is an admissions fee.

Overview gives a general description or notes items of interest about the area being walked.

Most of these walks can be taken at any pace. Where this is not the case, city streets with lots of traffic lights, for instance—we make a note of the unusual circumstances.

Map—The directional information pertaining to the walks, is numbered and printed within the text in boldface type. In the text ☞ followed by a number refers to a number on the map. Each walk is accompanied by a map except for those in the optional section.

Much time passes from when one starts a book until it reaches the bookshelf and many changes take place during that time. Keeping the manuscript up-to-date on a book of this type is a problem. In the first edition, from the time we started the book until we sent in the manuscript, and again, between that time and when we got the manuscript back for final corrections, a street disappeared, buildings came down, and businesses closed or changed names. The changes between the first and second editions are too numerous to mention.

So, should you find you can't follow the map or the directions exactly—don't panic. Part of the fun of exploring on foot is getting off the beaten path. Most likely you will not be detoured more than a block or two and then you can pick up the tour from where ever the map and your path had to deviate. There's no telling what interesting thing you might discover along the way.

SAFETY TIPS

Just a few reminders:

1. When walking in the street, walk on the left side facing traffic.
2. Heed low water crossings. Don't try to cross swiftly flowing water.
3. When walking at night, wear light-colored or reflective clothing.
4. When we say do not walk in an area at night, it is because it really is not safe. *Don't do it.*
5. When we say it is okay to walk in a small group (four or more persons), it is because we felt a little uncomfortable walking there as a twosome.

Some reviewers, friends, and relatives expressed doubts about walking on the Eastside and the Westside. "Is it safe?" they asked.

In the first edition we stated that we felt comfortable walking in these two neighborhoods. We still do on the Eastside, although not alone. It feels better with a walking partner. If you are still hesitant, go with several people. This precaution is simply to make you less vulnerable.

As for the Westside, we do not recommend walking that neighborhood at this time. Conditions deteriorated there after the book first came out, and, although they have begun to improve again, and hopefully will continue to do so, we just don't feel comfortable enough about walking there to recommend it. We are leaving it in the book because it offers so much that is interesting and because it is possible to drive to each of the major attractions: drive to the Stockyards and Produce Terminal to stop and take the tours, then drive through Cassiano homes to view the murals. Hopefully, before our next update it will once again be possible to walk in this very interesting neighborhood.

Remember, just follow a few common sense rules—rules that apply to walking in any big city. Most people are friendly and not out to get you. In our experience, if you make eye contact with a person, smile and say hello, they'll usually nod or smile and say hello too.

When walking in the neighborhoods and on the college campuses, please be considerate of both the privacy and property of the residents and display common courtesy in the public buildings featured on the walks.

1 Downtown I

Features: The Alamo, San Fernando Cathedral, Spanish Governor's Palace, Market Square, Southwest Craft Center, and side trips to Chapel of Miracles and a painted church.

Distance: 3.3 miles + Side Trip A, 2.0 miles (5.3k + 3.2k)
Side Trip B, 1.4 miles (2.2k)

Time: 2 hrs. 10 min. + Side Trip A, 40 min.
Side Trip B, 45 min.

Night: Alamo to Market Square only. See Comments.

Wheelchair Accessible: Yes

Restrooms, Water, Phones: At start

Restaurant: Many along route.

Getting There: Start in front of the Alamo.

Comments:

As with all our walks, the distance and time listed do not include browsing unless it is a specific part of the walk. In the case of this walk, which has so many tourist attractions, allow at least an hour extra, more if you plan to go through the shops at Market Square.

At night the route from the Alamo is the only feature of this walk worth taking. Everything else is closed. Commerce Street is busy with cars and people and is well patrolled, but still 9:00 P.M. is about as late as we feel comfortable walking there. If you wish to return to the Alamo from Market Square at night, the trolley runs until 10:30 P.M. in the summer and 8:00 P.M. in the winter.

The Alamo is open Monday-Saturday from 9:00 A.M. to 5:30 P.M. and on Sunday from 10:00 A.M. to 5:30 P.M. The Spanish Governor's Palace is open Monday-Saturday from 9:00 A.M. to 5:00 P.M. and on Sunday from 10:00 A.M. to 5:00 P.M. (admission charge). Market Square is open Monday-Sunday at 10:00 A.M. and closes at 6:00 P.M. in the winter and 8:00 P.M. in the summer. The restaurants are open late. The Navarro Historic Site is open Wednesday-Sunday, 10:00 A.M. to 4:00 P.M. (admission charge).

This is a slow-paced tourist walk. Except on the side trips, there is nowhere to pick up any walking speed.

Overview:

San Antonio has been referred to as one of the most romantic cities in the United States. Possibly more songs have been written about it than about any other American city. There have also been many battles fought in and around it.

There is evidence that Native Americans camped along the river that still runs through the city. The Spaniards came in 1718, accompanied by the padres who founded missions. A settlement grew around one of these, Mission San Antonio de Valero. Later, this mission (the Alamo) was used as a fort and figured importantly in the fight for Texas's independence from Mexico. The Republic of Texas, established in 1836, accepted statehood in the U.S. in 1845, then seceded to join the Confederacy in 1861.

By the time of the Civil War, European immigrants outnumbered those in the Mexican-American community, and a few Anglo-Americans controlled the political power. With the advent of the railroad in 1877, San Antonio soon compared to New York and San Francisco in offering the latest in fashion and culture. It was the crossroads of the Southwest. A wave of Mexican immigration into Texas came during the 1910 revolution in Mexico. The Mexican-American population is now over fifty percent. Once again Mexican-American names are prominent in the political arena. This is a fiesta city, an all-America city. Houston and Dallas have now taken over as the "big" cities in Texas, but San Antonio is still the jewel of the state.

It's almost impossible to walk downtown without spotting something that looks interesting enough to entice you off your planned route. That can lead to something else, and soon you've wandered many blocks away. Although all the major downtown tourist attractions are included in our walks, we also take you off the beaten path to places you might not have gone otherwise.

Walking through downtown San Antonio is like walking through a history book. We include bits and pieces of that history, and we tell some stories we've heard and read.

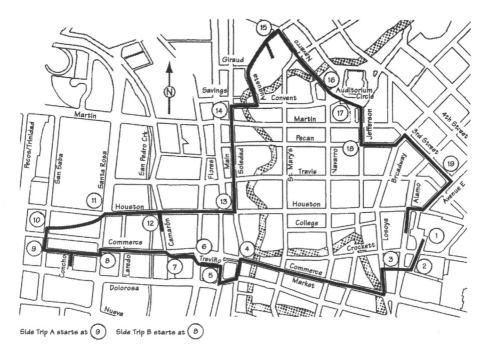

Side Trip A starts at (9)   Side Trip B starts at (8)

What everyone recognizes as "The Alamo" is the chapel of the original Mission San Antonio de Valero. Secularized in 1793, it lay abandoned until 1810, when Spanish soldiers from Alamo de Parras in Northern Mexico camped here, giving it its present name. Inside the grounds you can visit the Long Barracks where displays and a film describe what took place here.

To get some idea of the size of the original complex, stand with your back to the Alamo. The west wall ran along where the shops are across the street. (A portion of this wall can be seen under a glass window to the left of the Visitor Information Center.) The north wall reached to the doors of the post office on your right, and the wall around the grassy area across the street to your left marks the approximate southern boundary. A bronze model of the original complex is in the corner of this area along Alamo Street.

In the late 1800s, Hugo Schmeltzer used the walls of the Long Barracks, then a two-story building, to build a store in the image of a wooden castle. His store was so well stocked he could boast, "If you can't find it here, you can't find it anywhere!"

Still standing with your back to the Alamo, you will see across the street directly in front of you the Crockett Block, 317-23 North Alamo Street, designed by Alfred Giles in 1882.

On April 20, 1891, President Benjamin Harrison was scheduled to visit San Antonio. Because April 21 was the anniversary of the Battle of San Jacinto, when Texas won its independence from Mexico, the town ladies decided a parade was in order. They patterned it after the Battle of the Flowers Festival one of them had seen in Mexico. President Harrison spoke, but, owing to rain, the parade was held a few days later when, according to one newspaper report, a crowd of 10,000 onlookers watched as "marshals, cavaliers, damsels on horseback, bicyclists, mounted police, and the ladies themselves in flower-decorated carriages," came down Avenue E (then Nacogdoches Street), to Alamo Plaza, where the ladies proceeded circling and pelting each other with their flowers. When the carnage ceased, they headed home. Thus was Fiesta San Antonio born. The Battle of Flowers Parade is still held each year during Fiesta although it is less lethal now being simply a competition for the best-decorated floats.

1. Starting in front of the Alamo, turn left toward the bandstand.

The original bandstand, which dated from 1888, was moved to San Pedro Park in 1920 and replaced with a plain, concrete bandstand complete with restrooms. During a renovation of Alamo Plaza for the 1976 Bicentennial, this almost exact duplicate of the original was erected.

On the left is the Menger Hotel, the oldest hotel west of the Mississippi. When it opened in 1859, it offered baths and ice water, both luxuries at that time. Teddy Roosevelt recruited his Rough Riders in the bar. The magnificent suite retained by Richard King (of the world famous King Ranch) is a favorite of honeymooners. O. Henry, a frequent visitor to San Antonio, referred to the Menger in some of his stories. The Menger Brewery operated behind the hotel. A network of tunnels under the hotel was used to roll barrels from the brewery to the hotel and to connect the wine cellars and the underground storage vaults to the kitchen. Step inside the old portion of the hotel (iron grill work) to see the Victorian lobby with its stained-glass canopy. A self-guided tour of the hotel is available at the desk.

Next to the Menger is an entrance to RiverCenter, a three-story enclosed shopping, dining, and entertainment complex on the river. The Dillard's there now was, until 1987, Joske's Department Store, a long-time San Antonio landmark. Many San Antonians and visitors to the city will remember seeing a neon cowboy twirling a lasso on the roof of the building facing Alamo Plaza.

2. Turn right, cross Alamo Street by Dillard's. Go through the passage by the Crosswalk Deli to Losoya.

In the passage, a mural by Roland Rodriquez traces the San Antonio River from its headwaters in Brackenridge Park through downtown. The blue ring marks the headwaters, the yellow rings each mile (see Walk 3, River Walk North, for details).

3. Turn left on Losoya, right on Commerce.

On the left side of Losoya is a block of buildings dating from the late 1800s that have been nicely restored.

From the Commerce Street Bridge you can view part of the Big Bend area of the River Walk with its restaurants and shops. Across Commerce Street, on the bridge, is the bas-relief statue *First Inhabitant* by Waldine Tauch, originally a fountain.

As you cross Presa, No. 314 on the left is the old Alamo National Bank Building, literally picked up and moved back twenty feet to widen Commerce Street in the early 1900s. The top three stories were added later.

On the right (No. 315), the 1891 Romanesque Revival Stevens Building, designed by Gordon and Laub, and the 1894 Staacke Brothers Building, designed by James Riely Gordon in the Renaissance Revival style, were painstakingly restored in 1983. An exhibit of photographs inside the entrance shows their deteriorated condition prior to restoration, but unfortunately the entrance is now secured. The Staacke brothers operated a carriage business here and are credited with bringing the first automobile to San Antonio in 1905.

After crossing Navarro, No. 239 on the right was the First National Bank, founded by George W. Brackenridge. It is said he had a ticker tape line connected from his office here to Fernridge, his house on the grounds of what is now University of the Incarnate Word, so that he could conduct business at home.

At St. Mary's Street, cross Commerce to No. 154 and go inside to see the stained-glass window above the door.

Just past the bank you cross the flood control bypass channel to the San Antonio River.

4. At Soledad (Main Plaza), turn left. Walk around the Plaza.

The original name was Plaza de las Islas Canarias for the Canary Islanders who settled here in 1731. In 1749, the Spaniards and Apaches consummated a peace treaty in the Plaza by burying not only their instruments of war but also a live horse. Like most treaties, it didn't last.

On the northeast corner of Commerce and Soledad stood the home of Samuel Maverick, a pioneer Texas businessman and one of the signers of the Texas Declaration of Independence. The term "maverick" dates from a time in the mid-1800s when the businessman acquired some cattle that he turned loose on a piece of land he owned. The calves were never branded so they were always being rustled. His neighbors began referring to unbranded cattle as "Maverick's." The term caught on and eventually came to be used all over the west for unbranded cattle.

On the north side of Commerce also stood the Jack Harris Vaudeville and Gambling Hall. In 1882, Harris was killed during a fight over a poker game between his partner, Joe Foster, and Austin Marshal Ben Thompson. Acquitted, Thompson left town but made the mistake of returning later, which resulted in a big shoot-out. When the air had cleared, both Thompson and Foster were among those killed. You can see Harris's grave on the Eastside cemetery tour (Walk 12).

On the northeast corner of Market and Main Plaza, the Catholic bookstore stands on the site of the Council House, where the business of government was conducted during the Spanish, Mexican, and Republic of Texas eras. There is a historical marker around the corner.

The Bexar County Courthouse, constructed of red sandstone and granite and designed by James Riely Gordon, dates from 1891. Although the architecture is strikingly different, the new Justice Center across Main Street picks up on the color and arches of the old courthouse.

Continuing around the Plaza, the Gothic-Revival facade of San Fernando Cathedral was built in 1868 around the original parish church, begun in 1738 and not completed until 1750. French settler and architect François Giraud drew the plans for the present edifice. (He also designed the Ursuline Academy, now the Southwest Craft Center). The dome of the parish church is considered the geographic center of San Antonio. San Fernando is the oldest cathedral sanctuary in the United States and served the Presidio and the Villa Rica de San Fernando de Béjar settlement. A plaque in the church claims that the white marble coffin under the left bell tower holds the remains of Davy Crockett, Jim Bowie, and William Travis, but some historians dispute this. Walk up the center aisle to see the gravestone mounted in the floor. If there are no services in progress, walk behind the altar to read the burial plaques on the wall that supports the dome. This wall is the only part of the original parish church that still exists.

5. **Exit San Fernando Cathedral, turn left then left again on Treviño (along-side the cathedral).**

The part of the cathedral that has been stuccoed is the restored original church.

On the right, the San Antonio City Council Chamber is in the old Frost National Bank Building designed by J. P. Hayes in 1922. Note the round bas-relief sculpture panels set between the double-height arched window openings. They are copies of U.S. coinage.

6. **Coming out on Flores (City Hall), cross to Military Plaza.**

City Hall now dominates this plaza where once the Spaniards built their presidio. By the 1850s, the Plaza had become a marketplace. The chili queens reigned here in the evening after the market closed. The men and boys set up tables while the women and girls prepared chili and tamales. Until the early morning hours young señoritas served the people who gathered in the plaza for music, dancing, and cockfights.

City Hall, built in 1889, was a more imposing structure before the clock tower and turrets were removed to add a fourth story. It sits on the site of the old city jail and courthouse known as the Bat Cave, so called because bats roosted there, and often flew around the courtroom.

Continuing along Commerce, on the corner of the plaza, a statue of Moses Austin commemorates his negotiations with the Spanish governor in 1820 to allow Anglo-American colonists. However, the statue is in the wrong location as this event actually took place at the Council House on Main Plaza.

Cross to the Spanish Governor's Palace, home of the commandant of the presidio until the governor arrived in the 1760s. Although not our idea of a "palace," it is typical of the finer homes of the period.

The block of buildings to the left of the Governor's Palace dates from the 1880s. One of them housed the Fashion Theater, which at the time was the most elegant theater west of the Mississippi.

(Panchito's, in the basement of this group of buildings, is a good Mexican restaurant.)

7. **Exit the Palace, turn left, then left again on Commerce.**

San Pedro Creek (the ugly concrete ditch) has its headwaters in a once-abundant spring in San Pedro Park, the first location of Mission San Antonio. There are proposals to restore and beautify the creek.

Just past the creek, the San Antonio Metropolitan Health District office occupies the old Continental Hotel building.

Ox carts once traveled to and from the interior of Mexico along Laredo Street, known then as the Camino Real de Arriba del Río Grande (Upper Royal Road of the Río Grande).

Market Square (Photo by Celia Wakefield)

8. **Cross Santa Rosa, and jog left to the entrance of Market Square.**

   To take Side Trip B to painted church and tortilla factory (1.3 miles, 2.1k) go to Step 25.

The main market area of San Antonio moved to this location at the turn of the century when it was decided to build the new city hall at Military Plaza.

Walking down Produce Row, on the right is Centro de Artes, originally a meat and fish market. It is now used for meetings, receptions, and exhibits. Botica Guadalupana on the left is the oldest drug store in San Antonio. Until late 1989, it had a doctor's office attached, a custom from earlier days. After 93 years, in which three generations of the same family of doctors served generations of the same families of patients, the current doctor moved to a modern medical building across the street. The Botica no longer fills prescriptions, but it still has a stock of herbal medicines.

(La Margarita is a good place to people watch while eating fajita tacos.)

Down the side street to the left (Concho) are Galeria Ortiz (formerly the DaganBela Gallery) and other interesting shops. The last of the shops dating from the early market days, Casa Ramirez, moved out of this row in 1995.

Back on Produce Row, the large building on the right is El Mercado, a collection of import shops. This was the wholesale produce market until the new Produce Terminal Market (see Walk 15) was built on Zarzamora in the 1950s. This building replaced the magnificent Victorian market designed by Alfred Giles.

Don't miss the Mexican baked goods at Mi Tierra Cafe and Bakery.

Across San Saba at the end of Produce Row, Farmers Market Plaza (another collection of shops and a food court), is located on the site of the old Hay Market.

9. Turn right on San Saba. Cross Commerce Street to Milam Park.

You have three options at this point:

    a. **If you've had enough walking for today, take the trolley back to Alamo Plaza.**

    b. **Or take side trip A at Step 20 (2.0 miles, 3.2k), to Chapel of Miracles and an old train depot (daytime only).**

    c. **Or continue the walk at Step 10.**

10. Turn right through Milam Park.

A statue and grave marker of Ben Milam stands at the near end. The park was renovated in 1995 to make it more people friendly. At that time San Antonio's sister city, Guadalajara, Mexico, donated the bandstand, and a group of volunteers constructed the children's playground. Unfortunately, a monument was removed which commemorated Campo Santo, a cemetery of San Fernando Cathedral, that existed here from 1808-1860.

Across the street on the left is Santa Rosa Hospital and Children's Hospital, begun in 1889, through the efforts of three nuns from France. Open to all ethnic groups, the complex had a charity ward, a paying patient ward, and a ladies' ward.

11. Exit the park at Santa Rosa and Houston.

The block of Houston past Laredo Street is reminiscent of earlier days. Mexican music blares from the House of Tapes. The Librería Española offers Spanish-language newspapers, magazines, and books and, until it closed, the Alameda Theater featured Mexican movies.

An interesting curiosity here is the tile mural and fountain by the House of Tapes. The picture shows a man drinking from the springs. We weren't able to find out whether the springs went dry or the fountain was turned off. Customers of the music store tell of drinking from the fountain "not too many years ago."

The Alameda is an art deco gem which opened in 1946. It was the last grand movie palace in operation in the United States when it closed in the summer of 1990. It has recently been purchased by the City of San Antonio and is in the process of being restored. The interior and penthouse of the adjoining building retain some of the original art deco decor.

12. Turn right on Camarón. Continue to the middle of the block, then return to Houston, and turn right.

On the left side of Camarón, an old county jail built in 1878 now houses the climate-controlled Bexar County Archives. On the right, the Palace Livery Stable has been restored as law offices.

On the corner at Houston, the El Tenampa Bar is believed to have been the location of an early Budweiser distribution center.

The southwest corner at Flores (the parking lot), was the location of Albert Friedrich's Buckhorn Saloon, where ranchers gathered to hear the latest prices on longhorn steers. It is said that cowboys could ride their horses into the bar as long as they didn't buck or pitch. The bar and Friedrich's collection of horns can be seen at the Lone Star Buckhorn Museum, 600 Lone Star Boulevard until August, 1998. After that it will be relocated downtown at Houston and Presa Streets.

At 100 E. Houston, step inside the Rand Building to see the award-winning modernization of a 1913 open-atrium building that was saved from demolition by the San Antonio Conservation Society.

13. Turn left on Soledad.

On the corner of Travis, the Milam Building, built in 1929, was the first centrally air-conditioned office building in North America.

14. Turn right on Convent (at the three-story yellow-and-red-brick building), left on Augusta over the iron bridge.

At Giruad Street, on the right, is the iron-gated original entrance to the Ursuline Academy, the first girls' school in San Antonio, established in 1851 by Bishop John Odin with the help of a small group of French nuns. Bishop Odin hired French architect François Giraud to design and supervise the building of the Academy and Convent. The original building is one of the few remaining examples of rammed-earth construction in the United States. This building was renovated by the nuns in order to open their school. Other construction took place between 1851 and 1882. Notice the wooden toure (roundabout), used by the nuns to feed the hungry and to receive anything from the outside without opening the door. The buildings were saved by the San Antonio Conservation Society and are now home to the Southwest Craft Center.

Continuing along Augusta, the enchilada-red building on the left is the 1996 San Antonio Public Library designed by Ricardo Legorreta of Mexico. It is a spectacular building and well worth a visit.

At the first set of steps on the right enter the Craft Center grounds.

In the old dormitory are a gift shop, gallery, and the Copper Kitchen Restaurant (open for lunch only). Exceptionally helpful and friendly volunteers in the Garden Room (open 10:00 A.M. to 2:00 P.M.) can give you more details and take you on a tour of the grounds which also include an exhibit gallery.

Notice there is no clock on the north face of the clock tower. One story says the nuns couldn't conceive of the town developing in that direction. Another says the builder refused to "give the time of day" to the "damn Yankees."

On the other side of the parking lot, also in buildings from the Ursaline Academy, is Club Giraud, a private club formed to raise money to support the Craft Center.

Annual French Market, Southwest Craft Center

15. Exit the grounds where you entered, turn right, continuing on Augusta. Turn right on Navarro.

KMOL-TV (Channel 4), the first television station in San Antonio, began broadcasting in December 1949 as WOAI. With only twenty-five television sets in town, it was quite a gamble. At first local newspapers refused to print the TV schedule because they considered television a competitor.

16. Turn left on Auditorium Circle.

The Municipal Auditorium was built in 1926 in the Spanish Colonial Revival style popular at that time. It is a memorial to those who died in World War I.

Across Jefferson at Buñuelos you can buy this favorite Mexican sweet fresh from the factory.

17. Turn right on Jefferson towards the flagpole.

In front of the telephone building, with its elaborate Spanish-Baroque terra cotta embellishments, are Korean and Vietnam war memorials.

On the right at Pecan Street is St. Mark's Episcopal Church, started before the Civil War but not completed until the mid-1870s. Robert E. Lee, a parishioner, laid the cornerstone. It was here that Lyndon B. Johnson married Lady Bird in 1934.

Travis Park across the street is home to Friday brown-bag concerts in the summer, and a jazz festival in September.

18. Turn left on Pecan. At Broadway turn left, then right on Third Street.

At Avenue E, above the door of the *Express-News* Building, is a frieze by Pompeo Coppini, the noted sculptor whose studio was in San Antonio. Further up the street on the right is the Scottish Rite Temple Cathedral whose bronze doors, also by Coppini, honor Texas as a Republic with an image of Sam Houston, and Texas as a State with an image of George Washington; both heroes were Masons. The Cathedral's 1924 Möller organ has approximately 5,000 pipes that range from the size of a pencil to thirty-two feet in diameter. Visitors are welcome to go inside where a guided tour is usually available (just ask in the office).

19. Turn right on Avenue E, and go back toward the Alamo.

On the left is the 1926 Medical Arts Building, now the Emily Morgan Hotel. It is necessary to look up from across the street to see the elaborate Gothic embellishments and chateauesque mansard roof around the top.

Coming alongside the Alamo, the *Cenotaph,* again by Pompeo Coppini, dates from 1939, and honors the men killed in the battle for the Alamo.

Side Trip A

20. Side trip A to Chapel of Miracles. From step 9, continue ahead on San Saba, past Santa Rosa Hospital, cross Martin Street, and turn left under freeway. Turn right on Leona.

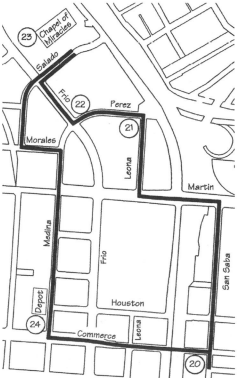

On the left along Leona is the University Health Center, part of the Bexar County Hospital District.

21. Turn left on Perez.

On the right in the vacant lot are two old buildings typical of those built in this area in the 1800s. The one-story house is constructed of mud and cedar in the German method called *fachwerk,* adopted by the Mexicans. These two buildings are owned by the city, which hopes to renovate them at some time.

22. Turn right on Frio by the post office, then right on Salado (the next street).

At the end of Salado, surrounded by freeway, apartments, and a city park, is a small house and chapel. Chapel of Miracles was built in the 1870s by the Ximenes family to house a wooden cross believed to have come from Mission San Antonio de Velero. Legend says that although the previous buildings that housed this cross were destroyed by fire, the cross always survived. People come here now to pray at the wondrous cross for miracles, attested to by the many *milagros*, the silver symbols you see pinned to the various saints in the chapel. You buy a *milagro* that represents the part of the body that needs healing, pin it on the skirt of the patron saint of that illness, and then say a prayer and make an offering. A donation box is also available for the upkeep of the chapel.

23. **Exit the chapel, turn right on Salado, cross Frio, and continue ahead. Turn left on Morales, then right on Medina.**

After crossing Martin, you come to Scoby Storage. The truck painted on the brick wall of the dock area dates from 1935, when Scoby began its affiliation with Allied Van Lines. Past this, the huge brick building on the right is the Bexar County Jail, which opened in 1989. Nine days after it opened, three prisoners escaped by using nail clippers to cut through some lightweight grating wire covering a window.

The magnificent domed building at Houston Street was the International and Great Northern Railroad Depot, which opened in 1907, when San Antonio was the largest city in Texas. (The city never had a union station; each rail company had its own depot.) From here, the Texas Eagle ran daily to Laredo. In 1970, with only one daily train left, the station closed. After the depot closed, the eight-foot, hammered-copperplate Indian on top was stolen, and then returned anonymously in response to a city-wide plea. The building stood empty and deteriorating until the City Employees Credit Union bought it and renovated it in 1988. Most of the stained-glass window had to be replaced, using for reference photographs and shards of glass found on the ground. Feel free to go inside the building and look around. Exit by the side door to read the historical plaque.

24. **Continue on Medina, then turn left on Commerce to go back to Milam Park.**

On Commerce between Medina and Frio, the red brick building on the right is the SAMM shelter (San Antonio Metropolitan Ministry), a well-run facility that ministers to the social and educational needs of the homeless, and provides as well a place to bathe and sleep.

Future renovation is planned for the abandoned buildings in this section known as Cattleman's Square. At Leona, down the street to the left are the offices of the Alamo Community College District, which are built around the old Talerico homestead. Talerico was at one time one of the largest wholesale produce distributors in the Southwest.

Down the street to the right is the new downtown campus of the University of Texas at San Antonio.

(Pico de Gallo Restaurant to the right on Leona is a good Mexican restaurant.)

Back at Milam Park you may continue the Downtown walk at Step 10.

Side Trip B

25. **Side Trip B to Immaculate Heart of Mary painted church, the Sanitary Tortilla Factory, and the Navarro Historic Site.**

From Step 8 continue down Santa Rosa. At Durango, cross and turn right. Turn left on Urban Loop.

On the right along Urban Loop is Father Flanagan's Boys Town of San Antonio.

Further down, on the left, the Immaculate Heart of Mary School no longer holds daily classes, but is used for seminars and retreats.

The Sanctuary of the Immaculate Heart of Mary, designed in 1911 by architect Leo Dielmann in the Romanesque Revival style, is an island standing alone in a sea of progress. The Mexican-American neighborhood around the church was removed for the expressway. Faithful parishioners still come back, but not so much the younger generation. The grotto in front of the church shows Our Lady of Guadalupe as she appeared to Juan Diego, a story much revered in Mexico as well as San Antonio. The church is open daily until 4:30 P.M.

Walk around to the side of the church to enter.

When you see the interior with its intricately painted designs you will understand why we included this side trip.

A long forgotten artist from Los Angeles first decorated the interior of the church in 1942. Father Alberto Domingo began a restoration of the painting in 1988, but failed to finish before his retirement a year later. His successor, Father Gamm, determined to get the work done, asked a man painting the church gutters if he could do it. The man said he had never done that sort of painting before but would try. The Father then went to the day-labor pickup point nearby and hired an assistant. We admire the faith Father Gamm had in the ability of these men, and they did not let him down. No sooner had they finished the restoration than one night an arsonist set fire to the sacristy. The whole church might have been destroyed had there not been a retreat in progress at the old school building next door. Firefighters arrived before it had progressed beyond the sacristy. While the painting over the sanctuary vault was badly blackened, the rest of the church suffered only minor smoke damage. Again the painters went to work.

The marble altar came from St. Michael's Polish Catholic Church, torn down along with its neighborhood, for development of HemisFair '68, San Antonio's world fair.

Exit church and walk back to the Sanitary Tortilla Factory.

Established in 1925, this is, as far as the owner can determine, the first tortilla factory in the United States. To introduce the non-Mexican population of San Antonio to tortillas, the owners would cook up chicken, roll it in tortillas, and give these tacos away free. The machines were brought from Tampico, Mexico and with them came Genaro Mariscal, then age fifteen, to keep them running. He modified the machines to make the thinner tortillas local people preferred. The two original machines, now about seventy years old, are still in use. Señor Mariscal, however, retired in 1995 at the age of eight-six after seventy years in which, we are told, he never missed a day's work tending his machines. Between 5:00 and 10:00 A.M. daily, you can watch the tortillas being made on these old-style machines.

26. **Exit the factory and walk straight ahead to Santa Rosa. Turn left onto Santa Rosa, continue until you reach Nueva.**

As you turn, the two-story yellow brick building behind the church serves as living quarters for the priests. It was the first structure on site in 1904, and included a chapel which was used until the church was completed.

27. **Cross Nueva, turn right, then left on Laredo.**

On the corner of Laredo is the José Antonio Navarro Historic Site. Navarro was one of the signers of the Texas Declaration of Independence. We have seen a photograph that showed the two-story building in 1940 painted red with a big black and white sign "Jacalito Inn." This is an interesting museum and the only house of its era open to the public in the downtown area. (Admission fee.)

28. **Continue up Laredo. Turn left on Dolorosa, then right on Santa Rosa to starting point.**

2 Downtown II

Features: Hertzberg Museum, Tower Life Building, La Villita, HemisFair Park, Alamodome, St. Paul's Square, Southern Pacific Depot, and RiverCenter

Distance: 3.1 miles (5.0k)

Time: 2 hrs.

Night: No. See Comments

Wheelchair Accessible: Yes, some curbs to negotiate

Restrooms, Water, Phone: At start and ☞ 6, 11, Depot, and 14.

Restaurants: Several along the way

Getting There: Start in front of the Alamo.

Comments:

Parts of this walk are at a slow, tourist pace, but there are stretches where you can pick up speed.

Although the walk is not recommended at night, it is okay to wander around La Villita and HemisFair Park at night as long as there are other people around.

The Hertzberg Circus Museum is open Monday-Friday from 9:00 A.M. to 5:00 P.M. (admission charge).

Alamodome tours are conducted Tuesday-Saturday at 10 A.M. and 1 P.M. (admission charge).

1. **Start in front of the Alamo, walk ahead to Alamo Street, cross and turn left. Turn right on Crockett.**

The Crockett Street Bridge is one of three (of the original five) nineteenth-century iron bridges left downtown.

2. **Turn left on Presa.**

The Casino Club Building is now an apartment building. An on-site marker relays its history.

On the first block of Presa are shops and restaurants that also face the River Walk.

On the corner of Market and Presa, the Hertzberg Circus Museum offers a miniature three-ring tent circus, lots of memorabilia, a library, and Tom Thumb curios. It is a fascinating place to visit.

The museum is in a former central library building. In the nineteenth century there were several libraries in San Antonio, but, in spite of such names as Alamo Free Library and San Antonio Public Library, they all required membership fees. The first truly free public library, the Carnegie Library, opened in 1903 on this spot.

That original structure was replaced by this one, designed by Herbert S. Green, which opened in 1930.

> **3. Just past the bridge turn right under the City Public Service Building. Cross Navarro, continue down Villita Street.**

At Navarro, the gray stone building on the left, formerly the Federal Reserve Bank, is now occupied by the Mexican Consulate General.

Just past the parking garage is the Tower Life Building, formerly the Smith-Young Building. This San Antonio landmark, designed by architects Atlee B. and Robert M. Ayres in 1929, was declared a national monument in 1991. Circling the upper stories of the building are gargoyles, placed, according to legend, to protect the building from evil spirits.

Step inside from the side entrance. In the hallway to the left of the postal station is a photographic exhibit of the building in its earliest days when it was the city's first Sears and Roebuck Store. Until the 1950s, not only was it the tallest building west of the Mississippi River, but also the only octagonal building in the United States.

Walk down the hall to the left of the entrance to see the ornate lobby with its gothic arches. Exit by the lobby door.

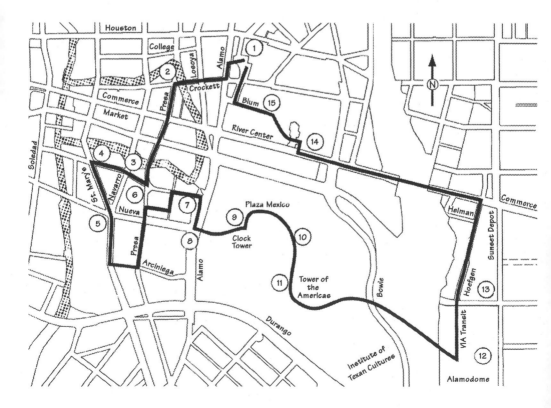

Across St. Mary's is Granada Homes, once the luxury Plaza Hotel, now senior retirement apartments. A passageway, now closed, connects it to the Smith-Young Building.

To the right of the Granada is the new International Center, home of the North American Development Bank, in the remodeled former central library. The spectacular new central library that opened in 1995 can be seen on the Downtown I walk.

4. Turn left on St. Mary's.

Between Villita and Nueva, the beautifully tiled building across the street on the right sat unused for many years. It reopened in late 1996, and once again is a parking garage. Because of its early Mexican influence, San Antonio is blessed with much tile work. It is interesting that this was used frequently on parking garages. The Nix Garage on College Street off Navarro is an outstanding example.

On the next block, on the right, Hermann Sons is a fraternal organization begun by German immigrants in New York City in 1840 and named for the German folk hero, Hermann of Cherusker.

5. Cross Nueva Street. Turn left into the alley marked Arciniega, then left on Presa.

The two houses along the alley and around the corner on Presa that comprise the Arbor House Hotel were built by a Swiss cabinet maker in 1903. The hotel opened in 1995. South on Presa are houses renovated as attorney offices. No. 401, on the corner, the last private residence, is the caliche block Tynan-Rice Cottage built in the late 1860s by the great-grandfather of the present owner. It is for lease now.

Across Presa is the back of the Plaza San Antonio Hotel, built on the grounds of the old German English school.

6. Back at the CPS building, cross Presa to La Villita.

La Villita (The Little Village) has an interesting history. During the Spanish period, when the Alamo had become a military outpost, La Villita was a village of primitive huts for the soldiers and their families. After a heavy flood in 1819 more substantial homes of stone and adobe were built. In the mid-1800s German and French immigrants moved in. Eventually the houses fell into disrepair and the area became a slum until a city ordinance in 1939, backed by Mayor Maury Maverick, Sr., ordained that it be rehabilitated and established as an arts and crafts center.

To the left is the Villita Assembly Hall. The seals around it represent the six countries that ruled over Texas: (from left) the United States, the Confederacy, the Republic of Texas, Mexico, France, and Spain. (Yes, that is George Washington sitting on his horse on the Confederacy seal. Southerners felt that, as a Virginian, Washington would certainly have been on the side of the South.) This site belongs to the power company and was the location of San Antonio's first electric power plant, Station A, in 1884.

Enter La Villita through the gate between the two cannons.

Fiestas and special events are held on the many plazas in La Villita.

Walk straight ahead. When the street ends at the yellow brick building, turn left.

Ahead is the entrance to the Arneson River Theatre and to its right, the Cós house where Mexican General Cós surrendered San Antonio to the Texans three months before the battle of the Alamo.

Turn right at this point.

The nondenominational Little Church of La Villita offers solace to the body as well as to the soul. Sandwiches and fruit are given to the homeless, and bread, rice, and beans to those who have cooking facilities. At Thanksgiving, the one hundred most needy families on the church records get food boxes, and at Christmas, the church serves dinner to about 1,700 homeless and needy.

The Starving Artist Show is held in La Villita each April to raise money for these projects. The Conservation Society holds its Night In Old San Antonio (NIOSA) here during Fiesta Week.

As you reach Alamo Street you will see the Little Rhein Steak House to the left. This was originally the German Working Men's Hall.

7. Turn right at Alamo Street.

On the left, before you reach Nueva Street, is a bust of Maury Maverick, a United States Congressman in the mid-1930s, who later became mayor of San Antonio. He promoted the restoration of La Villita.

Across Nueva Street is the red brick 1906 Fairmount Hotel that made the *Guinness Book of World Records* in 1985 as the largest building ever moved on wheels. The 1985 yellow brick addition was designed to complement the original.

8. Cross Alamo Street at Nueva and enter HemisFair Park. Walk straight ahead toward the clock tower.

San Antonio's world's fair, HemisFair '68, created much of what you see here. Although many of the fine old homes in this area were torn down, a few were kept here along the former Goliad Street. The Tower of the Americas has become a landmark second only to the Alamo. On the far right as you enter the park, the large, unimposing two-story building (it looks better on the other side) is Beethoven Hall, built by the Beethoven Männerchor (men's choir) in 1894, and at one time the entertainment hub of the German-American community. Besides its premier performance hall, it had a bowling alley and a ballroom. Many political rallies took place here. The original German-Classic facade had to be

Replica of temple at Teothihuacan, Plaza de Mexico, Hemisfair Park

removed to widen Alamo Street. The interior has been remodeled several times so very little remains of the original except its fine acoustics.

Poet Sidney Lanier described his first visit to the Männerchor: "Seventeen Germans sat at a 'singing table' with long-necked bottles of Rhine wine. The leader rapped his tuning fork and led the singing." Lanier said he was so affected that he felt like crying and hugging them. As an amateur flutist he felt he had never played better than he did with the Männerchor. The hall is now owned by the City of San Antonio and used for concerts, especially during the San Antonio Festival.

Walk ahead to the clock tower.

To the right of the clock tower, which, oddly enough, has never had a clock, is a delightful playground built by volunteers with donated materials. Also to its right is a restored portion of one of the early *acequias*, or irrigation ditches. Originally much deeper, it was built sometime in the 1700s and used until about 1908.

Beyond the tower is a gift shop, and past that you can see the Federal Court Building.

9. Turn left into the Plaza México.

To the right, as you enter the plaza, is a replica from one of the pyramids at Teotihuacan. Behind it is the Mexican Cultural Institute, which has free exhibits, lectures, and concerts. A newer gallery is ahead on the left. Straight ahead is a branch campus of the Universidad Nacional Autonoma de México. To the left of all this is the Convention Center.

10. **Exit the Plaza to the right, then turn left toward the Tower of the Americas.**

To the right is a campus of the Texas A&M Extension Service and to the right of that the United States Courthouse Building.

This is also the beginning of the Water Park installed in 1988. The structure on your right with the cross beams is called, for lack of anything else, a "beam fountain." The water, when the fountain was first installed and in use, came down from under the beams. It was great to walk through on a hot summer's day. Unfortunately because kids will be kids, and parents don't always watch them, it was turned off for safety purposes. Possibly it will be fenced and turned back on. Some of the original Water Park features had to be removed for expansion of the Convention Center that is due to open in the year 2000. In its new configuration, the Water Park will recirculate approximately 800,000 gallons of water.

The Tower of the Americas is 750 feet high. The view from the observation deck and revolving restaurant is spectacular, day or night.

To the right of the Tower, between two sections of falls, is an arched, metal bridge. The path under the bridge leads to a branch campus of the University of Texas, and to the Institute of Texan Cultures, which has exhibits reflecting the many cultures that settled Texas. You can spend hours browsing there, however, so you might want to come back another time.

11. **Continue around the Tower. At the end of the falls turn right and then right again across the little bridge to Bowie Street.**

(Just before you cross the bridge there are restrooms to the left.)

Cross Bowie, carefully, and turn right up the ramp to the Alamodome.

The multipurpose Alamodome, with its cable-suspended roof, opened in 1993. Interesting behind-the-scene tours are given Tuesday-Saturday at 10 A.M. and 1 P.M.

12. **Across from the main entrance turn left between the VIA transit station and walk ahead toward Hoefgen Street.**

The Southern Pacific Depot, built in 1903, served AMTRAK until recently. The interior features a fourteen-foot stained-glass window, oak stairway and elaborately decorated ceiling. Sunset Station, a hotel/retail/entertainment complex incorporating the depot will open Summer 1998.

13. **Continue along Hoefgen. Cross Commerce Street and turn left.**

This old commercial area was redeveloped in recent years and christened St. Paul's Square, after St. Paul's Methodist Episcopal Church, located one block past Commerce Street, and now converted to law offices.

When the railroad came to San Antonio in 1877, this district began to grow. It reached its peak during World War II and the Korean Conflict, when servicemen arrived here by train. After that the area slowly deteriorated and became blighted. An earlier revitalization project gave the area its current name but not much prosperity. An owners' association works to retain the historical and architectural integrity of the area. It is hoped the new Sunset Station development will finally bring life back to St. Paul's Square.

(Aldaco's Restaurant serves good Mexican food in a pleasant setting at moderate prices.)

After you go under the freeway, and just before Bowie Street, across on the left is the Central Heating and Cooling Plant, the city's giant air conditioner. It serves the Convention Center, the Alamodome, and other city facilities. If you cross the street and peer through the windows you can see the huge waterworks in one room and the computer that controls everything in the next room. To the left of the plant is the Yturri house, which used to be a water museum with exhibits of early waterworks equipment, but it is now office space.

14. Just past the Marriott Hotel enter RiverCenter.

You are on the second level of this shopping, dining, and entertainment complex. Once inside turn left through the door to the bridge spanning the river. Standing on the bridge look to the right to see the barge turnaround and the stage area. The lower level is mostly restaurants; the second and third levels are shops.

> **Continue across the bridge, turn right, and then left at the central escalators, exiting through the glass doors onto Blum St.**

In the early days of the Menger Hotel this was the wagon yard for stagecoaches, carriages, and horses.

15. Walk straight ahead alongside the Menger Hotel. Turn right in front of the hotel to return to the Alamo.

The Menger is the oldest hotel west of the Mississippi. (We discuss it more in the Downtown I walk. At the desk you can pick up a self-guided tour of the hotel with much historic information.)

This is a story we found reference to: On January 9, 1895, the Concatenated Order of Hoo-Hoos, whose membership consisted of the cream of San Antonio society, had an initiation ceremony of nineteen "kittens" (initiates) here. First, they had to answer a series of questions as to hat, shoe, collar, and cuff sizes. Then they had to pay, in exact change (or suffer dire consequences), a $9.99 initiation fee and $0.99 for dues. At nine minutes after 9:00 P.M. hoots and hollers were reported erupting from the room. Then the "kittens," hooded and standing with their hands on the shoulders of the one in front of them, formed a line, and took an oath. They finished by dancing on tacks, sitting in a tub of ice water, stepping in coal scuttles, and hitting their heads on doorknobs.

With that we leave you back at the Alamo.

3 River Walk North

Features: River Walk north of the Big Bend and side trip to San Antonio Museum of Art

Distance: 2.5 miles + 1.8-mile side trip (4.0k + 2.9k)

Time: 1 hr. + 40-min. side trip

Nights: Yes, but see Comments

Wheelchair Accessible: Yes, but see Comments

Restrooms, Water, Phones: At start, ☞ 2, and Museum of Art

Restaurants: Along the river and ☞ 2 and 5

Getting There: Start in front of the Alamo.

Comments:

There is not much foot traffic on the River Walk in the evening except around the restaurant area so it is best to go beyond Houston Street only in small groups.

Although this entire walk cannot be taken in a wheelchair, portions of the River Walk are accessible. There is a River Walk accessibility map available at the Visitor Information Center across from Alamo Plaza.

The San Antonio Museum of Art is open Monday and Wednesday–Saturday from 10:00 A.M. to 5:00 P.M., Tuesday from 10:00 A.M. to 9:00 P.M., and Sunday from noon to 5:00 P.M. There is an admission charge except on Tuesday from 3:00 to 9:00 P.M.

Overview:

San Antonio exists because of its river, so it is only right that the river has become one of the city's major attractions. This was not always so. After a disasterous flood in 1921, water rose as high as twelve feet over the streets of downtown. To control future flooding, the city built the Olmos flood-control dam. A bypass channel and flood gates controlled the amount of water entering the big horseshoe bend through downtown. Later the city adopted the beautification plan of architect Robert H. H. Hugman to enhance the river. Work began in 1939. The San Antonio River Walk was born.

Hugman envisioned restaurants, shops, and apartments along the walk. He planned the three-and-a-half foot depth to prevent drownings and to accommodate poled gondolas for a slow, quiet, romantic atmosphere below the bustle of the streets above. Hugman told the story of describing his dreams to a public official, a smart businessman with little formal education. Hugman spoke of "gondolas quietly gliding on the water." Ever conscious of cost, the man said he

thought the entire idea was fine, but added "We won't have to buy all those gondolas. We can buy a pair and raise our own."

Hugman planned each detail of the River Walk. No two of the 31 stairways
are alike. His concept combined commercial areas with restful parks. He even
made sure the walkways could be navigated by women in high-heeled shoes.

The war distracted attention from river development, and the River Walk remained primarily a park for years. Servicemen liked to take their sweethearts
canoeing or strolling along the walkway, but the area developed a tainted reputation and became so unsafe that it was declared off-limits. Commercial development did not begin in earnest until HemisFair '68. At that time an extension of
the River Walk created a convention center accessible by boat. Another extension in 1988 brought the river to the RiverCenter/Marriott Hotel complex.

Ever hopeful for the future of the river, Hugman had opened his office on the
river level of the Clifford Building. A friend told him, "I knew you were a
dreamer, but now I know you are also a fool. You'll be drowned like a rat in your
own hole." That "hole" has never flooded, but on the day in 1990 that a plaque
finally honoring him as "Father of the River Walk" was unveiled at Hugman's
former office, an unusually heavy rain brought the water almost to the walkway.

The Big Bend is drained each January for cleaning. Being a fiesta city, San Antonio takes advantage of this event by holding a River Bottom Mud Parade,
complete with Mud Queen and Mud King. Other major parades are the Christmas Parade on the Friday after Thanksgiving, the Fiesta Parade in April, and a
St. Patrick's Day Parade in March when the river is dyed green.

The San Antonio River Walk is internationally known and is a model for river
development in other cities. We have divided the walk into two sections and put
the San Antonio Museum of Art on one end and the Blue Star Art Space on the other.

After your walk on the river, the Crosswalk Deli in the passageway between
Alamo and Losoya Streets is a pleasant place to rest while viewing a mural of the
river by San Antonio architect Roland Rodriguez. The mural was commissioned
by Hap Veltman in 1986. Elton Moy, owner of Crosswalk Deli, who says he
constantly sees new things in the mural, took time to relate to us what the artist
told him.

In the upper lefthand corner, the large "G" represents the hand of God throw-
ing a bolt of lightning down to the blue ring, which represents the "blue hole" in
back of Incarnate Word College, where the San Antonio River comes gurgling
up. The small "g" with the small bolt of lightning represents the hand of George
Brackenridge, the first man to control the flow of the river. Yellow lines and dots
outline the Brackenridge estate.

The blue ring starts the river and the yellow rings, which actually belong over
the fish heads, each represent one mile of flowing river. The Berlin Bridge is one
of several built by the Berlin Bridge Company of East Berlin, Connecticut, that
you will see throughout the map.

The black to darker grey area on the map is called the Quest for Knowledge as
it is the location of Trinity University, Incarnate Word College, and San Antonio

College. The first of three eyes that watch over the City of San Antonio is the Eye of Truth, represented by a dead fish because truth is like a dead fish: nobody wants it around.

Throughout the map Rodriguez has noted places of interest and public art, marking them with a red triangle and referencing them in the lower center panel. He has located Hap Veltman's house on River Road with a blue star that you will find repeated later at the Blue Star Gallery, which Veltman started. (Veltman was a major player in downtown redevelopment in the 1960s and 1970s.) A photograph marks the studio, in a former pumphouse on the banks of the river, where Mount Rushmore artist Gutzon Borglum built the first scale model of that mammoth piece.

The darker grey to lighter grey area is called Respect for Nature and is watched over by the second eye known as Anima. The San Antonio Museum of Art and the Humane Society are located here.

The lines of small black and white dots along the map represent *acequias*, or irrigation ditches, that the first settlers built. Much of San Antonio grew up along these waterways. The historic districts are outlined with lavender broken lines. Rodriguez included all of the twenty-two large trees that grow on the banks of the river. Green gridwork areas show where the course of the river has been altered for flood control.

Moving from the grey area to the white area, the third eye, the Eye of Order, which includes the banks, the courthouse, and the various centers of justice watches over the part of the city Rodriguez has called Love of Beauty.

1. **Starting at the Alamo, cross Alamo Street toward the Hyatt Regency Hotel, and go down the steps to the left of the Visitor Information Center. Walk through the lower level of the Hyatt. Exit onto the River Walk, and turn right.**

The area from Alamo Street to the river that goes past the waterway and the Thomas Stell mosaic mural is a city park. The hotel is built around and over it.

Once on the River Walk, just before the Navarro Street bridge, notice the yellow brick high-rise on the right with the terra cotta ornamentation. This is the Nix Medical Center, the first high-rise in the city to have hospital, doctors offices, and parking garage all in one.

Just past Navarro, on the right, is La Mansión del Río Hotel. It is built around the former 1853 St. Mary's Institute, the first boys school in San Antonio. From the street level on College Street you can see the mansard roof of the stone original. The school was poor and payments were often made in cattle, produce, and land. Some boys, arriving at school by boat, enlivened their mornings by capsizing each other's crafts.

St. Mary's Institute grew, and in 1891, it became St. Mary's College. In 1894, an additional campus opened on Cincinnati Street in the Woodlawn district as St. Louis College. Both schools offered high school and college classes. In 1923, all the collegiate classes moved to the Cincinnati campus. Eventually the high

Mark crossing one of many footbridges (Photo by Celia Wakefield)

school split off and became Central Catholic High School, which you will pass later on the side trip to the San Antonio Museum of Art. In 1927, St. Louis College became St. Mary's University. The Law School was the last to remain at this location.

The water cascading into the concrete basin beside the hotel and in other locations you will see along the way is recirculated from the river. This system aerates the water to maintain the quality. Water empties from the storm drains in times of heavy rain.

Just past St. Mary's Street is the Petroleum Commerce Building, for many years the City Public Service (the local power company) headquarters, now being converted into a luxury hotel. The John Twohig home that stood on this site is now on the grounds of the Witte Museum. A footbridge connected the house to Twohig's bank on Commerce Street. Twohig was known as the "Breadline Banker" for his custom of giving free bread to the needy each Saturday evening.

Over the steps, where the river bends to the right, is a tile plaque. The twin cypress tree referred to couldn't have been the tree you see here, however, because this tree isn't old enough. To the left is the bypass channel put in for flood control. A footbridge crosses over the sluice-type floodgate.

Across the river from the Holiday Inn River Walk South was the location of the 1820s home of Don Juan Martín de Veramendi, a member of one of San Antonio's wealthy Spanish families. The large house was luxuriously furnished in the Spanish Colonial style of the Spanish Governor's Palace and was the center of aristrocratic society. Veramendi's daughter married James Bowie, who died at the Alamo. Ben Milam was fatally shot near the house during the Battle of Bexar three months before.

At the Houston Street Bridge you can see the facade of the old Texas Theater on the front of the former Republic Bank Building. This magnificent atmospheric theater was designed by John Eberson, one of the most prolific theater architects of the 1920s, who also designed the Majestic Theater on Houston Street. There was much controversy about tearing down the Texas Theater. The developers won with the "compromise" of leaving the facade. Perhaps it is poetic justice that the bank went belly-up a few short years after the building opened.

About where the Travis Street Bridge crosses the river was the Laux Mill back in 1873. Rising above the bridge is NationsBank on the right and the Milam Building on the left.

As you approach the Lexington Street Bridge, to the right is a boat ramp. The river parades that start downtown on St. Mary's Street end here. The church steeple rising above the ramp crowns First Baptist Church. At the present time the River Walk ends just under the bridge. There are plans to extend it to Brackenridge Park. Although the route we take now does not lack in interest, when the River Walk is complete it will be a more pleasant route to the Museum of Art. Still it is worth leaving the lovely river to see the museum.

2. **To skip the side trip to the museum, turn around and retrace your steps, picking up the text where it reads "Back on the river, the tower . . ." under Step 5.**

   To take the side trip (daytime only), go up the stairs, turn right across the river past the hotel, and then right again on St. Mary's Street.

Towards the left as you approach St. Mary's Street you can see the clock tower of the Southwest Craft Center and the new "enchilada-red" central library.

St. Mary's is one of several streets that branch out from the center of town along the course of the river, which is why we come upon it so many times. Future river development may include a flood conrtol dam and lake up river from Brooklyn Street. On the left, Providence High School is a Catholic girls school (run by the Sisters of the Divine Providence, who also run Our Lady of the Lake University). Beyond it, Central Catholic Marianist High School (Mark went to school there) is an offshoot of the first boys school mentioned earlier. A historical marker gives some of the school's background.

3. **Turn right on Dallas Street at the fire station, and then right on Jones.**

The castle-like building on the left is the San Antonio Museum of Art, which is located in the old Lone Star Brewery complex built in 1904. The building, especially the chrome and glass elevator, is well worth seeing. Local people will remember Old No. 300, the 1913 electric streetcar that rode on the tracks down

Looking north alongside La Mansión del Río Hotel

the middle of Jones. It is now on long-term loan to a city in Oregon that is restoring it. On the right is the Humane Society, which explains why, on the river mural in the crosswalk downtown, you see a dog sitting on top of the museum.

Continue walking on Jones to the bridge. To the right of the bridge is where the dam is proposed that will create a lake. A plaque on the bridge designates it as the Grand Avenue Bridge. (Grand Avenue was the name of this street a hundred years ago.) Three blocks ahead, about where Interstate 37 passes overhead, was the Galveston, Houston, and San Antonio Railroad Depot.

4. Turn right on Avenue B.

To the right at Tenth Street is the former Scott Petty mansion, now the site of the oldest VFW lodge in Texas.

At Brooklyn, across to the left, is Alamo Fiesta Floats, where many of the parade floats are made.

At 6th Street, in front of the Valero Building is a marker commemorating the First Chinese Baptist Church in San Antonio.

5. **Turn right on Fourth Street. Go down the same stairs you came up to return to the River Walk.**

The red-brick church on Fourth Street is First Baptist Church. Weekdays between 11:00 A.M. and 2:00 P.M. the 4th Street Inn across the street, which is run by the church to raise funds to aid the homeless, serves a generous meal for a very small price in a most pleasant dining room. The red-domed building on the left is the Municipal Auditorium.

Back on the river, the tower rising behind the Richmond Street Bridge belongs to KMOL (Channel 4), the first television station in San Antonio, which began broadcasting under the call letters WOAI in 1949.

6. **At St. Mary's go up the steps, cross St. Mary's, and go down the steps on the right to the other side of the river.**

In the center of the bridge is an old drinking fountain that no longer works. Look around to the back and see where it drained into the river.

Back down on the river, to the right, is Club Giraud, a private dining club whose members are generally the older, more established members of the business community. The club occupies buildings from the Ursuline Academy, as does the Southwest Craft Center next to it. Club Giraud was founded in 1981 to provide funds for the preservation of the Ursuline complex and to help support the Craft Center. Just past the gazebo are steps leading up to the Southwest Craft Center (see Walk 1). The Ursuline Academy for Girls was founded in 1851. The old limestone buildings, art galleries, gift shop, restaurant, and gardens are worth seeing (See Walk 1).

Just past the Houston Street Bridge, across from the Holiday Inn River Walk South, is a high stone wall with some carved and textured stones that could be from the Veramendi Palace and other long-gone landmarks.

7. **Go up the stairs when the walkway ends at Commerce Street. Turn left over the bridge, then left again, and go down the stairs. Turn right.**

This bridge took you over the bypass channel.

8. **Cross under the Presa Street Bridge. Go up the next stairs to the Crockett Street Bridge, turn left, and continue straight ahead on Crockett Street back to the Alamo. (For more about these iron bridges see Walk 5, Bridges.)**

4   River Walk South

Features: The Big Bend, King William Historical District, Convention Center and RiverCenter extensions, and side trip to Guenther House and Blue Star Art Space

Distance: 4.5 miles + 0.7-mile side trip (7.2 k + 1.1k)

Time: 2 hours + 20-min. side trip

Nights: Yes. See Comments

Wheelchair accessible: Yes. See Comments

Restrooms, Water, Phone: At start, Guenther House, Convention Center, and River-Center

Restaurants: On the River Walk, at the Guenther House, and RiverCenter

Getting There: Start in front of the Alamo.

Comments:

The downtown part of this walk has heavy tourist traffic, which makes it safe to walk alone well into evening. The King William area should not be walked after dusk.

Although this entire walk cannot be taken in a wheelchair, portions of the River Walk are accessible. There is a River Walk accessibility map available at the Visitor Center across from Alamo Plaza.

Guenther House is open seven days a week. Blue Star Art Space is open noon to 6:00 P.M., Wednesday through Sunday.

See Overview for River Walk North, for a general description.

1. **Starting at the Alamo, cross Alamo Street, and go down the steps to the left of the Visitor Information Center. Walk through the lower section of the Hyatt, and exit onto the River Walk. Turn left.**

The sidewalk that comes down from the Alamo to the river, including that which goes under the Hyatt Regency, is under the jurisdiction of the city parks department. When you emerge onto the river, you are on the flood-protected portion of the River Walk known as the Big Bend. It is the commercial hub of the River Walk.

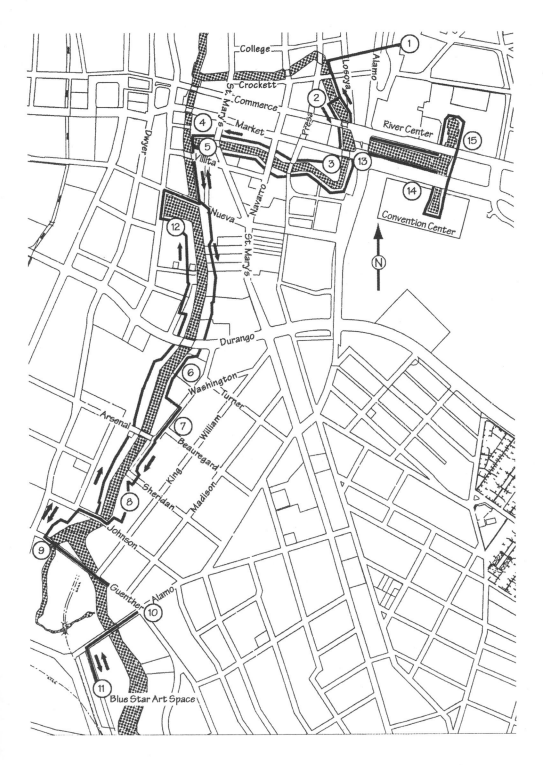

2. **At the first arched footbridge, cross over to the other side of the river. Turn left.**

Just before the Commerce Street Bridge, notice the Clifford Building, designed in 1891 by James Riely Gordon. It has survived with few changes. Robert H. H. Hugman, who designed the River Walk, had his office on the lowest level. In July 1990, the plaque was unveiled honoring Hugman as the "Father of the River" and a replica of his office sign was installed on the curve of the roof line.

Just past the Market Street Bridge is the river barge ticket booth. During World War II, canoe and rowboat rentals were profitable on the river. Many retired sevicemen on Mark's tours have said they appreciated the three and one half-foot depth of the river when their canoes capsized.

Dinner cruises are popular on the river. We've seen everything from raucous groups to a romantic candlelight dinner for two. (Contact any River Walk restaurant.)

3. **Just past the ticket booth, at the water tank, go up the stairs on the right, and turn left (walking behind the tank and the Arneson River Theater). At the first steps on the left, go down.**

Between Presa and Navarro Streets is an island near the site where the Lewis Mill was built in 1847 and where the Spaniards built a dam to supply the Concepción Ditch in the 1700s. Along this section of the Big Bend, in 1889, the steamer "Hilda" carried tourists past such signs as "Beowulf Dreisehn," "Schlagen und Vertragen's Bier Halle," and "Schooner, Pretzel, and Weiner—5¢."

Across the river on the left is City Public Service, San Antonio's city-owned gas and electric utility. On the right, just before Navarro Street, a ceramic plaque commemorates the old mill crossing.

On the other side of the bridge, to the left, is more City Public Service facilities. Beyond them rises the Tower Life Building.

After you go under the St. Mary's Street Bridge, the sidewalk ends. The tall building on the left is Granada Homes retirement apartments, which at one time was the Plaza Hotel and later the Hilton Granada.

On the right, in the remodeled former central library, is the new International Center, home to the North American Development Bank. Restaurants and shops will enhance the river level. In the 1870s this was the site of Fire Station No. 1.

Under the building, a channel leads into one of the two marina facilities that service the barges. Before a river parade you can see floats lining up at the St. Mary's Street Bridge. They are lowered to the river by crane. Note also the "traffic" light at the entrance to the bypass channel for the benefit of the barge drivers.

4. **At the end of the walk go up the stairs to the crossover. Cross over the river.**

From the crossover, looking down on the left, you can see the floodgate separating the Big Bend from the man-made flood control bypass channel coming in from the right.

This is a drawbridge-type floodgate. If you look down at the waterline, you can see the scoured-out, semicircular, silvery portion where the gate is raised and lowered. The gate is metal and totally automatic. On the right side of the crossover is the electronically controlled stream-flow measuring station antenna that controls the gate.

5. **Once across the river, go down the steps on the left, turn left, and then left again.**

You are now on the King William section of the River Walk, which was opened in 1984. Note the yellow cable strung in eyehooks at water level. Because this is a deep channel, the cable is there to grab onto should you fall off a barge. The barge drivers sometimes joke, "Just hold onto the cable and the next boat coming by will pick you up, but be sure to have another fare ready."

Under the Nueva Street Bridge is the main marina. Just past it at the main floodgate, a huge iron slab controls the water level upstream. Barges are prevented from going any further by rows of cables. Watch the gate for a few minutes

View of downtown from the Johnson Street Bridge (Photo by Celia Wakefield).

from street level, and you may see it going up and down.

This stretch of the river has been widened and straightened for flood control purposes. Because the San Antonio River had so many twists and loops, the Native Americans called it by a name meaning "drunken old man going home at night."

At the Durango Street Bridge the tower for the Spanish-language television station, Channel 41, rises above the river. On the left, just past the bridge, you can see the backs of the houses in the King William Historic District. When these homes were built in the late 1800s, lawns sloped down to the banks along a narrow river lined with trees, a place for birdwatchers or for itinerants to camp out. The walls and iron fencing are new, part of the River Walk development.

In the 1890s this neighborhood was predominantly German-American and German was the language heard most often; the area was known locally as "Sauerkraut Bend."

On the right, the old U. S. Army Arsenal is now corporate headquarters for H.E.B. Supermarkets. A historical marker gives the building's background.

6. The walk comes up off the river as you approach the Arsenal Street Bridge.

In the little park, notice the tree-filled "hole" that is surrounded by a stone wall. This is the partially restored Guenther's Upper Mill, built in 1868. You will get a better view of its millrace from the other side of the river where there is a marker.

King William Street is one block to the left of the park if you would like to browse through this area of lovely old homes (see Walk 2).

7. Descend back to the river. Turn left. Go under the Arsenal Street Bridge.

In 1893, Jacques Handline murdered a Mr. Maddux and threw the body into the river from the Arsenal Street Bridge. They say Maddux's ghost can be seen on the bridge on dark, stormy nights.

Immediately past the bridge, across the river to the right, is a house completed in late 1989, the first new house built along the river in many years. Its design takes good advantage of the river and downtown views considering that it is built on a very small lot.

Some of the houses along the right bank have recently been renovated.

8. Where the sidewalk ends on this side, go up the stairs to Johnson Street. Cross the bridge, and then turn left, staying on the walk above the river.

The Commerce Street "O. Henry Bridge" was moved here when they widened Commerce Street in 1912. Then, at the time of a widening of the river here, the bridge was stored. All but one spire and a few parts were inadvertantly sold for scrap. The spire was duplicated and the bridge reconstructed in the style of the original. After you cross the bridge and turn left, you are walking past the

San Antonio River Authority, which has responsibility for the development of the river, flood control, and sewage treatment. The River Authority works with the U. S. Army Corps of Engineers on some projects. The actual maintenance and operation of the river is contracted to various city departments. The River Walk itself is a city park.

To your left across the river, the light-colored brick building at the back of the Steves Homestead (open to the public for a fee) is the natatorium Mrs. Steves had built in 1910, when she was seventy years old. She loved to swim and had read of New Yorkers who had indoor pools and could swim whenever they wished. She had her son Ernest, a driller, put in a well to supply water for the pool. Her neighbors were welcomed to use the pool but each day at 2:00 P.M. she rang a bell which meant everyone out so she could have her swim. Neighborhood legend says she swam every day for the rest of her life, which must have been good for her because she lived to age ninety, dying, the legend says, the first day she didn't go swimming.

9. **To take the side trip (1 mile, round trip), go to the end of the sidewalk, cross Guenther Street, and turn left along the sidewalk to the entrance to the Guenther House. To skip the side trip, descend the steps back to the river, and turn left. Pick up commentary at Step 11.**

Carl Guenther, a German immigrant, built his mill in San Antonio in 1859. He opened a second mill in 1868 at Arsenal Street. The Guenther House is now a museum. There is a gift shop and a restaurant that features baked goods made with the mill's Pioneer brand mixes.

10. **Turn right on Alamo Street, and cross it to the Blue Star Art Space (☞ 11).**

In 1986, a group of artists founded this project, which includes galleries, studios, and apartments in an abandoned warehouse district.

Walking along the river through the parking lot back toward Alamo Street, you can see the last of the flood control gates under the Alamo Street Bridge. There are plans to develop the river as far south as the missions.

11. **From the Blue Star Art Space retrace the route by turning right on Alamo and left on Guenther, heading back to the river. Descend the steps, and turn left remaining on this side of the river.**

Past the Arsenal Street Bridge you get a closer view of the Arsenal. H.E.B. offers tours of its facilities to groups.

Guenther's Mill, across the river, was razed in 1926 to widen the river. When this portion of the River Walk was developed, a portion of the mill and millrace was reconstructed. A marker here tells about it. The mill, hanging over the bank of the river alongside the stone dam with its cascade of water, was a favorite subject of artists for decades.

12. At the Nueva Street flood control gate, cross over on the footbridge, descend the steps on the right, and turn right on the walk.

Shortly before Navarro Street is the spot where the Spaniards built a dam that channeled river water into the Pajalache (Concepción) Ditch. It was later utilized by Nat Lewis for his mill. This ditch effectively cut off a peninsula of low-lying land, known as Bowen's Island, where the Tower Life Building now stands. A marker describes how this peninsula became an "island."

Before the advent of piped water, public and private canvas bathhouses floated on pontoons in the river.

A little way past Presa Street is the Arneson River Theatre, named after Edward Arneson, River Walk engineer and district director of the Works Progress Administration (WPA) in the 1930s.

Beyond that is the Hilton Hotel, built in 1967 for the upcoming HemisFair '68. Contractor H. B. Zachry vowed the hotel would be finished in 200 days by using the revolutionary modular construction method. Each room module was built and completely furnished in a factory on San Antonio's south side, then transported here on trucks and lifted into the building frame. He missed his deadline, however; it took 202 days.

13. Come around the bend, and go under the Market Street Bridge. Turn right onto the RiverCenter/Convention Center extensions. Keep to the right, and follow the path to the Convention Center Basin.

The extension to the Convention Center opened in 1968, as part of the Hemis-Fair '68 project. When you get to the Convention Center, you will see on the left the Lila Cockrell Theater for the Performing Arts, which is faced by the mosaic mural *Confluence of Civilizations* by Mexican artist Juan O'Gorman. The right half shows the culture, technology, and history of the Old World, the left side that of the New World. The two meet in the center where they form a new civilization. Surrounding the turnaround basin are meeting halls. The outdoor area was designed to be used as a reception area. On the right, inside the door to the River and Patio rooms, is a two-story mural by Carlos Mérida.

14. Walk around the basin, and head back on the other side. Follow the path to the right around the hotel and under the arched steel bridge to the RiverCenter extension.

(Restrooms, phone, and food are located in the RiverCenter.)

This extension opened in 1988 to serve the new Marriott Hotel and River-Center, a shopping, dining, and entertainment complex. RiverCenter is located on the site of the old Degen Brewery, which was owned by the Menger Hotel a century ago.

15. **Walk around the RiverCenter turnaround, and continue on to the right back to the Big Bend, turning right to return to the Hyatt.**

Just past RiverCenter is a statue of Saint Anthony, patron saint of the city and of the river. On June 13, 1691, a troop of Spanish explorers camped on this river while on their way to found missions in East Texas. The padres celebrated mass and named the small stream "El Río San Antonio de Padua," the Saint Anthony of Padua River, because it was the Saint's feast day.

Diane on the Johnson Street Bridge, formerly the "O. Henry Bridge" that spanned Commerce Street. (Photo by Celia Wakefield)

5 Bridges

Features: Another walk along the river, this time with some bridge stories

Distance: 3.7 miles (5.9 k)

Time: 1 hour and 30 minutes

Nights: No

Wheelchair Accessible: Yes. See Comments

Restrooms, Water, Phone: At start and RiverCenter

Restaurants: Many along the route

Getting there: Start in front of the Alamo.

Comments:

Although this entire walk cannot be taken in a wheelchair, portions of the River Walk are accessible. There is a River Walk accessibility map available at the Visitor Center across from Alamo Plaza.

1. **From the Alamo turn right and walk towards Houston Street, go left on Houston, and turn right on Jefferson.**

After you turn on Jefferson, you pass Travis Park; St. Mark's Episcopal Church, whose carillon marks the quarter hour; the Bell Telephone / AT&T Building with its rococo terra cotta ornamentation; the Vietnam and Korean Veterans memorials; and the Municipal Auditorium.

On the right across from the auditorium is the old Maverick-Carter house, now law offices. Mrs. Carter, an astronomer and Texas poet-laureate, added the observatory. At 4th Street, the First Baptist Church is on the right. Across from it, the 4th Street Inn serves a generous, inexpensive lunch from 11:00 A.M. to 2:00 P.M. weekdays in an attractive, friendly setting. This restaurant is run by volunteers. The proceeds are used to support programs for the homeless.

2. **Cross Fourth Street. Turn left to the bridge.**

To test the strength of an iron bridge built here in the late 1800s, the builders assembled a U. S. cavalry troop at the bridge and then had the soldiers charge across it at full gallop. Fortunately, the bridge held. Many of the bridges have been replaced over the years. Only three of the original five iron bridges remain downtown. One has been moved to the King William Historic District and another one to Brackenridge Park.

3. Go down the stairs to the river. Turn left.

Each bridge is different. The first bridge, at Lexington, is a simple concrete design.

The Richmond Street Bridge, with its blue and orange tile, dates from 1930, and is of steel and concrete construction.

Navarro Street crosses the river three times. This gives you some idea of how both the river and the street twist and turn. Louise Lomax wrote in *San Antonio's River:* ". . . one could see it [river] at so many different places within so few city blocks." And Peyton Green in *San Antonio, City in the Sun,* said that in one mile the river passed under thirteen bridges ending up less than 800 yards from where it started. St. Mary's Street also crosses the river three times, and Presa does so twice. With the advent of the river extensions to RiverCenter and the Convention Center, both Commerce Street and Market Street now cross the river twice also.

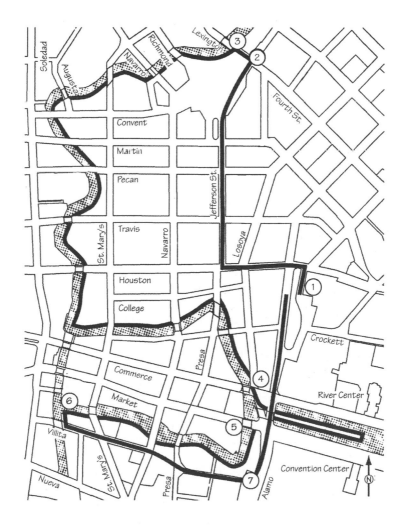

The river was spanned at the first of the three St. Mary's Street crossings in the late 1920s to extend the street toward Brackenridge Park. At that time St. Mary's Street north of the river was called Oakland Street. This bridge has built-in drinking fountains at street level. If you look up, you can see the spout where the fountain drained into the river. The fountains no longer function.

The 1890 Augusta Street Bridge is one of three iron bridges remaining downtown built by The Berlin Bridge and Iron Works of East Berlin, Connecticut. The cast-iron end posts of this and the former Commerce Street Bridge that is now on Johnson Street in the King William Historic District were unique to the bridges that the company constructed in San Antonio. The company also had to plan San Antonio's bridges so that they did not obstruct the parade floats San Antonio had even back then. You can cross this bridge to get to the Southwest Craft Center in the old Ursuline Academy (Walk 1).

The 1898 Berlin Bridge and Iron Works catalog states, "Although we are prone to think of Texas as a partially populated state of cattle ranges and agriculture bordering on the wild and wooly ideas of civilization and advancement, nevertheless, the people of that vast empire of a state are more advanced in their ideas of what constitutes good bridges than many . . . who have never crossed the Mississippi River nor stepped foot within her borders. Bridges with plank floors are relegated to the past in this enterprising place, and only bridges with solid iron and concrete floors are given consideration." The San Antonio Berlin bridges may be the only surviving ones in Texas; they are certainly among the few remaining in the United States.

The support trusses on the iron bridges were constructed with a system of triangles (that shape being the most resistant to distortion) called king posts, which are the bridges' most distinguishing feature. The simple king post truss, as seen on this bridge, can span only a short distance. Longer distances are spanned by overlapping triangles. In the early 1900s, it was found that by turning the triangles on the side and forming a "K," the system would support a span of eight hundred feet.

The Convent, Martin, and Pecan Street bridges are simple concrete expansions. Pecan Street once had a narrow, wooden footbridge barely visible behind a dense growth of trees and shrubs at either end; it was known as "Lovers' Bridge." Many a couple met there, and, so one report says, one young lover took her life there in the arms of the man who had betrayed her affections.

Near the Travis Street Bridge, there was a dam in the 1870s that provided power to the four-story Laux Mill (on the site of the present Milam Building).

Houston Street in the late 1880s was the end of the run for the tourist river steamer "Hilda," which started from the Old Mill at South Presa near Market.

The walk makes a 90-degree turn at the bypass channel. Before you turn, note the sluice-type floodgate under the footbridge which controls the amount of water coming into the Big Bend of the river.

Crockett Street Bridge looking south along the Big Bend

The next bridge is the second of the St. Mary's Street crossings. The first of San Antonio's iron bridges spanned the river here in 1869, giving the boys attending St. Mary's School (now La Mansión del Río Hotel) direct access so they no longer had to detour by way of Commerce Street. That bridge is now in Brackenridge Park.

At the second crossing of Navarro Street is a 1922 steel and concrete bridge.

The Presa Street Bridge is also made of steel plate and concrete and was built in 1925 using a simple truss.

At Crockett Street is an 1891 Berlin bridge. The netting under this and the previous bridge, as you may have guessed, is to keep birds from roosting on the support beams in this very popular tourist area. Otherwise it would be almost impossible to walk along here without receiving an undesired souvenir of the River Walk.

Officially, the bridge over Commerce Street is not the Commerce Street Bridge but the Jones Bridge, named for Augustus Jones, mayor of San Antonio from 1912 to 1913, who died in office the year before the bridge was completed. (However, should you refer to it as the Jones Bridge, some people might think you meant the bridge on Jones Street by the San Antonio Museum of Art, which is actually the Grand Avenue Bridge. Many streets changed names throughout the city's history.) The present Commerce Street bridge survived the 1921 flood that destroyed many of the downtown bridges.

There has been some sort of bridge at Commerce Street since a wooden one in 1736 connected the civilian and military communities of San Fernando (present day Main and Military plazas), to the religious and learning center of Mission San Antonio (the Alamo).

There seems to be a propensity for nicknaming Commerce Street bridges for writers. An 1870s masonry bridge was known as "Lanier's Bridge." Poet Sydney Lanier moved to San Antonio for his health and wrote lovingly of his adopted city: "One may take one's stand on the Commerce Street Bridge and involve oneself in the life that goes by this way and that." This is still true today.

The first iron bridge in San Antonio, and possibly in the state of Texas, was built here in 1880. It became known as the "O. Henry Bridge" after the author mentioned a bridge in his story, "A Fog in Santone." A sign prominently displayed on this bridge gave strict warning, in the three major languages of San Antonio:

> Walk your horse over this bridge, or you will be fined.
> Schnelles reiten über diese Brücke ist verboten.
> Anda despacio con su caballo o teme la ley.

That iron and wood plank bridge, with its cast-iron abutments, now spans the river at Johnson Street in the King William Historic District.

The drinking fountain, titled *First Inhabitant,* on the present 1914 concrete Commerce Street bridge was the first commission for a public work for Waldine Tauch, a protégé of Pompeo Coppini.

4. Turn left onto the RiverCenter/Convention Center extension.

The first two bridges, Losoya and South Alamo Street, date from 1967, when the River Walk extension was excavated to the new Convention Center.

From the first footbridge, facing toward the Convention Center extension, you can see the Market Street Bridge. It gained fame in 1985 when the Fairmount Hotel, the largest building ever moved on wheels, was towed over the bridge to its present location on South Alamo Street. It was not certain whether the bridge could bear the load so a scaffold support system was built under it. To test how well they did their job, one of the workmen wedged an empty beer bottle into a space between the scaffolding and the bridge. If the bridge sagged at all, the bottle would break. It survived intact, but we'll never know whether it was because of the scaffolding or the strength of the bridge itself.

The series of footbridges connecting RiverCenter, the Marriott, and the Convention Center were completed in conjunction with the RiverCenter extension in 1988.

(Restrooms, phones, and food are located at RiverCenter.)

> **Cross footbridge and turn right on other side of river to return to main channel.**

5. Turn left on the main channel (the Big Bend).

The Market Street Bridge at the Hilton Hotel dates from 1926.

A plaque on the footbridge leading to the Arneson River Theater stage honors Rosita Fernandez, who sang here in the Fiesta Noche del Río show for many years.

The 1890 Berlin bridge at Presa Street is the oldest of these bridges still in its original location. Here you can see in detail the cast-iron rosettes you may have noticed on some of the other iron bridges.

Presa means dam in Spanish. A dam here in the mid-1700s channeled water into the Concepción (Pajalache) Ditch to Mission Concepción to the south. During the American era prior to the War, Nat Lewis built a mill on the river near here.

The first English-language San Antonio newspaper, "The Western Texan," was published in the Old Mill building in 1848. In those days, with virtually no American settlement between San Antonio and El Paso, San Antonio was the "western edge of civilization." Hence, the paper's name.

The next bridge, a 1922 concrete structure with three lovely arches, spans Navarro Street at its third crossing of the river and is known as the Mill Bridge. The lamps on this and other bridges along this stretch of the river are a recent addition. A tile plaque across the river commemorates this as the fording spot used by all who passed this way: the Native Americans, the Spanish priests, the soldiers, the explorers. It was here, at the wide, shallow part of the river, that you washed your buggy a hundred years ago.

Around the bend from the Navarro Bridge is a historical marker that tells about Bowen's Island. Past that, note the circles in the concrete railing alongside the river. Robert H. H. Hugman, architect of the River Walk, designed the circles to represent millstones as a visual reminder of the Old Mill.

The last St. Mary's Street Bridge is made of concrete, and was built in 1915.

While the red sandstone courthouse rises as ever behind the bridge, the area right of the bridge underwent many changes in 1996–97. On the east side, the San Antonio Drug Company building that stood empty for so many years is now a hotel. On the west side of the bridge, the former main library building is now the International Center due to open in 1998.

6. **At the bypass channel, go up the staircase, turn left and then left again on Villita.**

Heading back to the Alamo, you walk past the Granada Apartments (once a luxury hotel, now senior citizen apartments), the Tower Life Building, then under City Public Service, and through La Villita.

7. **Turn left on Alamo Street, and walk back to the start.**

6 Mission Trail North

Features: Mission Concepción with side trips to Yturri-Edmunds Historic Site and the Lonestar Buckhorn Museum.

Distance: 6.0 miles (9.6 k) + 2.0-mile (3.2 k) side trip to Buckhorn Museum. See Comments
1.4 miles (2.2k) side trip to Yturri-Edmunds Historic Site. See Comments

Time: 3 hrs. 30 min. + 1 hr.-side trip + browse time at Buckhorn
.5 hour side trip + browse time to Yturri-Edmunds

Night: No

Wheelchair Accessible: Yes, to mission. See Comments

Restrooms, Water, Phone: At start, mission, and side trips

Restaurant: Several near start

Getting There: **Car:** Park in the lot at Mission County Park, off Padre near White Street.
Bus: No. 42 Roosevelt. Get off on White, cross Roosevelt, and walk past the drive-in theater to Padre. Turn right to park entrance. To return get back on the bus on the opposite side of Roosevelt.

Comments:

Mission Concepción is open every day from 9:00 A.M. to 5:00 P.M.

The Yturri-Edmunds Historic Site changes its hours from time to time. Call 543-8237 for current times (admission charge).

The Buckhorn Museum is currently located in the old Lone Star Brewery and is open from 9:00 A.M. to 5:00 P.M. daily (admission charge). It will relocate downtown at Houston and Presa Streets in August, 1998 (admission charge).

This is a long walk without much shade. In hot weather, it is best taken early in the day. Carry water. Walk distance may be cut in half by taking two cars and leaving one at your final destination: the Mission, Yturri-Edmunds, or Buckhorn Museum. While the Yturri-Edmunds Historic Site and the Buckhorn Museum are both well worth a visit, the walk to get there is not particularly scenic. You might want to drive over.

1. **With your back to the park recreation building, walk to the right around the children's playground to the paved footpath leading off to the right.**

The San Antonio River channel has been widened and straightened so that it will contain a flood so severe it occurs on average once every one hundred years.

The City of San Antonio, with the help of Federal funding, is beginning a project to improve the banks of the river and install a hike/bike trail from the Alamo to the missions.

In the 1700s, mission farm lands, called *labores*, ran along the river. This side belonged to Mission San José. A dam, or *presa*, upstream channeled water into irrigation ditches called *acequias*. The Pajalache *acequia* for Mission Concepción went due south from a dam where Presa Street crosses the river and proceeded along what is now St. Mary's Street. The street was known as Garden Street in the 1800s because those who lived along it used the water to create lush gardens. Some references say the *acequias* were wide enough to float boats on.

Further along are the three graceful arches of the Roosevelt Avenue bridge whose massive pillars were built to withstand the pressures brought by flood waters that can last from a few hours to days—even weeks. Water flows from the confluence of Alazán, Apache, and San Pedro creeks into the river north of here.

After you pass under Roosevelt, you come to the Riverside Golf Course. At the end, where you come to Mission Road, note the separate bridge and tunnel connecting the two sides of the golf course.

2. Turn right off the footpath onto Mission Road.

Near here, on the other side of the river, water in the Pajalache Ditch flowed back into the river.

Mission Road connects all the missions south of the city, except Mission Espada, and is designated as "Mission Trail." The bridge, built in 1961, has embedded tile signs that give the traveler directions to the various missions.

To the left, upriver, the long-gone San José dam crossed the natural channel about 240 years ago. It backed water into the San José *acequia*.

To the right, on the other side of the river, golfers swing their way over the spot where Teddy Roosevelt drilled the Rough Riders in the spring of 1898. Huge, Victorian-style exposition buildings and a race track stood near the present clubhouse.

Further along Mission Road (at the end of the mobile home park), there is a historical marker under a stand of trees that tells about Mission San Francisco de la Nájera. The last record of this mission was in 1726.

The red brick building across from Mission Concepción is a Catholic children's home.

3. At Felisa Street, turn right to the mission entrance.

(Restooms are located in the visitors center.)

Most of Mission Nuestra Señora de la Purísima Concepción de Acuña (Our Lady of the Immaculate Conception of Acuña) is now gone. What remains is mostly original. Founded in 1731, the mission originally had single-story dwellings that surrounded a courtyard in front of the church. The well, with its original shaft, has never gone dry.

Inside the church, in the room to the right of the main door, is the baptistery with its baptismal font. The room to the left of the entrance is the confessional. When the mission was restored in the 1850s, wall paintings of saints and five depictions of Mary were plastered over. The church itself is still in use, belonging to the Catholic Archdiocese. The grounds and other buildings are under the auspices of the National Park Service.

Walk down the corridor of the *convento*. On the ceiling of the last room on the left is "The Face of God." Before being restored a few years ago, only the eye showed and was thus referred to as "The Eye of God." Standing in the arched breezeway outside these rooms in the summer is proof the Spanish priests in the mid-1700s knew about aligning breezeways and doors with the prevailing southeastern winds. A slide show in a room back here tells of the mission's history. An iron gate leads to a stairway where you can go up to a room that overlooks the altar.

4. From the mission, walk ahead to Mission Road.

The large grotto outside the mission was built in the 1930s with Edwards Plateau limestone from the Hill Country.

5. Turn left on Theo, following it to the monument at the corner of Concepción Park.

Just before Christmas, the local residents perform *posadas* that reenact the

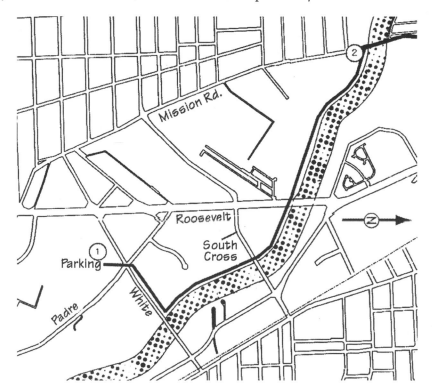

search by Mary and Joseph for an inn, a custom brought here from Spain and Mexico. The roles are traditionally handed down within families. Although performed in Spanish, the pageantry of the *posadas* goes beyond the need for language. The *posadas* are a moving experience, no matter what your religious beliefs. They are performed first in the mission and then moved here to the street.

Continuing down Theo, you come to a softball park built along an old bend in the river. A monument commemorates the Battle of Concepción that involved Jim Bowie and Stephen F. Austin. Descend the stairs next to it and walk about twenty paces where you will be standing in the channel of the river as it existed until the late 1950s. The line of trees curving off to the left was the old riverbank. The channel was straightened so it could carry more water than the natural, twisting river, thus alleviating flooding in this area.

Ahead at the corner of the park (just before the pool) is a monument to Richard Andrews, the first Texan to die in the Texas Revolution.

Across the street, the Mission Pump Station is one of two in San Antonio that gets water both naturally from artesian wells and by pumping.

6. **Retrace your steps back to Mission Road. To take the side trip, turn left and continue on Mission Road. To skip the side trip, turn right and retrace your steps back to the parking lot.**

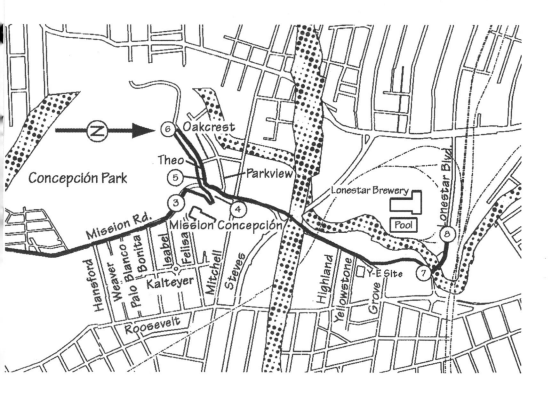

Mission Concepción (Photo by Celia Wakefield)

Note: See Comments before taking side trip.

Next to the mission is the former St. John's Seminary, which was built in 1915, and is now home to the Patrician Movement, a drug rehabilitation program of the Catholic Church noted for its high success rate.

The old mill at the Yturri-Edmunds Historic Site

At Mission Road and Grove Street is the Yturri-Edmunds Historic Site. The house dates from the mid-1800s and is one of the few remaining adobe brick buildings in San Antonio. The mill probably dates from the mid-1700s. Vincenta Yturri married Ernest Edmunds in 1861. Their daughter, Ernestine, who was a dedicated teacher in San Antonio for thirty-five years, willed the property to the San Antonio Conservation Society. Other buildings have been moved here for preservation. The millstone has been reworked so you can watch corn being ground just as it was in the past.

7. **Turn left on Lone Star Boulevard, and enter the grounds of the Lone Star Buckhorn Museum.**

The entrance fee to the Buckhorn Museum includes a tour and a free beer or root beer at the cherry and marble back bar from the original Buckhorn Saloon downtown. There are other exhibits on the grounds, including O. Henry's house.

8. **Turn around, and retrace the route back to the Mission County Park parking lot.**

7 Mission Trail South

Features: Mission San José, Mission San Juan Capistrano, and Espada Dam and Acequia

Distance: 9.7 miles (15 k) miles round trip. May be taken in shorter segments. See Comments

Time: 5.0 hrs. round trip. See Comments

Nights: No.

Wheelchair Accessible: Yes

Restrooms, Water, Phone: At start and at missions

Restaurants: At Mission San José, across Roosevelt Street, there are several restaurants. Picnic facilities are found all along the walk.

Getting There: **Car:** Park in the lot at Mission County Park, off Padre near White.

Bus: No. 42 Roosevelt. Get off at San José Mission. Begin walk at Step 4. To return, get back on the bus across the street.

Comments:

The Missions are open daily from 9:00 A.M. to 5:00 P.M.

Because there is little shade on this walk, in hot weather it is best taken early in the morning. Carry water.

This is a very long walk if taken round trip. It can be shortened by taking two cars and leaving one at your final destination. Here is a breakdown of distances: from park to San Jose Mission is 1.8 miles, 45 minutes walking time, plus .6 miles, 45 minutes to tour mission (does not include time at Visitor Center). San Juan Mission from San Jose Mission is 2.7 miles, 1.5 hours. Add .4 miles to walk nature trail and grounds. Total distance one-way is 5.5 miles, 3.5 hours. The return trip, being more direct, is approximately 4.2 miles, 1.5 hours.

For those who enjoy walking the Mission Trail, news of the construction of a hike/bike trail from the Alamo to Mission Espada, federally funded through the Intermodal Surface Transportation Efficiency Act (oh the titles they come up with!), or ISTEA ("ice tea"), is as refreshing as the drink. There will be a "wet" road that runs alongside the river designated as a hike/bike trail, and a "dry" vehicular road running at street level. Plans to extend the River Walk from where it ends in the King William Historic District all the way to Espada Dam are still in the discussion stage.

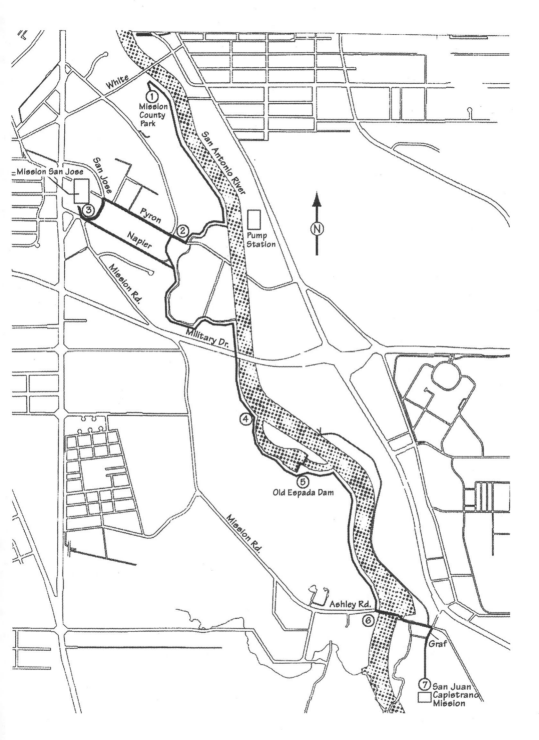

1. **Standing in the parking lot with your back to the park recreation buildings, turn left, and walk along the fence line. Turn to the right along the
   river. Down by the dam, stay on the paved path that veers to the right.**

On the other side of the fence from the parking lot, on weekends especially,
you might see the charros practicing. Charros are the country gentlemen of
Mexico. When the Spaniards brought the horse to the New World, it became a
status symbol. Until the 1910 revolution in Mexico, haciendas existed in a type
of feudal system where generation after generation of families served the ranch
owner, who took care of all their needs. The rancher took pride in his horse-
manship, showing off to family and friends on weekends. He spent huge sums
of money for ornate saddles and adopted a style of dress that included tight
breeches, a short, tight jacket, and big sombrero (called a *cocula*) that was often
ornamented with silver.

A charreada, then, is an exhibition of riding and cattle-working skills that
tests the rider's control of his mount and his use of the lariat. It differs in several ways from our rodeo: the rider stays on the bull until it stops bucking or
bucks him off. The charro brings down a calf by grasping the tail and winding
it around his own ankle, pulling the calf off balance. There are death-defying
riding exhibitions. The charro rides for honor, not money.

When you turn right alongside the river, one of the first things you may notice is that it looks like a big ditch. It has been widened and straightened for
flood control purposes. Trails and landscaping will some day soften this stark
appearance.

Across the river, the beige-colored brick building with the collapsed roof is
the old Hot Wells Resort. Some drillers back in the early 1890s, looking for oil,
tapped instead into a source of 104° F sulphur water 2,000 feet deep that flowed
300,000 gallons a day. A spa soon developed. Mule-driven trolley cars brought
people from town to a three-story, Bavarian-style hotel. With its galleries, fountains, and wicker furniture, the hotel's amenities and the healing powers of the
water made Hot Wells world-renowned for many years. It was destroyed by
fire in the late 1940s. Now that modern doctors are more likely to prescribe
medications than hot mineral water therapy for people's various ills, nobody
has wanted to take on the expensive gamble of rebuilding the resort, but the
well is still there.

Farther along, the baseball field on the right is Spencer Field.

Beyond Spencer Field is Padre Park. At this point, on the other side of the
river, is a new limestone-block pump station. The river channel on this side of
the pump station has been narrowed to force the water into a pool deep enough
for the pump to work. Water is pumped out of this channel into the original
channel, which is out of sight. The original channel carries water to San Juan
Mission where it will be used to irrigate the living history museum farm fields
planned for the mission.

Past the pump station as the path veers right, you will see mustang grape
vines crawling over the pecan and black walnut trees. With its high acid and

low sugar content, this grape doesn't make the best wine, but the pioneers used it for that purpose. On your left now is the original channel of the river. The elephant ear plants are not native. They were probably brought from Mexico but have now gone wild.

2.   **Where the path comes up to Pyron and Padre roads, turn right on Pyron, left on San José Street, and right on Napier to the Mission San José Visitor Center.**

The Visitor Center, opened in 1996, has interesting, well-laid-out displays. A beautifully produced film depicts the arrival of the Spaniards, and the changes they wrought. It also shows how the missions looked when they were brightly painted—giving the effect of tile. A fiber optic diorama shows the history of development along the San Antonio River. This Center is a welcome addition to the mission.

From the Visitor Center walk to the entrance of the mission. Turn left.

Except for the original limestone walls of the church, the mission is completely rebuilt with sandstone quarried in the 1930s. As you tour, assume everything is rebuilt unless otherwise stated.

On your left are typical living quarters of the Native-American converts brought into the mission. The original area probably had earthen floors and certainly didn't have railroad ties as headers above the doorway. The furniture in the model is probably quite authentic. Outside the quarters is a typical oven. You build a fire inside to get the rocks hot, remove the fire and ashes, and put the bread in. All the small rooms were living quarters for the natives who were here basically to become lower class citizens of the Spanish empire. They had to learn Spanish, convert to Catholicism, and learn how to take orders.

As you walk down the row of living quarters, notice the rain spouts. These were important because they drained rainwater quickly from the thatch and earthen roofs.

Within the compound are trees and plants typical of the Spanish era, all useful in some way. The huisache has an edible seed pod. The natives used yucca, also known as mother-in-law's tongue, as needle and thread. The leaf fibers can be separated by pounding with a rock. The holly-like agarita bush has edible berries. Acorns from the live oak, although edible, are not tasty. There are also pomegranate trees on the mission grounds.

Each corner of the mission compound has an entrance. It is believed that the one by the granary was the main gate. Before the restoration, Roosevelt Street ran through here. Also before the restoration, nothing of any of the buildings showed above ground except for the church. The foundation stones were located under ground and built upon.

The walls of the granary are supported by flying buttresses. A display at the far end gives an audiovisual story of a typical day at the mission.

Beyond the granary, the series of smaller rooms were originally work-rooms for weaving and other crafts. Now they represent the priests' quarters. The type of stove you see in the kitchen is still used in Mexico. As protection against Indian attack, there are no windows in the outside wall. In the living room, above the shelf, is an example of the much used conch shell design. In Roman mythology, Neptune caused Venus to be reborn, pictured as rising out of the ocean on a shell. Christians substituted Mary being reborn in Christ, and shells have become a religious symbol.

When you exit under the grape arbor, immediately turn left to go outside the walls. To the right, the bottom half of the wall is of light-colored stones, possibly some of the originals found here. The stones above are darker and rather long and thin, quarried in the 1930s. Further along the path you cross over the Acequia Madre, the mother (or principal) ditch. The water flowed from the left through this irrigation canal. A dam between here and downtown backed up enough water for the natives to use their canoes. The women fished and did their wash in the *acequia.* Near the bridge you can see some of the steps.

Walk over to the old mill, which has a historical marker. Go down the steps to the bottom to see the wheel. When you come back up, walk to the other side of the building. This is a norse mill. There is a gate that could be pulled up to allow water from the *acequia* to flow into this hole. The narrow opening in the mill's wall probably held the pulley or rope that the person inside could pull to close the outlet below so the hole could fill with water. The amount of water in the hole, when released, provided the pressure to turn the wheel. The reason for locating the mill here just outside the walls, rather than putting it more conveniently four blocks away on the river (which would have eliminated the necessity for going through this laborious process) was that in case of danger, you were close to the protective walls of the mission.

Across the path from the hole is a stone-lined excavation where sugar was processed from the cane grown here.

Continue along the path, turning to the right at the corner. (Restrooms and vending machines are located here.)

At the entrance to the church, the uppermost statue is St. Joseph (San José), the one on the left is St. Dominic, and the one on the right, St. Francis of Assissi. Just above the doorway is Our Lady of Guadalupe. St. Joachim on the left and St. Ann on the right are the parents of Mary. We ran across an 1854 reference to soldiers who "did not fail to improve the opportunity for showing at the same time their skill in arms and their contempt for the Mexican belief (Catholicism) . . .," by using the statues for target practice.

Reconstruction of the church in the 1930s was done from the original plans and drawings and from remembrances. The graffiti around the door (don't add to it!) dates as far back as the 1840s.

Above the left bottom window, you can see traces of the brightly colored geometric designs that originally decorated the front of the church. The original doors were still here in the 1870s to 1880s, although hanging askew. A story says that one of the big railroad magnates came here to see the ruins of the missions. He made what seemed a generous offer to the people who attended church here: he would take the doors back to New York and have the finest craftsmen restore them, and then he would return them. He said it was a beautiful church and they were deserving people, and he wanted to do this for them. Naturally, they agreed. He took the doors away, and they were never seen again.

As you walk through the church, notice the water stains on the very porous walls, which get damp in a heavy rain. The dome and roof of the main sanctuary collapsed in 1868. After this, services took place in the sacristy next to it.

Inside the sacristy, above the doorway, you can see another example of the scalloped conch shell design. The doors leading outside are original, although some panels (uncarved) had to be replaced. The artist who did the copies of the front doors used this door, as well as photographs, for reference.

San José Mission is popular for its Mariachi Mass, which is held every Sunday at noon.

Immediately after exiting the sacristy, turn left. Look up to the left to the second-story door. Bordering the door are thin, irregular, obviously handmade Spanish bricks.

The columns outside are the remains of the priests' quarters, or *convento*. The structure had two stories. The fact that some arches are pointed (Gothic) means they are not the original Spanish construction. When Benedictine priests came here from Pennsylvania in 1859, they saw cracks in the arches and were afraid the structure might come down, so they built a reinforcement, putting in these Gothic arches of American factory-made brick. Except for the new arches, the *convento* is original. If you look closely, on the underside of some of the arches, you can see the remnants of the Spanish painted designs. Above the fourth arch away from the church, on the inside corner, is a gauge that the National Park Service installed to measure the width of the crack. With this information they know what needs to be strengthened. In 1984, when we had a bad drought, the crack was wider than two of Mark's fingers.

Go up the stairs and to the right. On the bell tower side of the church is the famous Rose Window, also known as Rosa's Window. One very romantic story says that Spanish emigrant and stonemason Pedro Huizar, upon hearing of the death of his beloved Rosa at the hand of English pirates as she sailed to the New World, carved the roses on the window and named it in her honor. This tale says he took a vow of celibacy and died unmarried, and beloved by all. The facts, however, show that Huizar was born in Mexico, had two wives (neither of them named Rosa), and fathered many children. (His descendants still live in San Antonio.) Besides, the National Park Service historians say the flower design probably represents pomegranate flowers, not roses. It is more likely that the window got its name from the early 1800s custom of the priest giving a benediction from in front of the window on the feast day of St. Rose of Lima, Peru. St. Rose was the first New World Catholic saint.

The top half of the bell tower collapsed in the early 1900s and has been rebuilt. Inside are the original hand-hewn, solid log steps.

Continue around the mission compound. This is a national park, although all the buildings and grounds belong to the Catholic Church. Everything other than the church itself is run by the National Park Service.

The gate next to the church is open on Sunday for mass. The building outside it provides quarters for the parish priest. Along this wall, on both sides of the sidewalk, are the foundations of other buildings that were not rebuilt. Stone, thatch, log, and adobe buildings occupied the whole of the mission's interior courtyard.

Go inside the corner bastion. Here a cannon would be moved around to fire through any of the bottom holes. Soldiers on the ledge would shoot from smaller holes with their muskets. Thousands of people going through here since the 1930s have had a guide tell them the dome was to keep off flaming arrows. Mark has asked his own tour groups what they thought it was for, and that's what they have come up with. However, the Native-Americans in Texas never shot flaming arrows—except in movies. Actually, archaeologists have found there was never even a dome. Instead of a ledge, there was a complete floor, probably with a stairway. Similar structures in Mexico show this is most likely how it was.

As you head back along the south wall, there are two rooms with photographic exhibits.

3. **Exit the mission. Walk straight ahead down Napier Avenue. At footpath, turn right along river.**

As you walk back towards the present river channel, you cross two wooden suspension bridges over the original channel. Because these narrow, twisting channels caused so much flooding, the U. S. Army Corps of Engineers widened the river for flood control. Fishing is permitted in the river with a license. Although swimming is illegal, in hot weather, the kids cannot resist taking advantage of the river's coolness.

4. **When you reach the big dam on the left, cross the road to the right down to Espada Dam.**

Espada Dam is the best preserved of the Spanish Colonial diversion dams in the United States and was completed between 1735 and 1740. It is constructed of layers of brush weighted by loose rock and gravel and earth thrown in front, the rock cemented together gradually by deposits of lime salts from the water. Some experts say the dam was designed incorrectly. However, Spanish dam building at that time was considered to be without equal. In his report on Espada Dam, National Park Service historian Arthur Gomez says there is ample evidence that the dam was intentionally slanted downstream, its purpose being to raise the level of water and divert it into the *acequia*. It is believed this also protected it against long-term erosion. Dams built for modern reservoirs slant upstream.

To the right is a stone monument describing the dam. From the monument, looking to the opposite side of the river, you can see a bit of the mission *acequia*. The water backed up by the dam represents the original channel of the river, now bypassed by the flood control channel behind you. This *acequia* is the only one still flowing. The dam was dedicated as a National Historical Site by President John F. Kennedy the day before he was assassinated. As a memorial, a tree from the Kennedy estate in Hyannisport was planted here. It didn't survive. A new tree was dedicated by Ted Kennedy. Unfortunately, it failed also, that variety not being able to adapt to the South Texas climate.

5. **From the Kennedy Memorial, walk along the path, through the parking lot, cross the suspension bridge, and continue to where the trail ends at Ashley Road.**

After you cross the suspension bridge, across on the left is the Howell Oil Refinery, the only refinery in San Antonio.

The concrete raceway in the flood channel at this point leads to two openings. This is what carries the natural flow of the river. Flood waters will not fit through these openings; they'll go down the widened channel, thereby not endangering the mission.

6. **Turn left on Ashley, crossing the flood channel and then the concrete bridge. Turn right on Graf, and follow the visitor parking signs to the mission entrance.**

After you turn onto Ashley, the ruin in the field on the left is Berg's Mill, a three-story mill uncovered in 1959 during the channel widening. At various times it was used as a sawmill, a grist mill, and a wool scouring mill.

The second bridge on the right goes over the original river channel that is upstream from the nature trail you'll go on next. Looking down on the left, you can see the water coming from the tunnel put in by the Army Corps of Engineers.

To the left side of the parking lot at the mission is a field that the National Park Service will develop as a demonstration farm that grows crops common to the Spanish Colonial period.

The San Juan Woodlands Trail (one-third mile long) behind the mission offers a glimpse of how the river looked in its natural state. This woodland is a galaría forest, a term used to describe a narrow band of trees along a river rather than an extended woodland. The river flows rapidly here. At the water's edge grow native bamboo and mustang grape vines. What fun the young natives must have had swinging out over the river on these vines. There are inviting swimming holes along here, but there is also a "No Swimming" ordinance in effect. Because the river runs fairly swiftly and straight, and because of the tremendous number of trees and bushes with their extensive root systems into the banks, there is little erosion along here, resulting in steeper banks than at other

San Juan Capistrano Mission (Photo by Celia Wakefield)

places. Notice the thick stands of bamboo. Del Wineger in his book, *Explorers of Texas*, tells of the early Texas pioneers coming upon bamboo thickets so dense and extensive they had to detour for miles. You no longer find such growths because the pioneers burned them.

7. **The entrance to the San Juan Capistrano Mission is straight ahead as you come off the nature trail.**

As you emerge from the arches, the portion in the right corner was the first church. These walls replace it. Straight ahead, past the well, is the foundation of the first real church, which was exposed a few years ago by archaeologists.

Walk to the corner of the compound, and turn left to the ruins of an unfinished church. Though small, it was to have had a domed roof and domed octagonal sacristy. A great smallpox epidemic in the 1750s left over half the native population dead, creating a labor shortage. A few years ago, when archaeologists excavated the floor of the church, they found a mass grave attributed to this period.

Cut across the courtyard to the present church. The parishioners will tell you that the largest of the three bells is original; the National Park Service says that it is not. When you enter the church, go up to the altar. This is the only mission in San Antonio to have three original statues. At the back of the altar is a small statue of St. John of Capistrano. Made in Mexico, it had been in East Texas in the 1690s and came to this mission about 1740. The church at that time was the one whose foundation stones are exposed outside. To the left and right of the altar are statues of Jesus and Mary, which are estimated to be about 450 years old. Under the figures' skirts, Jesus has only one leg and Mary has no legs. This was the custom in the Mexican village where they were made; they were formed this way so they could be carried on poles in processions. The secret to their realistic appearance is the corn shucks and the mashed corncob glue they are made of in a process resembling that of making papier-maché. The statues' eyes heighten the impression of reality.

On the steps to the altar, on the right side, look for the clay tile plaque in the floor. The Coahuitecan remains referred to are those of the mission's native inhabitants. They had been on display in the museum next door until federal law deemed such remains had to be buried. When you exit the church, head back to the entrance, stopping by the museum along the way.

The two shingle-roofed buildings past the church look old but were built in 1968 by the Catholic Church as residences, using stones from the old walls.

Leaving the mission (omit the jog to ☞ 3), retrace your steps back to the start.

As you walk back, you are following the same route used 250 years ago between Missions San Juan and San José.

The Espada Dam after a heavy rain.

8 Fort Sam Houston, The Quadrangle

Features: The Quadrangle with its menagerie, the stables, and Staff and Infantry Posts

Distance: 3.5 miles (5.3 k)

Time: 2 hours

Night: Yes, but Quadrangle not open

Restrooms, Water, Phone: Inside the Quadrangle

Restaurants: At ☞ 7 (walk to during the day only)

Getting There: **Car:** Park in the Staff Post Lot on Liscum Road off Grayson.

  Bus: No. 11 Broadway. Stops in front of Quadrangle.

Comments:

Although this is a tourist-paced walk, there are some stretches where you can pick up speed.

This is a military reservation and is run by federal regulations. Observe all signs (e.g., No Trespassing, speed limits). Violation of the law is a federal offense.

There may be occasions when an area is closed off for some military reason and you will be asked not to enter it. You must obey. In times of national emergency, the fort itself could be closed.

Overview:

U.S. Army troops, the 2nd Dragoons, arrived in San Antonio shortly before Texas entered the Union in 1846. For the next thirty-five years the Alamo served as a supply depot, and the Vance Building, on the southeast corner of Market and Main Plaza, as headquarters. Colonel Robert E. Lee was a ranking officer.

In the 1870s, to keep the army post from moving to Austin, the City of San Antonio gave the federal government some land outside the city located on what became known as Government Hill. The Quadrangle was begun in 1876, and the army moved in soon afterward. In 1890, the post was designated Fort Sam Houston; by 1910, it had become the largest army post in the country. In 1975 Fort Sam Houston was designated a National Historic Landmark. As such, it can never be destroyed. You might see buildings posted "Facility programmed for disposal" These have no historic or aesthetic value. The United States Modern Pentathlon, still held in San Antonio, was once headquartered at Fort Sam Houston.

1. **From the parking lot, turn left on Liscum Road, then left on Staff Post Road.**

Staff Post was built in 1881 to provide headquarters for the senior officers of the Department of Texas (a military district roughly equivalent in organization to the United States Fifth Army). Building 48, the Sam Houston House was the first permanent hospital on the post and is now Distinguished Visitors' Quarters. Some of the houses have historical markers. They were designed by architect Alfred Giles. Stone used to build the houses was quarried from the pits in what is now Brackenridge Park.

2. **Turn right on Stanley Road, then left on Wilson. If the gate on Wilson is closed to vehicle traffic, it is okay to walk around it.**

Just before the gate is the Pat Memorial. Prior to the late 1930s, the Army was mobilized by horses and mules. All officers, including those in the infantry, had horses. Teams of six horses hauled artillery behind caissons loaded with the gun crew and ammunition. Occasionally, a group from Fort Sill, Oklahoma, reenacts this activity. It's a great sight to see horses pulling such a rig when they brake from a full gallop. Pat was one of these horses and a favorite of the 12th Field Artillery. When the army motorized the unit, Pat was too old to sell. Rather than have him destroyed, they got permission to retire him, because at the age of thirty they didn't think he had too many years left. But the sturdy old workhorse lived to be forty-

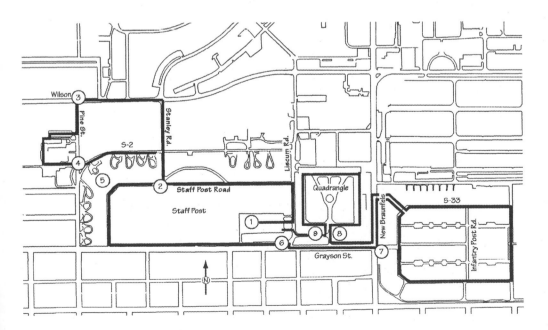

The Pershing House (Photo by Ceclia Wakefield)

five and made "Ripley's Believe It or Not." This memorial to Pat represents the significant contribution that horses and mules made to the army's history.

3. **Turn left on Pine (first street on the left). Turn right into the driveway, just before the Veterinary Hospital (Bldg. 2186) and the old wooden stables (Bldg. 2183), just over the creek. Continue walking left around the stables and the brick Veterinary Hospital building.**

The stables used to cover the area between the Quadrangle and the row of barracks on Stanley Road. Fort Sam Houston's ceremonial unit, the Fort Sam Houston Mounted Detachment, used to be headquartered here. They dressed in the manner of the 1840's 2nd Dragoons, the first troops to ride into Texas. The unit took part in parades and other special events.

The primary duty of the post Veterinary Corps is meat inspection. It also takes care of the horses, the K-9 Corps, the animals in the Quadrangle, and the pets of those stationed on the post.

4. **Come back out on Road S-2. The stables will be on your left. Continue straight ahead, crossing Pine. Back at Stanley, turn right, and then right again onto Staff Post Road.**

After you cross Pine you will be walking between the former pasture and some cream-colored buildings, the old carriage houses, which are now garages for Staff Post residences. Walking here has more of the feel of a small country town than a military installation. Live oak and pecan trees abound. In the summer, cicadas hum while mockingbirds flit about. In the evening, flocks of starlings come to roost.

No. 6 Staff Post Road, at the curve of the road, is the Fifth Army's commanding officer's quarters, named in honor of General John J. Pershing, who lived here in 1917, before he was summoned to Washington, D.C. by President Wilson to command the United States Expeditionary Force in World War I.

5. Continue walking around Staff Post Road.

As you parallel Grayson, the stone house across the street with the turrets and arches is known as Terrell Castle. Alfred Giles designed the house for Edwin Terrell, who served as U.S. Minister to Belgium (he would now be called Ambassador), for several years during the McKinley era. Terrell so liked the architecture of Belgium he had his house designed in that style. It is now a bed and breakfast.

The money to build St. Paul's Episcopal Church was donated in the mid-1800s by a Philadelphia woman whose nephew was stationed at Fort Sam Houston.

The residential section adjacent to the fort was a neighborhood of fine homes until Interstate 35 was built. This split the area and began a period of decline.

Further up the road, the large white house belonged to General Bullis, the famous Army Indian fighter. It was built in the early 1900s of factory-made concrete block that looks much like stone. It is also a bed and breakfast with a youth hostel attached.

6. At Liscum, cross, turn right, then left to walk along Grayson Street. Cross New Braunfels.

Unfortunately, the New Braunfels gate to Infantry Post is now closed. Inside, to the left, Bldg. 688 is where young 2d Lt. Dwight D. Eisenhower brought his bride, Mamie, on July 1, 1916. These brick apartments, built between 1886 and 1906, have recently been renovated. Note that the undersides of the porch ceilings are painted blue. This supposedly fools wasps into thinking it is sky so they won't nest there. This was a common practice in the days before air conditioning when people sat on verandas.

7. Turn left and enter Infantry Post at the first break in the fence. Follow the driveway, bearing right, until you get to the sidewalk that goes around Infantry Post. Turn right.

The homes on the outside perimeter of the post were built between 1885 and 1894. At the lower bend of the road are the first post headquarters (Bldg. 616) and permanent barracks (Bldgs. 601-613). The thick shade makes this a pleasant place to walk on hot days. The rather dreary yellow brick duplexes in the center, built during World War II on the site of the original parade field, destroy the ambiance of Infantry Post. An effort is underway to remove them.

(There are soft drink machines and restrooms behind the Sally Port, the stone arch dated 1887.)

Quadrangle tower (Photo by Celia Wakefield)

Turn left on S-33.

The yellow brick building on the right is the former Band Barracks built in 1893 for the regimental band.

At the last bend of the road is the Stilwell House (Bldg. 626), built in 1888 as the Infantry Post commander's quarters. It is named for Lt. Gen. Joseph W. (Vinegar Joe) Stilwell, who lived here prior to World War II. It now belongs to the Fort Sam Houston Museum, which hopes to find funds for its restoration.

Exit on Hood Street by Stilwell House. Retrace your steps back to the Quadrangle.

(If you're hungry when you reach New Braunfels again, Johnny's Mexican Restaurant and Johnny's Seafood Restaurant, two blocks to the left, are good and inexpensive. Walk there daytime only, however.)

8. Enter the Quadrangle.

The Quadrangle is the oldest building on the post, built in 1876 as a supply depot for the U.S. Army Department of Texas. Note the sign over the entrance "San Antonio Depot." The post was designated Fort Sam Houston in 1890. The windows are a later addition when the storerooms were converted to offices.

(Restrooms inside the Quadrangle.)

In the compound, the fort's menagerie wanders at will. Nobody knows how the first animals came to be here, except that it was a common practice to keep pet deer. Over the years, Post Commanders have added to the collection. There are white-tailed deer, geese, ducks, peafowl, rabbits, and exotic breeds of chickens. The deer and rabbits, and most of the fowl, are tame enough to pet— especially if you have food in your hand. Please, only feed them the special food that is available in the gift shop.

The tower was a lookout point and housed the cistern (where the clock faces are now). The water came from the Alamo Ditch to the west of here. Geronimo and some of his warriors were held captive in the Quadrangle in 1886.

Behind and to the right of the tower are two plaques honoring some of the officers' pets that are buried here. The Quadrangle is open from dawn to dusk.

9. Exit and turn right back to the parking lot.

9 Fort Sam Houston, The Parade Ground

Features: A good walk workout, two museums, and side trip to the San Antonio Botanical Gardens

Distance: 4.6 miles + 3.4-mile side trip (7.4k + 2.2k)

Time: 1 hr. 30 min. + 2-hr. side trip

Nights: Yes, except side trip

Wheelchair Accessible: Yes

Restrooms, water, phones: When open: Road Runner Community Center and museums

Restaurants: Taylor Road

Getting There: **Car:** Park in the lot at Reynolds Road

Bus: No. 15 Fort Sam Houston. Get off at Reynolds Road.

Comments:

This long loop, with few cross streets and the option of walking on sidewalk or grassy parade ground, is a good place for aerobic walking. Because of its length, we start in the middle so it can be taken in two sections.

This is a military reservation and is run by federal regulations. Observe all signs (e.g., No Trespassing, speed limits). Violation of the laws is a federal offense.

There may be occasions when an area is closed off for some military reason and you will be asked not to enter it. You must obey. In times of national emergency, the fort itself could be closed.

The two museums are free. The Fort Sam Houston Museum is open Wednesday to Sunday from 10:00 A.M. to 4:00 P.M. The Medical Museum is open Tuesday-Sunday from 10:00 A.M. to 4:00 P.M. The Botanical Gardens are open Tuesday to Sunday and holidays from 9:00 A.M. to 6:00 P.M. (admission fee).

1. With back to parking lot, turn left.

The Community Support Center (Bldg. 367), serves the entire San Antonio army community including Camps Stanley and Bullis.

Most of the trees along the walk are Arizona ash, live oak, or persimmon.

Shortly past the community center, across the street and behind the flagpole, is a marker commemorating the birth of military aviation on March 2, 1910 during a celebration of Texas Independence Day. On that date Lt. Benjamin Foulois was the first American military man to fly an American military plane. The biplane had been built by the Wright brothers, who sold it to the army after it had been wrecked and repaired. It arrived here in 1909 in seventeen crates. Lt. Foulois and a sergeant put it together and learned to operate it. Foulois knew the Wright brothers and had flown in their planes, but it is believed he never formally completed his training and learned to fly mostly through correspondence.

On this side of the street is the marker designating Fort Sam Houston as a National Historic Landmark.

(At Taylor Road is a U.S. Post Office. Down the street one block to the right is an Arby's Restaurant, open daily, 10:00 A.M. to 10:00 P.M.)

(Just past Schofield, restrooms are located inside the Road Runner Community Center.)

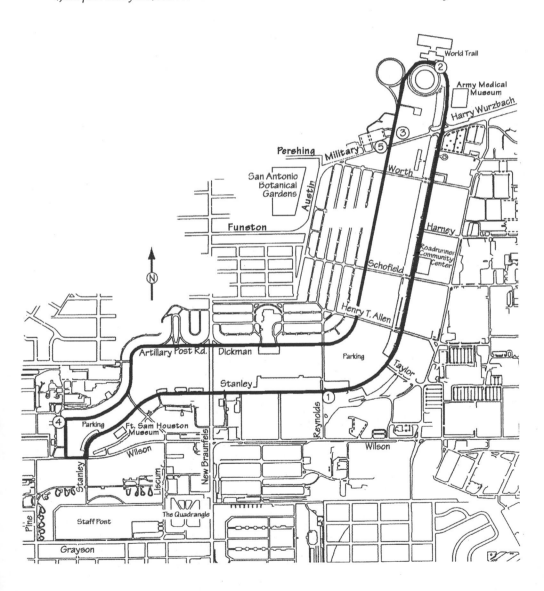

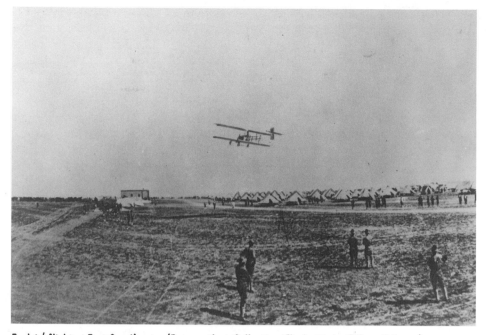

Foulois' flight at Fort Sam Houston (Express-News Collection, The Institute of Texan Cultures).

Just past Worth Road is the U.S. Army Medical Department Center and School (Bldg. 2840), formed in 1972 from the Medical Field Service School and the Medical Training Center. This is the army's principal medical training facility.

The only regular parade on the parade grounds these days is held in conjunction with the Academy's graduation ceremony.

Just past the Academy, you get an excellent view of USAA Towers, the condominiums built by the United Services Automobile Association for retired military personnel. USAA is a member-owned insurance company founded in 1922 by a group of army officers to solve the problem they had insuring their cars because they moved around so much. Those of you who are retired and living in motor homes can appreciate this problem.

At Harry Wurzbach is the Army Medical Department Museum which traces military medical history from 1775 to the present. Well-laid out and interesting, the museum is rather grisly too. Until World War II, when antibiotics became available to fight infection, amputation offered the best chance for survival to a soldier with a limb injury, as evidenced by the number of saws in the field medical kits. A series of seals representing the various medical services decorates the front of the museum. From the left, they are: Medical Corps, Army Nurse Corps, Dental Corps, Veterinary Corps, Medical Service Corps, and Army Medical Specialist Corps. There is also a gift shop in the museum.

A U.S. Army Rail Unit is on display beside the museum.

2. **The road curves around at the former Brooke Army Medical Center and becomes Dickman Road on the other side.**

The building at the apex of the curve is the former location of Brooke Army Medical Center (popularly known by its initials "BAMC" and pronounced bam-cee). It was built in 1937 as part of the New Post development. BAMC was named for Roger Brooke, a brigadier general in the Army Medical Corps from 1878 to 1940 and serves both active and retired military personnel. The world-renowned burn center at BAMC is open to civilians. BAMC also serves as a regional trauma center. BAMC moved to new, modern facilities further east in 1996. Just under the red-tiled roof at the top of this building are the two rooms used by President Lyndon B. Johnson, especially in the years after he returned to Texas. He was flown here by helicopter from his ranch in the hill country. The building will be renovated for a new use.

Past the hospital and past where the "Guest House" sign overlooks the San Antonio Country Club golf course, is a panoramic view of the San Antonio River valley. It gives you a good idea of how advantageous this high point was as the location for a fort.

3. **To take the side trip to the Botanical Gardens (1.4 miles round trip plus 2.0 miles minimum to view gardens), go to Step 5.**

To skip the side trip, continue on Dickman.

To the right as you continue along Dickman is officer housing.

At the bend in the road, between Allen and Reynolds, to the right, is the former Division Commander's Quarters, presently quarters for the commanding general of the U.S. Army Medical Command.

At Road S-16 E is the Officers and Civilians Club (civilian refers to civilian employees, not the general public).

At New Braunfels the street name changes to Artillery Post Road. The houses here are not as large or as old as those on Staff Post Road near the Quadrangle. Colonel and Mrs. Dwight D. Eisenhower lived at Bldg. 179 in 1941. Major General Walter Krueger, who rose through the ranks to become commander of the Sixth Army during World War II and is acknowledged as an architect of the modern U.S. Army, lived at Bldg. 167. The Foulis House, Bldg. 107 (named in his honor, not because he lived there), was originally bachelor officers' quarters and now is Distinguished Visitors' Quarters.

4. **At the end of the Parade Ground turn left at the white crosswalk and then left again at the end of the houses (Wilson). Turn left on Stanley, circling back to your car.**

The additions of the Artillery and Cavalry posts to Fort Sam Houston from 1905 to 1912 made it the largest U.S. Army post of its day. The section to the left, once the polo grounds, is now a soccer field. Before World War II, when horses were still part of the active army, every officer had to have a horse and had to ride it well. To keep in practice, they played polo.

The Fort Sam Houston Museum (Bldg. 123) is behind Bldgs. 122 and 124 and traces the history of the post and the U.S. Army in San Antonio from 1895 to the present.

Bldg. 142, was originally Regimental Headquarters.

Between here and New Braunfels, on the right, the windows and porches of the brick barracks, built before air conditioning was invented, take advantage of the prevailing breeze. These are offices now.

On the other side of New Braunfels Avenue, Camp Travis was built as a training facility for troops during World War I. The New Post, begun in 1928 and built in the Spanish Colonial Revival style, replaced Camp Travis. Army policy dictated that buildings reflect local architectural styles. Someone decided that "local" in San Antonio meant "Spanish."

On the corner of Stanley and New Braunfels is the former guardhouse.

On the Parade Ground, just past New Braunfels, in what looks like a two-story house (now offices for the post exchange), is the old pigeon roost. Before the days of field radios, military commanders used pigeons to report back to the command post. The pigeons lived upstairs, and the men who handled them lived downstairs. These men were excused from KP duty.

Behind the post theater, the gray-domed building is the Gift Chapel, so named because it was built with donations from the post's soldiers and the citizens of San Antonio. President Taft dedicated it in 1909. The chapel serves all denominations. It is well worth a visit.

5. Side trip to Botanical Gardens.

To take the side trip, turn right on Military Highway (Old Austin Highway), which becomes Funston.

There are no sidewalks, but there is sufficient shoulder to walk on. We included this side trip just to introduce you to the Botanical Gardens. You might want to make it a separate excursion. Allow a minimum of one hour just to breeze through it!

The thirty-three-acre Botanical Gardens opened in 1980. As you walk along Funston and approach the entrance, you will pass the Texas natural vegetation section. Ahead you will see the geometric glass domes of the conservatories, each housing a different type of habitat: desert, rain forest, a palm court, and an ever-changing exhibit. One garden features touch and smell for the visually impaired. Other specialty gardens include Japanese, herb, sacred, rose, and an old-fashioned garden such as our forefathers might have had. The native Texas area includes representative plants from the Hill Country, East Texas, and South Texas. The limestone walls of a former five-million gallon 1890's reservoir, fed from the pump house in Brackenridge Park, creates an outdoor theater. The Sullivan carriage house, designed by Alfred Giles in 1896 and long a downtown

Houses along Artillery Post Road

landmark, was moved here, stone by stone, from Fourth Street and Broadway. It is now a gift shop, tearoom, and lecture hall.

Retrace your steps to Dickman at Step 3.

10 Fort Sam Houston, The Training Area

Features: The business end of Fort Sam Houston

Distance: 2.1 miles (3.4k)

Time: 1 hour

Nights: No

Wheelchair Accessible: Yes. See Comments

Restrooms, Water, Phone: At start during library hours and at Mini Mall, No. 5

Restaurants: At Mini Mall, No. 5

Getting There: **Car:** Park at the library on Harney and Chaffee.

Bus: No. 11 or 15 to Ft. Sam, get off at New Braunfels and Grayson, transfer to No. 508 which runs about every 40 minutes. Get off 508 at Garden and Binz Engleman and start walk from there at Step 1.

Comments:

Remember, this is a military reservation and is run by federal regulations. Observe all signs (e.g., No Trespassing, speed limits). Violation of the laws is a federal offense.

There may be occasions when an area is closed off for some military reason, and you will be asked not to enter it. You must obey. In times of national emergency, the fort itself could be closed.

The area is wheelchair accessibile except you might have to be in the street at times—but there is little traffic.

While there are phones and vending machines scattered throughout this area, the only restrooms available are at the Mini Mall, except when the library is open.

The library is open Wednesday-Sunday, 11:00 A.M. to 8:00 P.M.

Overview:

In this training area, it's fairly quiet on the weekends. The action is during the week when troops march to and from classes, the mess hall, and the barracks. *Always give them the right of way.* Watching the troops march along in cadence to the Jody calls is part of what makes this walk interesting.

The benefits of marching in cadence have been known since early times. It improves the efficiency of the troops and boosts their morale. The Jodies as we know them today began during World War II and are credited to an African-American soldier named Willie Duckworth. The Duckworth chant is more popularly known as "Sound Off."

No one knows for sure when the term "Jody" came into being, but a Jody is the guy or gal back home ever ready to take your wife, husband, girlfriend or boyfriend. Jody enjoys the comforts of home while the soldier is training in the field or stationed overseas. Many Jodies were extremely vulgar and sexist, but they have been modified with the advent of male and female troops training together. Even so, the language we've heard is not what one would always use in "polite" company.

In a Jody, the drill leader sings a line and the troops either repeat that, answer with their own verse, or count cadence. Marching cadence is 120 steps or beats per minute, and double time is 180. The words of the Jodies reflect the different

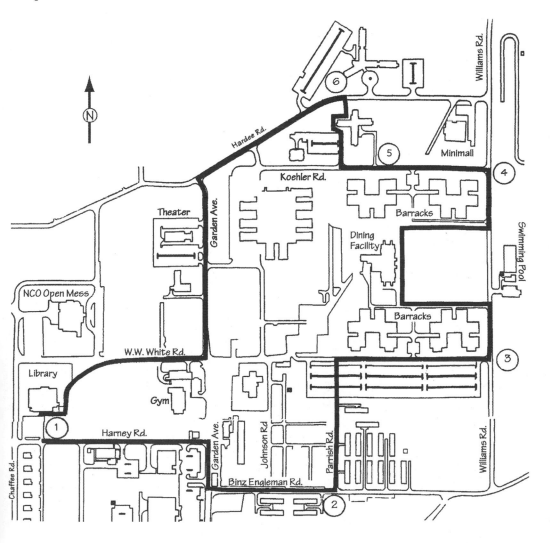

branches, units, posts, and events, and they often change to fit particular situations. As we stepped off the sidewalk to let a group on the way to the mess hall pass, we heard, ". . . if you don't get out of the way, we're going to walk all over you . . ."

The history of cadence marching and the Jodies is quite interesting and has been collected by Sandee Shaffer Johnson in two books available at the post library: *Cadences: The Jody Call Book, No. 1* and *No. 2*.

There's even a San Antonio Jody, credited to Peggy Sexton of Austin. We changed it slightly to make our own Jody:

> I gotta friend in San Antone
> She ain't got no telephone.
> I gotta friend in San Antone
> She don't like to walk alone.

1. **With back to parking lot, turn left on Harney, right on Garden, left on Binz Engleman.**

The metal buildings on your right on Binz Engleman are classrooms.

Down the hill, somewhere in the area where the road forks off through the golf course, is where the infamous 13-drop gallows stood. In 1916, some troops of African-American soldiers under Fort Sam Houston's command were sent to guard against pilferage of equipment on the building site of Camp Logan in Houston. There they met with racial abuse, to which they were not accustomed at Fort Sam Houston. Tensions mounted. One night the soldiers rioted. One hundred twenty-five men marched into downtown Houston, shooting. Several people were killed. There is some evidence of mutiny in the affair as an officer had ordered them to lay down their guns.

Sixty-nine soldiers were returned to Fort Sam Houston for military court martial, the largest single trial ever held in the United States. The men were held in the post jail, and the trial was held in the Gift Chapel. Thirteen were found guilty and sentenced to hang. There was a lot of controversy afterwards because it was a military rather than civilian trial, and because the accused were tried and hung so quickly without recourse to an appeal. The fact is, though, at the time there was no appeal in the military system. It is this case that effected the change in military law: an appeal can now be made to the President of the United States. The thirteen men were buried in the vicinity of the gallows; their remains were later moved to the National Cemetery on post when it opened.

2. **Turn left on Parrish Road (the small road running alongside more classrooms). Cross the parking lot, turn right on W. W. White Road.**

The buildings to the left on W. W. White are barracks. The open area underneath provides a recreation area and allows the troops to form up no matter what the weather.

3. **Turn left on Williams, then left, right, and right again around the ball field, and left again back onto Williams.**

Just after you turn onto Williams, looking down the hill on the right you can see, set among the trees, two of the outdoor lecture areas used to demonstrate tactics. The trees run along Salado Creek.

The building at the back of the ball field area is the mess hall. At mealtime, troops march here in formation. We found ourselves walking along in cadence as they sang out, "Hey, hey, Captain Jack, meet me down by the railroad tracks. Go left, go left, go left, right, left . . ."

Further along on Williams, across on the right, is an obstacle course used in training.

4. **Turn left on Koehler.**

(The Mini Mall has restrooms and a food court, but the post exchange is for military only.)

Along Koehler, each building is posted as to which army unit is housed in the barracks.

Barracks provide a covered, open space for both recreation and training.

5. Go past Murphy Barracks, Bldg. 1380 on the left. At the end of the barracks turn right into the driveway to the parking lot and walk around to the front of the yellow brick building.

The yellow brick building past the parking lot (Bldg. 1382) is the U.S. Navy Hospital Corps. It also serves the air force and the army with training in laboratory sciences, physical therapy, respiratory therapy, and neuropsychology. There is an interesting dedication marker at the entrance.

Across the street, the large yellow apartment building houses Visiting Officers' Quarters.

6. Turn left on Hardee Road, left on Garden, right on W. W. White. When you get alongside the NCO Club turn left across the paved area on your left and march, in cadence of course, back to your car.

> Pick 'em up and put 'em down
> We'll be marching round and round
> Body straight and shoulders square
> Marching proud and with a flair
>
> Sound off 1-2, sound off 3-4
> 1-2-3-4, 1-2—3-4.

The post library is available to the public for browsing, but not to check out books.

11 Alamo Heights

Features: A quiet, shady, older neighborhood with slight hills. Includes Olmos Dam and a side trip to the McNay Art Museum.

Distance: 4.5 miles + 1.7 mile side trip (7.2k + 2.7k)

Time: 2 hrs. + 40-min. side trip

Nights: Yes. McNay Art Museum closes at 5:00 P.M.

Wheelchair Accessible: No

Restrooms, Water, Phone: At start, McNay

Restaurants: Several near start

Getting There: **Car:** Park at intersection of Broadway and Terrell/Patterson

Bus: No. 9 Broadway or No. 14 Perrin-Beitel. Get off at Terrell/Patterson.

Comments:

There are no sidewalks on parts of this walk, but the traffic is light.

Admission to the McNay Art Museum is free. It is open Tuesday-Saturday from 9:00 A.M. to 5:00 P.M., Sunday from 2:00 to 5:00 P.M.

Overview:

Now, as always, a quiet neighborhood of both large and smaller homes, Alamo Heights has become a very "in" address. It is said that "you get less house for your money here than anywhere else." The residents of Alamo Heights are referred to as "09ers," the local zip code. One of the earlier suburbs of San Antonio, the city has grown so much further north that Alamo Heights is more "near downtown" than suburb now. Its feeling of "small town" plus its convenient location and good schools draw people to it. It is a separate, incorporated city.

1. **Start at the covered bus stop on the northwest corner of Broadway and Patterson. Facing Broadway, turn left walking up Broadway.**

The bus stop is the work of Dionicio Rodriguez, who was born in Mexico in 1893. From an Italian artist there, who made imitation rock, he learned how to mix cement to the correct consistency for modeling without the use of sand and rock (concrete) and which chemicals to use for staining. He sculpted with his fingers and simple tools such as tableware and twigs and could duplicate many kinds of wood. Rodriguez was perhaps the most accomplished of the cement artists. He died in San Antonio in 1955. Sam Murray is the best known of his apprentices.

The H.E.B. across Patterson is that chain's second store; it was first located one block ahead, where Cappy's Restaurant is now. This H.E.B. is nicknamed "Gucci B," reflecting the lifestyle of its "09" customers..

The Luby's Cafeteria across Broadway is the second location for that chain. Robert Luby opened a cafeteria downtown in 1948, and this one a year later. Next to Luby's is the old art deco Broadway Theater which has been remodeled as a bank.

2.   Turn left on Mary D Avenue.

Cappy's Restaurant is a San Antonio favorite in the moderate to expensive price range. The Twig Bookstore next to it on Broadway is one of the city's few independent bookstores.

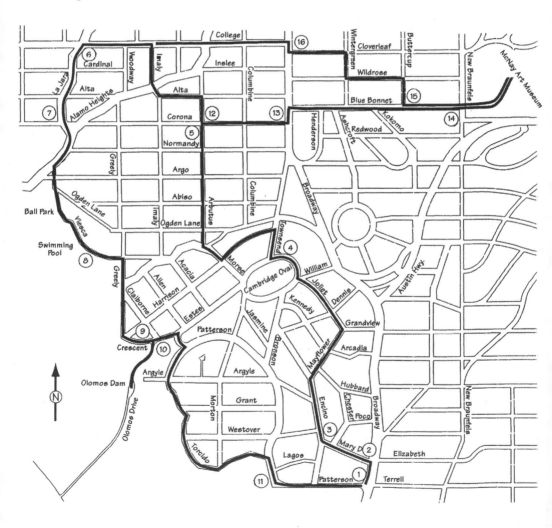

3. **Turn right on Encino, right on Mayflower, and left on Joliet. Turn right on Cambridge Oval.**

For this neighborhood we chose to just walk without a lot of commentary. It is quiet and pleasant with slight grades and can be approached either as a leisurely stroll or a good workout. There are any number of routes we could have followed. Perhaps you'll want to come back again and explore further.

On Cambridge Oval, the former 1922 Alamo Heights High School is now an elementary school.

4. **Turn right on Townsend, left on Harrison, and right on Morse (which becomes Arbutus). Continue on Arbutus to Corona.**

On Morse you cross a little creek, usually dry, as it passes through a small mesquite grove.

At the corner of Abiso, in the garage of the corner house on your right, is Barney Smith's gallery. Whenever Barney is at work the doors will be open inviting you in to see his collection of over 420 decorated toilet seat lids. Barney insists he will stop at 500. He is a retired plumber and a pack rat. Each of his works commemorates a special event, holiday, trip, or showcases some of his eclectic collectibles. Barney and his gallery have been featured on CNN and Bob Philip's *Texas Country Reporter,* as well as in newspaper and magazine articles.

At Corona, to take the side trip to the McNay Art Museum (1.7 miles), go to Step 12.

5. **To skip the side trip, continue up Arbutus, turn left on Alta, right on Imlay, cross Alamo Heights Blvd., and continue on Imlay to College. Turn left on College.**

Just after you turn onto College, on the left is a street named Woodway Lane. A glance down this lovely, shaded street and you know where it got its name.

At the end of College Street, until the early 1990s, was the campus of the Texas Military Institute, a coeducational college prep school operated under the auspices of the Episcopal Church. Its first campus opened in 1893 as West Texas Military Academy, across Grayson Street from Fort Sam Houston. A member of its first freshman class was Douglas MacArthur, whose father was then commander of the post. In 1926 the school merged with the upper level of San Antonio Academy and became Texas Military Institute. A landmark building located on the College Street campus was Old Main, in 1910 the first precast tilt-up structure in the United States. After the Institute moved to its new location in northwest San Antonio in 1989, Old Main and the other campus buildings were torn down, replaced by houses.

6. **Turn left on La Jara, keeping to left side of creek bed.**

We tend to forget we are in the city when strolling along this street, a favorite with walkers and joggers.

7. **At the end of La Jara cross Corona and walk on Alamo Heights Blvd. for a short distance. Cross Argo and follow Ogden Lane for a very short distance until it turns left. Stay straight ahead on what is now Viesca. Walk on the right shoulder to avoid blind curves on the left, traffic-facing side of the street.**

   (Unfortunately, these streets do funny, curvy things that makes giving, and following, directions complicated.)

   (Where a road on the right goes down to the ball fields, the restrooms will be open if games are in session. At other times they are locked.)

   Just past the ball fields is the pool. If you reach that you did everything right. If you don't come to the pool you did something wrong. Try again.

On Viesca, behind the pubic swimming pool, the land drops off into the Olmos Flood Basin, which is upstream from the Olmos Dam. Beyond the pool is the Jack Judson Nature Trail. The San Antonio Audubon Society offers a Beginners Bird Walk here on the second Saturday of each month (see Appendix D).

8. **Continue on Viesca, turn right at Greeley which becomes Crescent. Continue on Crescent past Harrison.**

Architect Harvey Page bought the property on Crescent Drive in the 1920s and built these houses. At the top of the hill, 202 Crescent intrigued us with its lintel over the entrance gate. *Caravanserai* means "inn for caravans." It appears we weren't the only ones. A former neighbor told us that people frequently

Dionicio Rodriguez bus stop on Broadway, 1929 (Photo courtesy of John K. Kight, The Institute of Texan Cultures Collection).

asked the Prassels what Caravanserai meant. Mrs. Prassel would say, "Oh, ask Dick." Mr. Prassel (Dick) would say, "It's just an old name for a welcome place for travelers." We looked it up. It is an Eastern word for a large building with an open court where caravans can rest at night. The Prassels, the neighbor said, were very hospitable people.

9. **To see Olmos Dam, turn right on Olmos Drive and go down the hill to the chained-off road going across the dam. Return to this point to continue (.3 miles round trip).**

As you go down the hill, where the wall on the right ends, look down below. This was the location of Worth's Spring. Some of the U.S. Army troops that accompanied General William Worth into northern Mexico in the Mexican-American War camped here in 1849. General Worth died here during one of the recurring cholera epidemics. Some local historians think that this spring was misnamed, and that General Worth actually camped at the San Antonio Springs on the University of the Incarnate Word College Campus.

Olmos Dam was built as a flood control measure after the devastating 1921 flood. Before the dam was built this was farmland irrigated from the springs.

With your back to the dam, look across the street and up the hill to the left. You can see the arches of one of the houses off Argyle Street. To the right of this is the USAA Towers, the 200 Patterson condominiums, the Southwestern Bell Telephone Building on Hildebrand, the 401 New Braunfels Building, University of the Incarnate Word, Fort Sam Houston on the hill behind it, and off to the right, the Tower of the Americas.

10. **Once back on Crescent, continue ahead a very short distance to the right, then turn right on Estes a short distance. Turn right on Patterson, which becomes Torcido on the other side of Argyle Street.**

Patterson Street is named for J.W. Ballantyne Patterson, an American who moved to England. He never lived in Alamo Heights, but, along with Charles Ogden and R.H. Russell, bought and developed property here.

The grand old house on the right at 934 Patterson is the Argyle Club. It is a private club noted for its fine dining. Colonel Charles Anderson built the house in 1859 on what was then his horse ranch. After he spoke out against secession, he was arrested and sentenced to die but escaped. During the Civil War the house was used as an arsenal.

Colonel Anderson had a reputation for hospitality and fine dining. Coincidentally, the house's subsequent owners have carried on this tradition. Two Scotsmen bought it and converted into a hotel, naming it the Argyle because the area reminded them of the rugged hills of their Argyle homeland. Their venture failed, and in 1893, Robert O'Grady, who was to become the first mayor of Alamo Heights, bought it. He placed his daughter, Alice, in charge of running it, which she did until 1940. They furnished the rooms with antiques and served meals family style. Alice O'Grady's "platters of chicken and ham, served with flawless sauces, artistically served vegetables, splendid cakes, and creative table decorations" earned her a national reputation. Next, the Argyle became a rooming house. Nothing is known about the quality of the food and hospitality during that period. In 1956 it was bought and restored by the Southwest Foundation for Biomedical Research, which operates it as a private dining club and uses the proceeds to fund their research. Club members are required to make an annual donation to the Foundation.

The house on the right at the corner of Argyle, 401 Torcido, is the Maverick-Zachry house designed by George Washington Smith (his only work in Texas), who created the Santa Barbara style based on Spanish Colonial architecture.

The beige brick house on the left at 400 Torcido is the Schoenbaum house, built in 1985. *Schoenbaum* means "beautiful tree," and the owners have built their home in a spot befitting their name. The gardens are an important part of the house with stone pathways leading through elm and mountain laurel. The walls are of handmade Mexican brick, and the architect, Isaac Maxwell, designed and made all the light fixtures, doors, and other architectural details. Notice the tin cutwork on the front door.

As you walk down Torcido, notice that the land to the right drops off into the Olmos flood basin.

Farther down the hill at 111 Torcido is the headquarters of the Episcopal Diocese of West Texas.

11. **Turn right at Patterson, staying on the right shoulder to avoid blind curves on the left side, and follow it back to the start.**

The condominiums at 200 Patterson are built on the location of a Native-American trash midden. There was much controversy about putting a high-rise into this low-rise community.

12. **To take the side trip to the McNay Art Museum (1.7 miles): Turn right on Corona.**

In the section of Alamo Heights we've just walked through and the one coming up, the homes range from modest bungalows to homes that are quite grand. As you approach Broadway, you can see the fire station with City Hall next to it. On the corner are the courtroom and council chamber.

13. **Cross Broadway at the light, and continue ahead on Bluebonnet.**

In the 1920s, when this section began to develop, it abounded with bluebonnets in the spring and thus received the name of Bluebonnet Hills.

14. **Cross New Braunfels Avenue (carefully), enter the gate to the McNay Art Museum, and follow the signs up the drive. When leaving, recross New Braunfels, and walk back along Bluebonnet.**

Marion Koogler McNay bequeathed her house and art collection to the City upon her death in 1950. The original house, designed by Atlee B. and Robert M. Ayres, had twenty-four rooms. The ten galleries, library, and support facilities were added later. The original collection has been expanded by the addition of works from the Oppenheimer, Lang, and Tobin collections. Behind the McNay, the former San Antonio Art Institute building offers an interesting contrast in architecture. Many pieces of sculpture enhance the extensive gardens surrounding the property.

15. **Turn right on Buttercup, left on Wildrose, right on Wintergreen, and left on Cloverleaf to Broadway.**

If the street names also represent flowers that once grew on these hills, perhaps the area should have been called Wildflower Hill.

16. **At Broadway, jog to the right, then turn left on College. Continue on college to La Jara at Step 6.**

Marian Koogler McNay Art Museum (photo courtesy of the McNay Art Museum)

12 Eastside

Features: 31 contiguous historic cemeteries and Dignowity Hill Historic District

Distance: 4.3 miles + 1.5 mile side trip. (6.9k + 2.4k) See comments

Time: 3 hrs. 45 min. + 40 minute side trip. See comments

Nights: No

Wheelchair Accessible: Yes. See Comments

Restrooms, water, phones: Unfortunately, there are no restrooms unless the maintenance people are at the office. There is a water fountain at Agudas Achim Cemetery.

Restaurants: Aldacos (Mexican) on Commerce Street in St. Paul Square

Getting There: **Car:**   Park in City Cemetery No. 6 on Commerce and Palmetto.

   Bus: No. 25 East Commerce. Get off at Palmetto.

Comments:

We feel more comfortable walking here with another person rather than alone. The cemeteries are safe, but because there is usually no one else around you are vulnerable. Go with a small group if that makes you feel even more comfortable. The Dignowity Hill neighborhood, while not "one of the best" these days, is safe to walk alone, but you will always feel more comfortable walking with a partner.

These are both daytime only walks.

Wheelchairs: In Dignowity Hill not all curbs have ramps, but there are driveways. The cemeteries have gravel or grassy paths that might be a bit bumpy but are navigable. The problem is the cables across some of the entrances we use. You might prefer driving to each of the cemeteries.

This is mostly an unshaded walk and, therefore, not recommended for a very hot day. Carry water.

The Jewish cemeteries are closed on Saturday.

The time given is for following our route, allowing time to try and locate the various grave sites mentioned. Allow extra time! Even following our route you will no doubt find yourself meandering, as we still do, through these fascinating old cemeteries, reading gravestones, looking for familiar names. Since it takes almost an hour to cover a mile, you might want to take it in two or more sessions. Before or after City Cemetery No. 1 is a good start and stop place as you are close to your car.

The Cemeteries

An accumulation of this many contiguous cemeteries, thirty-one of them (eight city-owned, and twenty-three private), is rare in the United States. (There

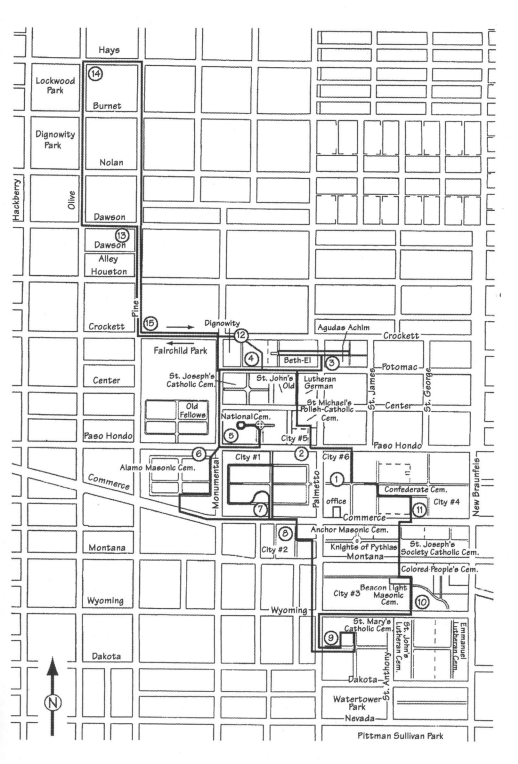

is some debate now about the exact number of cemeteries as some have been closed and grave sites moved to new locations here or to other cemeteries such as San Jose Burial Park.) A proposal has been submitted for a listing in the National Register of Historic Places. There are also plans to open a visitor center across the street and provide more security against vandalism.

A historical marker that you will see later says that the King of Spain originally granted forty acres of land to the City, which then sold off pieces to various groups. The oldest grave site dates from 1853. The size of this cemetery group is now 103 acres with approximately 85,000 burial sites. Approximately 27,000 grave sites have been identified, 75 percent of which predate World War II. These cemeteries once were so far out of town that funeral processions were accompanied by armed men to guard against Indian attack.

The cemeteries represent a diversity of ethnic, fraternal, and religious groups. Not all are still in use. The concrete log gravestones of the Woodmen of America, a fraternal benefit society founded in 1890, are abundant. The Jewish cemeteries, set up as perpetual care, stand out for their well-manicured appearance. Others are maintained by existing churches and organizations, and by individual families, while most of those associated with now-defunct lodges, churches, and other organizations have care provided by the city. Many iron fences around plots have been stolen or removed for ease of upkeep. At one time some sections of the cemeteries had reached such a state of neglect that they had become dumping grounds for dead animals and old couches. People sat on gravestones while waiting for the bus. Sadly, there has been an increase in vandalism in recent years.

We could fill volumes with the history of these cemeteries and about the people buried here. But that is not within the scope of this book. To make your walk interesting, we have located the burial sites of some persons of historical or local interest. To aid you in locating them, we have numbered them in the text and placed these numbers on the map in the approximate locations. The numbers do not appear in sequence because we have added some as we located them, as well as deleted some that proved difficult to find again. Hopefully you will be able to find the ones you are most interested in. If not, we feel you will be happy enough just wandering through this unique place.

1. **Start at City Cemetery No. 6 at the flagpole, facing north. Walk straight ahead.**

The office originally stored the cemetery records. They are now at San Jose Burial Park.

Before you start, note that with few exceptions graves in these cemeteries face east. Terry Jordan in his book, *Texas Graveyards, A Cultural Legacy*, says this is based on Christian symbolism: east is the direction of Jerusalem and of the second coming of Christ. In order to be facing Christ when they rise from their graves on Judgment Day they must lie with their feet facing east. You will note a few exceptions to this. Jordon says that those who have sinned extraordinarily are buried on a north-south axis, so that their debt to society will be paid on Judgment Day when they rise facing in the wrong direction. The origin to this practice is found in Europe, particularly England, and may have a pagan antecedent in sun worshipping cults that bury the dead to face the rising sun.

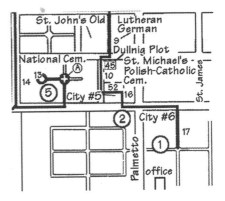

Another practice to look for is the wife buried to the left of the husband. This is principally a British Christian belief that Eve was created from the left side of Adam. In Texas it is found mostly in Anglo and African-American cemeteries, but not those of some ethnic groups such as German, Czech, Polish or Mexican.

Just north of the flagpole:

17. *Mattie Blackshere Winn*—The sculpture on Winn's tombstone is by Pompeo Coppini whose work you will find also on Walk No. 1.

    Exit onto Paso Hondo, turn left, cross Palmetto.

2. **Turn right into City No. 5 (the first break in the stone wall).**

16. *Nathaniel (Nat) Lewis Mausoleum*—Lewis owned the mill on the river near South Presa Street known as "The Old Mill" (see Walk 5, Bridges). This mausoleum has been vandalized in recent years.

    Walk ahead towards St. Michael's Polish Cemetery. At the chain link fence turn left to the service road.

52. Just before you get to the service road, on your right, are grave markers for the *Aylmer's*. Note the personal messages on each stone, carved out in each other's own handwriting.

    Turn right on service road.

10. The second plot on the right, behind the chain link fence, is the *Kotula plot*. Ed Kotula is remembered in several ways. He had a store on Military Plaza and was known as "the Wool King" because he sold so much of that product. His firm was noted for its upright, honest dealing. But, so it is told, Ed Kotula's history could have been different. Back in the mid-1800s, there were two Kotulas in San Antonio, Ed and Joe. Besides sharing the same name, they were of the same age and came from the same part of Poland. This caused so much confusion that one day in 1865, in the lobby of the Menger Hotel, they decided to flip a coin to see who would stay in San Antonio and who would move away. Joe lost, changed the spelling of his name to Cotulla, and moved south to the Nueces River, where he founded a ranching empire. When the railroad came through in the late 1870s, he gave them right-of-way with the

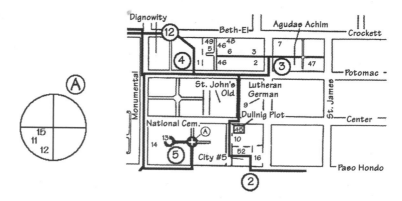

stipulation that the train would stop at his settlement. He sold plots of land and founded the town of Cotulla.

45. In the corner at Center Street, in the walled section, is the *Dullnig family cemetery*. The handsome nineteenth-century Dullnig Building is at Losoya and Commerce.

Cross Center Street. Walk ahead through St. John's Lutheran Cemetery towards Potomac.

This is the earlier of the two St. John's Lutheran Cemeteries.

9. *Beller*—Just inside, on the right in the second row, are two shell graves. In his book, *Texas Graveyards, A Cultural Legacy*, Terry Jordan gives much information on the use of shells on grave sites. The practice is too wide-spread, according to researchers, to be merely decoration. Some say it stems from pagan times in Mediterranean Europe, possibly as early as the Cro-Magnon era, 30,000 years ago. In the United States, it is definitely a Southern folk custom. All three of the major cultural groups that shaped Southern culture used shells in this manner on their grave sites. Shell-covered graves are found in Africa. Interestingly, although the custom may have been brought here from Spain, it is not found south of the border in Mexico. And although it is found among the German graves here in Texas, it is not found in Germany.

Continue towards Potomac, turn right on Potomac, then left on Palmetto.

3. **Turn right into the Agudas Achim Cemetery.**

7. *Karotkin*—This family had a downtown furniture store. The long-empty building on Commerce street still carries their sign.

47. *Gurwitz* monument: Although many of the grave markers in the two Jewish cemeteries have some inscriptions in Hebrew, this marker stands out.

Exit cemetery, cross street to Beth-El Cemetery.

2. *Finesilver*—This is the burial plot for the family whose work clothing factory is located in downtown San Antonio.

3. *Joske Mausoleum*—The Joske family founded the century-old department store downtown on Alamo Plaza that is now Dillard's.

6. *Landa Mausoleum*—Harry Landa gave his home on Shook to the city for a library and children's playground (see Walk 24).

48. Behind the Landa mausoleum is the *Zork family plot*. The Zork's were possibly the first Jewish family to settle permanently in San Antonio.

46. *Oppenheimer* and *Halff family plots*: On both sides of the center path are burial sites of these two families. The Oppenheimer's had a privately owned bank in San Antonio's early days and are noted for their philanthropic deeds. The Halff's are another of San Antonio's prominent early families. Brothers Solomon and Mayer built homes facing each other on opposite sides of Goliad Street. Both of these homes still exist in HemisFair Park. There were several marriages between the Oppenheimer and Halff families.

49. The walled plot in the back right corner is the *Feinberg family plot*. Note the grave marker with the bas-relief scene of a man in a stovepipe hat shooting another man. It is said that Feinberg had a quarrel with Benedict Schwartz over a dog, which resulted in a duel and Feinberg's death. His wife claimed he was ambushed. There is no record of the incident either in criminal or newspaper records. Schwartz was never prosecuted and went on to become a leading citizen. Ironically, he met his death by gunshot from a burglar. Feinberg's wife was so upset over her husband's death that she ordered a wall built around the family plot so there could be no chance of Schwartz being buried close to her husband. It was the Feinberg family that purchased the first piece of land here for a Jewish cemetery. The family then presented it to the Hebrew Benevolent Society, and in 1881 it became the Temple Beth-El cemetery.

5. *Hertzberg family plot*—Harry Hertzberg was a prominent attorney who is well known for the Hertzberg Circus Collection that he bequeathed to the city (see Walk 2). His brother Eli owned the Hertzberg jewelry store whose clock still stands downtown on the corner of Houston and Navarro.

Retrace your steps to Potomac, turn right.

As you walk down Potomac, on the left, past St. John's, is St. Joseph's German Catholic cemetery. A row of four iron crosses stands out. This cemetery has many iron crosses. You should be able to see others as you walk around the perimeter of the cemetery.

4. From Potomac, turn right up the steps and through the iron gate into the Dignowity Cemetery.

1. The *Dignowity family plot* is in the southeast corner. Anthony Michael Dignowity, newly arrived from Czechoslovakia, rode into San Antonio in 1833. After a short stay in Mississippi where he studied medicine, he returned to San Antonio in 1847, started a medical practice, and began buying property. He built his home, Harmony House, on a hill east of San Antonio in 1854. An outspoken opponent of secession, he had to leave town quickly one night

after being warned he was to be captured and hung. Returning to San Antonio in 1869, he spent the rest of his life trying to recover his property.

Dignowity sold off full blocks of property in this area to wealthy German friends, and, in the 1880s, Dignowity Hill became an early San Antonio suburb. With no trolley service and the expense of digging a well to supply water, this suburb was for the rich only. The advent of the trolley in 1903 and improved water, sewer, gas, and electrical service brought industry to the area. Smaller homes for workers appeared. The wealthy began moving to the newer suburbs north of the city, and Dignowity Hill began to decline.

On the death of her husband, Mrs. Dignowity bought this whole lot. Keeping this corner for her family plot, she sold off the rest of the plots.

If you wish to tour a portion of the Dignowity Hill Historic District at this time, go to Step 12. (The distance is 1.5 miles and will take about 40 minutes.)

To continue the cemetery walk, return to Potomac, turn right. At Monumental turn left, cross Center, then turn left on Paso Hondo.

Between Center and Paso Hondo Streets, on the right, is the Odd Fellows Cemetery, one of several that are not maintained. Because of its isolation we *highly* recommend that you do not go there.

5. Turn left into the San Antonio National Cemetery.

This was the first National Cemetery in San Antonio. When it became full a second one was opened in 1921 at Fort Sam Houston. On special occasions, ceremonies are held in the bandstand at the entrance. Note the strict floral code posted to the right of the entrance. A grave locator is in a red wooden box behind the flagpole.

11. *General John Bullis* is remembered as a famous Indian fighter. Camp Bullis, northwest of San Antonio, is named in his honor. His house near the Fort Sam Houston Quadrangle is now a bed and breakfast.
12. *Brigadier General Charles M. Terrell* was a brother of Samuel Terrell, who began the exclusive suburb of Terrell Hills.
15. *Captain Lee Hall*—A historical marker tells about this Texas Ranger.
13. *Harry M. Wurzbach*—In 1920, he was elected to Congress and was the first native Texas Republican to hold that office. He later became the first Texas Republican to be elected to more than two terms.
14. *Tomb of the Unknown Dead*—The plaque in front of the monument honors the resting place in this cemetery of some of the Buffalo Soldiers reinterred here from their first burial at Fort Concho.

Exit the National Cemetery. Turn right on Paso Hondo.

Inside the cemetery a grassy "road" goes in a circle around the cemetery. In the northeast quadrant is another shell grave.

41. In this quadrant are two stone historical markers. One is for *James Nathaniel Fisk,* who served in the Texas Army in 1836-1837, and the other for his wife, *Simona Smith Fisk,* daughter of "Deaf" Smith, Sam Houston's scout at the battle of San Jacinto.

43. Behind and to your left of these markers is one for *Julian Onderdonk,* a well-known San Antonio artist, who, among other accolades, is known as the first of the bluebonnet painters. His paintings hang in the state capitol.

42. *Sandra Ilene West* (under the clump of trees just before you get to the road in the next section), is buried in the West family plot sitting upright in her beloved powder blue 1964 Ferrari. The story made the evening news across the country. If you look closely, you can see the rectangular area to the left of the grave marker.

40. Just inside the Commerce Street entrance is the mausoleum of *Clara Driscoll.* A historical marker tells how she worked to save the Alamo from destruction.

51. Behind and to the left of the mausoleum, near the street is the grave site of *John Lang Sinclair*, who wrote "The Eyes of Texas."

City Cemetery No. 1, the Marriott RiverCenter is in the distance (Photo by Celia Wakefield).

Exit Alamo Masonic onto Commerce Street. Turn left.

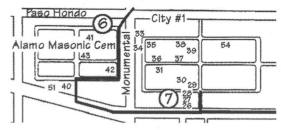

Just before Monumental Street, curbside, is a historical marker that tells about Powder House Hill.

7. Enter City Cemetery No. 1 at the stone entrance.

City Cemetery No. 1 has many grave sites of persons associated with San Antonio history. Here are some that we found.

26. Just inside the gate is the *Gustav Groos family* plot. The Groos' were an early San Antonio banking family. The home Groos built is on Washington Street in the King William Historic District.
27. Next is the family plot of his brother and partner *Carl Groos*, also a resident of the King William District.
28. Next to that is the *Steves Family plot*—The Edward Steves, Sr. home on King William Street is owned by the Conservation Society and is open to the public for tours.
29. Across the road is the burial site of another King William District resident, *Carl Guenther* of Guenther Mills, now Pioneer Flour Mills. His home is open as a museum, gift shop, and restaurant.
30. The *Jack Harris* marker (behind the Weise plot) tells the story of this Old West gunfighter.
31. Further back in this quadrant is the *Tobin Family* plot. John Tobin, son of William and Josephine Tobin, was mayor of San Antonio from 1923 until his death while in office in 1927.

     Also in the Tobin plot is a large, rough-hewn stone reportedly taken from Mt. Rushmore. It marks the burial site of *James Lincoln de la Mothe Borglum,* son of Gutzon Borglum who designed the Mt. Rushmore Monument at his studio on the grounds of what is now the Brackenridge Golf Course. The father died before completion of the monument. His son finished the project.

Cut across the center road to two tall pink granite monuments.

37. *Maverick family plot*—Samual Maverick settled in San Antonio in 1835. Members of the Maverick family figure often in San Antonio history. We refer to them on several of our walks.
36. *Edwin Holland Terrell*, once a U.S. Minister (Ambassador) to Belgium. His wife, Mary Maverick Terrell, was the daughter of Samuel and Mary Maverick. She died in Brussels at the U.S. Consulate.

Emerging on the back road, turn right.

34. *The Kalteyer family plot*—The Kalteyers founded the first cement plant west of the Mississippi, as well as San Antonio Drug Company, long a vacant building on the corner of Market and St. Mary's Street and now a luxury hotel. *Johanna Kalteyer* and her neighbor, Mrs. Edward Steves, Sr., were good friends who attended church together and shared a daily kaffee klatsch.

33. *Theodore Gentilz* was one of San Antonio's most noted artists. He taught at the old St. Mary's Boys School downtown, presently La Mansion del Rio Hotel.

35. *Ferdinand Herff* was long associated with Santa Rosa Hospital and founded a dynasty of medical practitioners. Dr. Herff performed his last surgery at the age of 87.

Turn right down the last road.

38. Two historical makers are located here. *Samuel S. Smith* was a member of the Wohl and Summerville expeditions, and *Charles Fredrick King* was twice a mayor of San Antonio.

39. *Alfred Giles* was one of San Antonio's most noted architects. We point out examples of his work throughout the book.

54. Albert Friedrick owned the Buckhorn Saloon.

Walk back towards Commerce and Palmeto.

Exit City No. 1.

If you've had enough for this trip, you are close to your car at this point.

8. **Cross Commerce Street, enter City No. 2. Walk through, bearing left to exit about the middle of the block on Palmetto. Turn right on Palmetto. Continue past Montana and Wyoming Streets.**

50. As you turn onto Palmetto, in the Anchor Masonic Cemetery across the street is the impressive statue marking the burial site of cattle/ oil baron *James M. Chittim*.

9. **Enter St. Mary's Cemetery.**

The east end of the cemetery is its earliest section. The east-facing orientation is very noticeable here, as is the one exception that we found facing north-south. One wonders what dastardly deed this poor fellow was guilty of.

21. Just inside the gate to the left is a historical marker for *Colonel Edward Miles*, who served in several wars during early Texas times.

At crucifix monument turn left. Towards end of road look for:

22. *Adina Emilia de Zavala* who once saved the Long Barracks at the Alamo from being torn down by barricading herself inside for three days.

23. Behind and to the left of de Zavala's burial site, a pink granite stone marks the resting place of *Marie Therese, Countess Skarzynska,* who died June 24, 1967. On a flat stone in front of this marker, half-covered with weeds, we found a touching bit of history. "Here with Marie Therese, ends the noble Polish House of Skarzynski, founded in 1410 for the valor of the First Count at the victory of Tannenberg." This grave site is sinking and these stones may one day be lost.

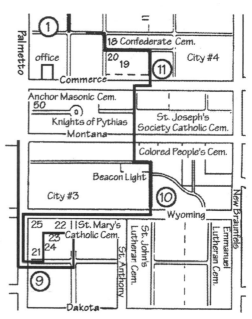

24. Next to the grave of the Countess is that of *Josephine and Gactano Lucchese,* parents of Sam Lucchese who founded the Lucchese boot business and whose grave site is ahead in the right-hand corner.

25. *Sam Lucchese,* his wife, and their daughters Josephine and Maria are buried here. As a bootmaker Sam Lucchese treated all his customers alike, be they Texas rancher, Pope John Paul II, President Reagan, or actor John Wayne. If you had the price of a pair of boots, that was all that counted. The company is now located in El Paso. Josephine became a noted opera singer.

Exit St. Mary's where you entered. Turn right, then right on Wyoming.

10.   Enter City Cemetery No. 3.

The section to the right at Montana and New Braunfels Street was the "colored people's cemetery." It is mostly broken into small cemeteries owned by different fraternal orders. In years past people waiting for the bus at the corner of Montana and New Braunfels used the tombstones to sit on. Reverent R. A. Collies at that time arranged with the City to use jail inmates to clean up and fence the area.

As we walked through we spotted some interesting homemade, concrete crosses, and one marker with punched tin on concrete.

Exit City No. 3. Cross Montana Street. Walk through Knights of Pythias. Cross Commerce Street.

11.   Enter City Cemetery No. 4.

Part of this cemetery is the Confederate Cemetery. Note the street signs. There are J.E.B. Stuart Way and Jefferson Davis Walk among others.

18. The Confederate Cemetery is described on a historical marker.

19. A pink granite marker honors *Hamilton T. Bee,* who served Texas in many ways.

20. Back and beyond the Bee marker, another pink granite marker tells the story of *"Rip" Ford*. He acquired his nickname during the Mexican-American War. He had the duty of writing letters to the grieving relatives of his men who had been killed in battle. He always signed these with the shortened form of "Rest In Peace." He too served Texas in many ways.

Turn left back to car.

12. **Side Trip. Refer to map on page 91. To tour a portion of the Dignowity Hill Historic District (1.5 miles), exit the Dignowity Cemetery onto Crockett Street and turn left. Turn right on Pine.**

The original grandeur of Dignowity Hill is evident in the remaining fine homes scattered throughout the area. We will tour a small section of the neighborhood.

Not along our route, but noteworthy is the city-owned Carver Community Cultural Center, at Hackberry and Center Streets. The facility is in what was once the "Colored Branch of the San Antonio Library and Auditorium," a major social, civic, and cultural center for the African-American community from 1929 until the late 1950s, when it closed due to desegregation and deterioration of the buildings. It reopened in 1977 as a cultural center featuring a performance hall, art gallery, ceramic workshop, and dance studio. Dance, theater, and art events of high quality, which draw on national and international artists as well as local talent, are presented here at affordable ticket prices. To receive a schedule of events, call 210-299-7211. Night parking is secure in the adjacent lot.

The first few blocks have mostly smaller homes. Watch for pieces of scroll work here and there on the older ones.

The 400 block on Pine has some nicely kept one-story houses, as well as a fine stand of old sycamore trees.

13. **Turn left on Dawson, then right on Olive.**

No. 805 Nolan, on the corner of Olive, is the turn-of-the-century home of air conditioning businessman Ed Friedrich, which has, among other features, an elevator. Some of the trees surrounding the house came from Oregon as a gift. As a hobby, Mr. Friedrich designed furniture from buckhorns, some of which may be seen at the Buckhorn Museum. It is listed in the National Register of Homes.

To the left, between Nolan and Burnet, is Dignowity Park, the site of Dignowity's mansion, Harmony House.

The block of houses across from the park are among the best preserved in this neighborhood.

No. 710 Olive is the Greek Revival home Friedrich had built in 1911 for his daughter.

No. 720 dates from 1909. During a 1995 survey of homes in this district it was found that descendants of the original family still live here.

No. 724, with its stately Corinthian columns, is a 1910 home with a two-story wraparound porch and a widow's walk.

No. 732 dates from 1875 and is perhaps an earlier Dignowity home.

The next block on the left is Lockwood Park, the original site of the Joseph S. Lockwood home. If you look towards downtown and imagine the view without power lines and high-rise buildings, you will understand why Dignowity and Lockwood chose these sites on which to build their homes.

14. Turn right on Hays, right on Pine.

At Pine and Hays is the former Calvary Baptist Church which dates from 1908. Note the brick gothic window arches and the outstanding stained glass windows. It is now the Childress Memorial Church. There is another large window on the other (parking lot) side of the church.

No. 821 Pine, with its Doric columns, is an impressive home.

No. 805 probably dates from the late 1800s.

No. 727 is the 1913 home of Richard Friedrich.

Ed Friedrich house

House on Olive Street

No. 702, at the corner of Nolan, dates from 1926 when it was Posey's Filling Station—architecturally one of the fanciest we have ever seen. Besides the lion crests there are carvings that we guess would be either Neptune and sea serpents, or dragons and wizards.

Also at the corner of Pine and Nolan, was Prassel's Drugstore, which reportedly made a great chocolate cream soda. Mr. Prassel, described as "...just the nicest gentleman around," dispensed "health maintenance" and was generous to anyone in need. This was possibly in the building with the black and white tile. The old sign on the roof of the corner of this building is for a pharmacy with a different name.

No. 711 Pine was the Prassel family home.

No. 328 Pine, at the corner of Crockett, is headquarters for the Delta Sigma Theta Sorority as well as the Myra Davis Hemmings Resource Center. It has a particularly lovely porch with carved medallions.

15. **Turn left on Crockett, then right on Monumental and left on Paso Hondo, to pick up the tour at Step 5.**

13 Hill Country Village

Features: Country suburban neighborhood

Distance: 5.1 miles (8.2 k)

Time: 1 hr. 45 min

Nights: No, too dark

Wheelchair Accessible: Yes. See Comments

Restrooms, Water, Phone: At start

Restaurants: At start

Getting There: **Car:** Park near the intersection of Bitters Road and West Avenue.

Bus: None

Comments:

There are no sidewalks, so walk toward the traffic (on the left side of the street).

As in all neighborhood walks, please be considerate of the private property and privacy of the residents.

If you park south of Bitters Road, be especially careful walking to and crossing Bitters. There are no shoulders, and the traffic is fierce.

On the walk itself, wheelchair accessibility is limited. There are no sidewalks, but there are good blacktop streets with little traffic. Shoulders, however, tend to be narrow and rough.

We took the long way around in this walk. If you wish to shorten it, the map shows other roads through the area.

1. **Cross Bitters Road at West Avenue, and continue straight ahead. West Avenue becomes South Tower on the other side of Bitters Road. Turn left on Powder Horn.**

The ball moss you see on many of the trees is not a parasite that kills the trees as many people think, but an epiphyte, an air plant that needs sunlight. Thus, it is found more often on dead branches with no leaves to block the sun. It also proliferates on power lines. Airborne spores land on the host object and grow anchors to attach themselves.

2. **Turn right on Winding Way.**

Throughout the walk, in addition to the fox squirrel, you might see the rock squirrel, which is darker, probably so it can blend with the weathered limestone. The black plastic covers on the power lines protect them from the squirrels, who have a tendency to gnaw through the insulation. Roadrunners are frequently seen on this walk also.

If it is springtime, there should be bluebonnets along the way.

3. Turn left on Tower.

There is more traffic along here but sufficient shoulder to walk on. This stretch of the route is heavily forested with younger trees, but there are some old live oaks and cedars scattered throughout.

4. Turn right on Hill Country Lane.

The first property on the left, 100 Hill Country Lane, has stables, so you might see horses grazing.

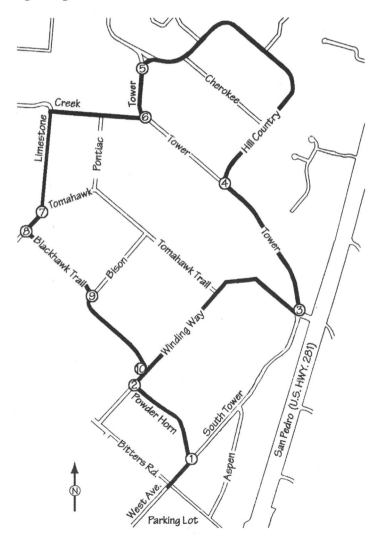

Horses graze on a rustic ranch at beginning of walk (Photo by Celia Wakefield).

5. Turn left on Tower Lane at the triangle intersection.

Notice that the blacktop here is laid down on a concrete base. This is more expensive initially, but in the long run it pays off as it prevents pot-holes and other types of road deterioration.

6. Turn right on Limestone Creek.

The water tower here is not as picturesque as old-time towers. The well goes down into the Edwards Aquifer.

The house at 313 Limestone Creek has a pond, not visible from the road, which is home to wild ducks that frequently can be seen flying around the property.

The road makes a sharp left-hand turn at one point.

7. Turn right on Tomahawk.

8. **Turn left on Blackhawk Trail.**

Signs are posted all along the way and offer a reward for catching anyone shooting deer.

9. **At Bison, jog right, and then pick up Blackhawk again.**

Along here you pass the Hill Country Waterworks, a private water distribution company with its own well.

10. **Turn right on Winding Way, and then almost immediately turn left on Powder Horn Trail. Turn right on South Tower to return to your car.**

A herd of shy goats runs from the photographer (Photo by Celia Wakefield).

14 Inspiration Hills

Features: Hilly, suburban neighborhood with some spectacular views

Distance: 2.7 miles (4.3k)

Time: 1.0 hour

Nights: Yes

Wheelchair Accessible: No, too hilly

Restrooms, Water, Phones: At Babcock and Hillcrest

Restaurants: No

Getting there: **Car:** Park at Midcrest and One Oak off Babcock and Hillcrest

 Bus: No. 90 Babcock. Get off at Babcock and Hillcrest.

Comments:

You don't have to walk far to get your daily dose of aerobics on this walk; it's all hills, from long, gradual to short and steep. This—and the spectacular views—are why we chose it. We have modified it from the first edition of the book, both by shortening it, and walking down instead of up the hill (High Sierra) that is so long and steep we recommended that you "Shift yourself into second gear . . .." You'll still get a good workout, but now the walk is within the capabilities of more walkers.

We enjoy this walk both day and night. Just before sunset is ideal.

Overview:

When Wilbur Fite and G.C. Thorne developed Inspiration Hills in the early 1950s they set aside seven acres for a park. Each house is different. Some restrictions existed as to size and materials used. Mr. Fite's father made the first attempt to develop the area. His efforts failed because of an impractical street plan. His son modified the grid and was able to sell the lots. Willowbrook is the highest point in the development and also its northern boundary. Our walk goes further north, however, because we wanted to include more views. At one time, we are told, this was known as Rattlesnake Hill. That seems to have been a popular nickname for San Antonio hills.

1. Facing Midcrest, turn right. Turn right on Glenview.

We start a block before Glenview to give you a chance to "warm up" before starting up the first hill, a long, gradual climb. Admittedly, it's not enough of a warm up, but better than nothing.

2. Turn left on Clubhill, then left on High Sierra.

Although we always recommend walking on the left, traffic-facing side of the street, when you turn onto Clubhill, and again onto High Sierra, get on the right side, sticking close to the curb and being very aware that traffic is behind you. This is because the upcoming views are, unfortunately, aligned to the right side of the street. Great if you're driving, but cut off if you're walking.

Didn't we say the view was spectacular!

Notice how the "Big Red Enchilada" (San Antonio Public Library) stands out. Okay, now get back on the left, safer side of the street.

3. Turn left back onto Clubhill, right on Crestline, then right on Hill-crest.

The area on the other side of Hillcrest was the former Sunshine Ranch where Albert Maverick settled his family in 1905. The entrance to the ranch was below on Babcock Road. Albert built a large, two-story house with a long porch and an upstairs gallery to catch the prevailing breeze and to take advantage of the view across the "wide spreading valley." Jane Maverick's Sunday suppers, where family (eleven children) and friends gathered, became legendary.

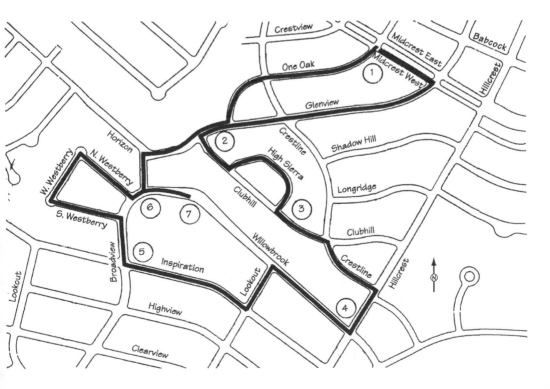

Sunshine Ranch built in 1905 by Alfred Giles, was the home of Albert and Jane Maverick (photo courtesy of Ellen Maverick Dickson).

Son Jim later turned the ranch into a profitable dairy farm. Another one of the Maverick boys, Maury, became a U.S. Congressman and a mayor of San Antonio. He took over a three-acre site on the ranch as his own. For twenty-five dollars he bought a derelict streetcar, had it hauled up the rugged hillside, and made it into his home, later adding an Army surplus hut as a living room. He called it "The Maverick." His son, Maury Jr., became a Texas legislator and civil liberties lawyer, and presently writes a Sunday column for the *Express-News*. (For the story on how the term "maverick" came to be coined from this family's name, see Walk 1.)

4. **Turn right on Willowbrook, left on Lookout, then right on Inspiration.**

There is one short "second gear" hill on Inspiration.

5. **At Broadview turn right, then left on South Westberry, right on West Westberry, and right on North Westberry.**

There was no reason to walk here except that we couldn't resist the opportunity to give such convoluted directions.

6. **Back at Broadview turn left, then immediately right on Willowbrook. Walk a short flat distance to view point.**

This spectacular panaramic view made Willowbrook a favorite spot for lovers to park.

View of downtown from High Sierra

7. **Turn around and walk back to Broadview. Turn right on Horizon, right
    on Glenview, then left on One Oak back to car.**

Shortly after turning onto Horizon it bears off to the left (at the white bumps).
This is where you turn right onto Glenview.

15 Jefferson/Monticello

Features: A 1920s-40s neighborhood, San Antonio's newest historic district, Jefferson High School

Distance: 2.6 & 2.7 miles (4.2 & 4.3k). See Comments

Time: 1.0 hour each

Nights: Yes

Wheelchair Accessible: Yes and no. See Comments

Restrooms, Water, Phone: No

Restaurants: Nearby on Fredericksburg Road

Getting there: **Car:** Park at intersection of Donaldson and Kampmann.

Bus: No. 89 Donaldson or 90 Babcock.

Comments:

The walk can be taken in two segments of 2.6 miles (northern half) and 2.7 miles (southern half).

This walk has some slight uphill grades from Kampmann that make it wheelchair accessible only to the hardy or motorized. We advise checking it out by car first.

Overview:

The Jefferson/Monticello area was part of the land developed by the West End Town Company that also developed the Woodlawn Lake area (see Walk No. 21). Most of the homes date from the 1920s to the 1940s, with the biggest spurt of development in the late 1920s. Monticello Park (the section north of Donaldson), was designated a Historic District in 1995, making it the eleventh in San Antonio.

There is a great diversity of architectural styles and detail, with homes ranging from modest bungalows to the palatial. It has always been a stable neighborhood and has been described by *Express-News* columnist Mike Greenberg, a local resident, as "respectably midfalutin."

There are two neighborhood associations here: Monticello and Jefferson. The Monticello Historic District is actually within the Jefferson Neighborhood Association boundaries. It is hoped that the scope of the historic district will be expanded to include both neighborhoods eventually. There are two home tours in the area each year.

The house numbers here are somewhat confusing. From Donaldson north to Quentin, the streets begin at Fredericksburg Road. Since that street is on a diagonal, and all the streets coming off it begin with the 100 block, by the time you get to their terminus at Kampmann Boulevard, the block numbers range between 300 and 600. As if that isn't confusing enough, the streets south of Donaldson all originate further east, so they line up with each other and are all 2200 at Kampmann. Oh well, aren't our crazy streets part of San Antonio's charm?

We mostly chose not to include details about individual houses here. We invite you to enjoy the diversity and charm of the neighborhood. There are many interesting architectural details and pleasant landscaping along the way.

1. Facing Kampmann Road, turn right. Turn left on Gramercy.

Remember to walk on the left side, facing traffic when walking on Kampmann, which has no sidewalks.

This section was developed as Woodlawn Terrace.

2. Turn right on Vollum, then right on Kings Highway.

No. 2235 Kings Highway is a classic Mediterranean style built in 1937 and is mostly original. It has one of those rare features in South Texas homes: a fully furnished basement.

3. Turn left on Kampmann. After it curves, turn left on Summit.

Kampmann makes a long, right-angle turn here. Even though you are facing traffic, part of it is a blind curve. The street is wide, but for safety walk single-file next to the curb and be watchful of cars.

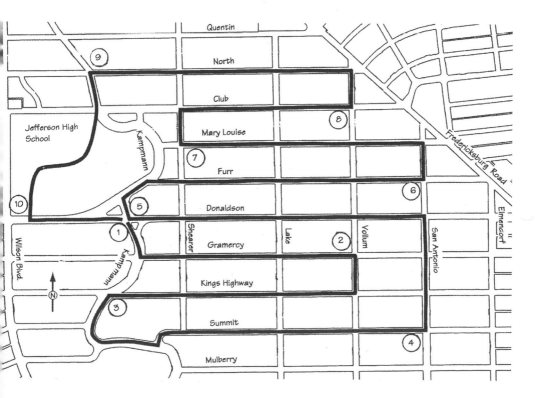

Interestng stonework on house in Jefferson neighborhood

4. **Turn left on San Antonio Avenue, continue ahead to Donaldson, then turn left again.**

No. 555 Donaldson has an elaborate, scenic, stained-glass window.
The house between No. 591 and No. 531 is a delightful "fairy tale" castle.

5. **At Kampmann you can stop, or continue by turning right on Kampmann, then right again on Furr.**

Donaldson to Quentin and Wilson to Fredericksburg Road is the area designated as the new Monticello Historic District. It was developed in the late 1920s as North Woodlawn Terrace.

House, Monticello neighborhood

6. Turn left on San Antonio, left on Mary Louise.

In 1928 the West Texas Chapter of the Architects Institute of America (AIA) chose fifteen local architects to design two houses each on Mary Louise. The assignments were given in alphabetic order starting with Atlee and Robert Ayres. The architects worked with two developers, American Building Company and C. M. Furr Company. These firms approved all plans before beginning construction.

No. 303, corner of Vollum, is a French Norman-style house that is one of the oldest in Monticello dating from 1926. Its original owner was Howard J. Shearer, one of the developers of this area. It is said he named the street for his daughter. The house features a step-down living room whose twenty-foot, oak-beamed, vaulted ceiling supports a large wrought iron chandelier. At one end of this huge living room is an ornate, walk-in fireplace. At one time, former mayor Lila Cockrell, was an owner.

No. 433 is a New Orleans Colonial designed in 1939 by N. Straus Nayfach, architect of the Alameda Theater. Nayfach is noted for building to suit his customer's budget. At whatever cost, he always left his "signature" on his homes: an octagonal window, low-hanging roof line, and facia board around the top.

7. Turn right on Shearer, right on Club.

No. 314 is described as an English Country Cottage. The Dickensian lamp post on the front lawn certainly adds to this look.

No. 326, and No. 329 across the street, both have colorful gardens. One is of real flowers, the other artificial.

8. Turn left on Vollum, left on North.

In 1928 the Davidson and English Company of developers opened English Village on North Drive. Their ads boasted that each of the twenty-two rock-and-brick homes had a different design and varied floor plans. The ads also said that by visiting the site while the homes were still being constructed, the buyer could observe the quality of the construction.

9. Turn left on Kampmann, cut through parking lot and across the sports field to the front of Jefferson High School.

In 1930 Jefferson was the third school built by the San Antonio School District. Architect Max Frederick of the Adams and Adams firm designed it in the Spanish Moorish style. It has its own coat of arms. The entrance was carved by an Italian immigrant, Hannibar Pianta and his son, who did the carvings for the Aztec Theater downtown. The interior features solid dark oak beams supporting a ceiling of stenciled acoustical tiles. The $1,250,000 it cost to build was considered extravagant at that time. Compare that with the 1988 restoration cost of $1.1 million.

The school has been featured in several magazines here and abroad, including a 1937 photo essay in *Life* magazine that described it as the most modern high school in the country. It was the first school in San Antonio to have asphalt tile floors, built-in lockers, its own gym, and an unheard of (at that time), 2,000 seat auditorium with an impressive presidium arch, sunken orchestra pit, and projection booth.

Segments of the 1937 movie *High School* featuring Jane Withers, as well as its sequel, *Texas Girl* were shot here.

In 1982-83 the school's student council raised the money and processed the paperwork, including a zoning change, to have the school designated a historical landmark.

10. Cross Donaldson, turn left back to start.

At the time the school was built it was on the outer edge of the city limits and sparked development of homes and businesses as well as street projects in the surrounding area. One of these, two blocks to the right at Donaldson and Manor, was Jefferson Village, established in 1948, the first shopping center in San Antonio. At one time named Best Suburban Shopping Center in the United States, it is now a meager ghost of its former glory. Plans exist to renovate it. Whether they will ever be carried out is questionable as the area no longer has sufficient traffic to sustain shops. Commercial redevelopment at this time is concentrated on

Railroad ties, rails, and wagon used as yard decor, Monticello neighborhood

Fredericksburg Road. A one-mile stretch there has been designated as the "Deco District."

(Restaurants: If you drive back to Fredericksburg Road and turn left you will find a wide variety including DeWese's Tip Top Cafe for down-home cooking, King's Wok, and several Mexican restaurants including Las Tortillas that began as a distributor for Sanitary Tortillas visited in Walk 1, Side Trip B.)

16 King William Historic District

Features: One of San Antonio's finest residential and historic districts

Distance: 2.4 miles & 2.5 miles (3.8k & 4.0k)

Time: 1 hr. 30 min. & 1 hr. 30 min.

Nights: Yes. See Comments

Wheelchair Accessible: Yes. See Comments

Restrooms, Water, Phones: At start. See Comments

Restaurants: At start

Getting There: **Car:** Park at Guenther and King William Streets

Bus: King William Streetcar, hopefully. No. 44 Pleasanton/Belaire. Get off at So. Alamo and Guenther.

Comments:

The walk is routed for two short or one long walk.

Although both sections of King William are quiet, residential neighborhoods, it is still recommended that you do not walk alone at night.

The sidewalks are not always good, or even passable in some sections, even on foot. Nor are there curb ramps for wheelchairs. But traffic is light, so there is no problem using the street.

We start this walk near the Guenther House which is a museum, restaurant, and bakery and has restrooms just inside the entrance. The house is open Monday-Saturday from 9:00 A.M. to 5:00 P.M. and Sunday from 8:00 A.M. to 2:00 P.M. The restaurant is open Monday-Saturday from 7:00 A.M. to 3:00 P.M. and on Sunday from 8:00 A.M. to 2:00 P.M.

Overview:

In the first edition of this book the King William Historic District was part of the Downtown South walk. We have moved it to neighborhood walks, where it should be, and added more of the historic district, the area known as Baja King William (Lower King William). This name probably came into use because it is "lower" on the map than the better-known section north of Alamo Street. Interestingly, the whole King William district was part of the *labor de abajo* (lower farm field), of the Alamo.

Most of the homes in the King William neighborhood date from the 1860s through the 1920s. It was the tradition at the time for the first builder on a street to name it. Ernst Altgelt named King William Street after the Prussian ruler Wilhelm I. For a time around World War I it was called Pershing Avenue. Some of the other streets in the area had earlier names also.

A lot of the houses, especially in the Baja section, had become rundown by the 1970s, many of the larger ones divided into apartments. The section that comprises the first part of our walk began to upgrade in the late 1970s, converting back to single-family homes. In most recent years several have converted to bed and breakfast establishments. Baja King William has seen a spurt of renovation in the 1990s.

We point out some of the more outstanding and interesting houses along the walk. For more information about the houses, we recommend the two excellent books by Mary Burkholder (see Appendix E) which describe the homes in King

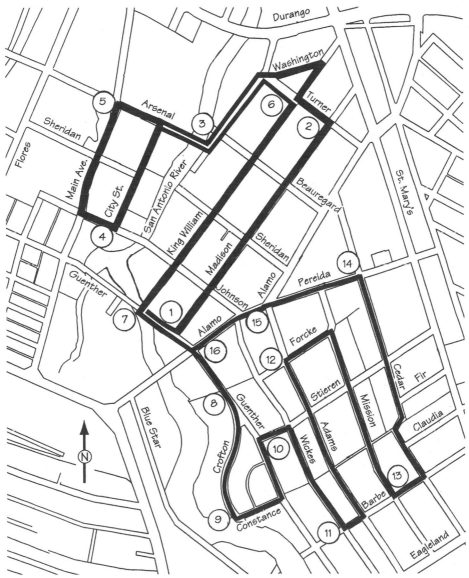

William in great detail. *The King William Area* covers the first section of the walk and *Down the Acequia Madre* covers the Baja King William area.

The San Antonio Conservation Society has a free pamphlet, available at their headquarters in the Wulff House, that provides details on some of the houses along King William Street.

It is not within the scope of this book to mention all of the houses. It was difficult deciding which few we could include. We point out our favorites, plus some of historic or architectural interest.

1.   Facing the Guenther House, turn left on Guenther, then left on Madison.

No. 219 Guenther is the Adolph Wagner house built around 1884-85. Note the superimposed A and W on the crest over the entrance. Mrs. Wagner was one of Guenther's daughters. At one time it was used for offices for the mill before being converted back into a residence.

No. 222 Guenther, on the left at Madison, dates from around 1886 and has an interesting "architect" history. Its designer and owner was architect Albert Beckmann, who was married to one of the Guenther daughters. It has been lived in by Beckmann's son, whose wife is the daughter of architect Alfred Giles. In 1965 it served as offices for architect O'Neil Ford. It is once again a private residence.

No. 403 Madison, the George Chabot house, has been added on to. Born in England, Chabot came here after working for the British foreign service in Mexico. The house dates from 1876. There is a marker.

No. 402 was built about the same time by a son of Chabot's.

No. 338 dates from around 1906 and is notable for its absolute symmetry.

No. 337 was featured in the "Historic American Buildings Survey." Built in 1872 as a one story, sometime after 1886 the second story was added.

No. 309 is the Jesse Oppenheimer house dating from about 1900. At one time it was a clinic and rest home.

No. 243 was built in 1995. Some like it, some don't.

No. 236 dates from 1892. Note the detail on the upper floor.

Nos. 213 and 217 have had additions to the original one-story houses. Built by stone mason Herman Wagenfuhr in the early 1870s, they are among the earliest stone houses in King William.

No. 209 was rented by architect Alfred Giles before he built his own house at 308 King William Street.

No. 202, dating from 1906, is the only house showing German influence in its design, despite the fact that many of the original King William residents were of German descent.

2. **Cross Turner and turn left. Turn right on King William and left on Washington.**

As you turn onto Turner, No. 117 Madison, across on the right, dates from 1896. From 1929-1946 it served as an exclusive girls school called Bonn Avon.

No. 130 King William is now headquarters of the San Antonio Art League.

At the end of King William Street, across on the left side, is the Anton Wulff house, headquarters of the San Antonio Conservation Society. Pick up a brochure at the front gate to use when we come back to this street of grand houses.

The gazebo in the park was originally located near the Commander's House on the other side of the river.

No. 209 Washington, the Ogé house, has a marker. It was originally one story with a half basement like No. 213, the house to its left. An 1882 remodeling by Alfred Giles resulted in this Deep South-style mansion. (Mark once lived here in an apartment under the front stairs.) The house has been renovated and is now a bed and breakfast.

No. 218 is a 1920 house that is notable for its fine brickwork.

House on City Street, King William

No. 231, the first of the Groos (of former Groos National Bank) family homes in the area, has delightful scrollwork as well as an interesting wood dowel fence. Why was there so much scroll work on houses of this period? Very simple. The scroll saw had just been invented.

No. 228, on the left, is built of caliche blocks and dates from 1866.

3. Turn right on Arsenal, cross the bridge, then left on City Street.

For all the interest in the River Walk and the King William Historic District, few people are aware of City Street that backs onto the river. This street was fairly rundown when we first came here. Now many of the houses have been renovated.

No. 103 City, on the right, has a great window on the Arsenal side which you will see on the way back.

No. 113 has a dormer turret and mullion windows, popular in Victorian architecture.

No. 204 is another house with turret and mullion window.

No. 212 has a pediment with nice scroll design.

4. Turn right on Johnson, right on Main.

No. 216 Johnson is a charming Victorian.

The apartment complex across on Main Street is run by the San Antonio Housing Authority.

At Arsenal Street, across on the left is that part of the former U.S. Arsenal that is still government property. The rest was sold to H. E. Butts and is that grocery

The Carl Gross house on King William Street.

chain's corporate headquarters. The lobby is open to the public (entrance on Main Street) and has exhibits of some of the arsenal paraphernalia.

Further down Main Street from Arsenal, the Commander's House, home to the commander of the arsenal, is now a senior center.

5. Turn right on Arsenal, left on Washington, right on Turner.

As you approach City Street again, note the large round stained glass window on the house we mentioned before.

6. Turn right on King William Street.

No. 217 is the Sartor House, designed by Alfred Giles in 1881. It has a historical marker.

No. 226, built in 1876, is the second King William house Ernst Altgelt built. He moved to San Antonio in 1866 from Comfort, Texas, a city he helped establish.

No. 236 is the 1867 house Altgelt built, the first on the block, that gave him the privilege of naming the street. A two-story addition was made to the first structure.

No. 241, built for Alexander Joske in 1892 around the original two-room house dating from 1881, had reached a terrible state of disrepair before its restoration in the late 1980s.

The first few houses on the 300 block still have carriage stepping stones at the curb.

Nos. 306 and 308 are two of the smaller homes that Alfred Giles designed.

No. 309, the Hummel House, is a good example of the L-plan, two-story house of nineteenth-century Texas. Some of its fireplaces have cast iron mantels, and it has a handsome circular stairway.

No. 335, designed by Alfred Giles for banker Carl Groos, is considered one of the outstanding Gothic Revival houses in Texas. Note the iron pipe columns on the porch and the deck and watchtower on the roof.

No. 401 started as a one-story house for owner Russell Norton. Edward Polk added the second floor. It was purchased and added onto again by rancher Ike Pryor. Walter Mathis restored it in 1968.

No. 419 is a simply designed house from 1867. It was the Ladies Boarding and Day School where Lucy Edmonds taught young ladies "literary, classical, and scientific knowledge, and polite and dignified deportment."

No. 422 is an outstanding house of Victorian Empire design dating from the mid-1880s and restored in 1974.

No. 425, an 1890s Romanesque Revival designed for George Kalteyer by James Riely Gordon, has a three-story-high stairwell topped by a skylight. Johanna Kalteyer and her friend Johanne Steves (Mrs. Edward Steves, Sr.) at No. 509 would ring a bell mounted on their porches to call each other to their daily kaffee klatsch.

No. 431 on the corner was a wedding present to Edward Steves, Jr. from his father. Note the difference in the stone used in the house itself and the carriage house behind it. The original carriage house was torn down when the river was widened, and this duplicate was built in the 1980s.

No. 504 across Johnson on the left, belonged to another Steves son, Albert.

At Johnson Street, to the right, is the old Commerce Street Bridge known as the "O. Henry Bridge" because it was that writer's favorite. The bridge was moved here when Commerce Street was widened in 1912. When they widened the river here the bridge was stored, then most of it inadvertantly sold as scrap. This bridge is a reproduction in the style of the original. Only one of the columns and a few parts are original.

No. 509, designed by Alfred Giles in 1876 for Edward Steves, Sr., is now owned by the San Antonio Conservation Society and is open to the public for a small fee, which includes a tour. All the doors and windows are spanned by rounded arches. The mansard roof reflects a French influence on the Gothic Revival architecture.

No. 516 is one of the newer houses in the district, constructed in 1927. The stone came from the original Pioneer Mill property, which is why it looks older. The iron fencing is old and was searched out piece by piece from San Antonio and surrounding towns.

No. 523, last house on the right, is the Carl Harnisch house built around 1884. Note the many porches and gables decorated with wooden scroll work. Mr. Harnisch and his mother-in-law, Mrs. Josephine Baer, owned Harnisch and Baer, one of the most elegant restaurants and confectioneries in San Antonio. The restaurant was decorated with potted palms, banana trees, and other plants, and featured fine cakes and pastries as well as their own ice cream. It was *the* place to go for gourmet food.

Across Guenther is the Guenther House and Pioneer Flour Mill. The house serves as a museum and is open to the public at no charge. There is a gift shop and a restaurant that serves breakfast and lunch at moderate prices. A good place to refresh yourself before and/or after the walk.

7. **Back at Guenther Street, to continue walk (2.5 miles), turn left, crossing South Alamo Street.**

Although there are homes on this side of Alamo as grand as the ones on King William Street, as a whole the homes are smaller. The neighborhood has seen an upsurge in renovation in the 1990s.

No. 409 Guenther is Miss Margaret's house, open to the public during Fiesta or by appointment for large groups. Built in 1891, it was bought in 1944 by Mrs. John S. Gething. Her daughter, Margaret, was a Broadway actress who used the name Nancy Allen in order to spare her scandalized family. After she gave up her stage career she studied interior design and became a noted consultant on historic preservation, working with Jacqueline Kennedy to restore the White House. This house is a Victorian gem, preserved just as Miss Margaret and her mother left it, and well worth a visit.

No. 503 was built in 1891 by developer C. A. Steiren for his own residence.

8. Bear right on Crofton.

The houses along here back onto the river.

Just as you turn onto Crofton is a newer townhouse complex.

No. 107 dates from 1892. At one time it had been turned into apartments. When we complemented the present owner on the fine job of restoration she said, "We worked hard. We love this old house."

No. 123 was the home of Albert Steves, Jr. and dates from 1908. The family frequently traveled by boat along the river between this house and the Steves' houses on King William Street.

No. 133 dates from 1892 and was probably designed by Albert Beckmann.

No. 151 was built in 1903 for Edward Hertzberg and remained in the family until 1971. It also has been restored in recent years. Note the Texas emblem in pebbles on the driveway and in stained glass at the entranceway. Note also the small shingles that have been painted multicolor. This treatment is not historical, but has become very popular. There are many examples throughout the area. Color, in fact, abounds in the restoration of homes in this area, ranging from subtle to outlandish.

No. 155 was built in 1890 by Theodore Hertzberg and sold in 1909 to Judge Sidney J. Brooks whose son Sidney, Jr. was one of the first cadets killed while training for World War I and for whom Brooks Air Force Base is named.

9. Turn left on Constance, left on Guenther.

No. 631 Guenther was bought new in 1901 by Hilmar Guenther, son of mill owner Carl Guenther.

10. Turn right on Stieren, right on Wickes.

Nos. 319 and 323 were built in 1891 by developer Axel Meerscheidt.

11. Turn left on Barbe, left on Adams.

No. 502 Adams, across Barbe, is a delightful stone cottage.

No. 434 was built by Widow Elmendorf in 1908 after the death of her husband, Emil. She lived here until her death in 1940.

No. 417 was sold in 1907 by Constance Barbe Ford to Clarence Barbe, then sold to Judge Luby whose family lived there for some 60 years. The house was called "Sans Souci."

No. 410 has a charming keyhole window on the second floor.

No. 332 was built in 1908 by Otto Meerscheidt who was related in some way to Axel and Paul Meerscheidt who developed much of the land around here. For some reason they didn't get a street named after them like the other big developers in this area. In 1955 the house was sold to Patterson Lodge No. 1177 A.F. and A.M. The lodge sign is gone now. Note the stained glass around the entrance and over the front windows.

No. 320 is a bed and breakfast. Built in 1889, it was bought by the present owner and her husband in 1954. The umbrella elm tree was planted in 1946 and may be the only one of its kind in San Antonio.

No. 302 is reputed to be the oldest house on Adams, built in 1888 for developer Paul Meerscheidt.

No. 221, the Schulze/Schilo house, has a historical marker. It dates from 1891. This is the Schilo family that owns the popular German restaurant on Commerce Street downtown.

12. Turn right on Forcke, then right on Mission.

No. 322 Mission is delightful with its onion dome over the corner of its gingerbread porch.

13. Turn left on Barbe, left on Cedar.

No. 311 Cedar is competing with the enchilada-red central library. Note also the shingles and the leaded glass entry way.

No. 201 is a caliche block (stuccoed over), two-room house built by owner Ernst Wehrhahn for his field hands.

14. Turn left on Pereida.

No. 318 is another stone and caliche house dating from 1887.

No. 317, the limestone block house across the street, dates from the early 1880s.

No. 412 is the 1892 home of Jens Jacob Olsen, a retired Norwegian sea captain. In 1887 he quit the sea, gave his ship to relatives in New York, and followed other family members to San Antonio. He had many businesses including hauling wood and coal. He kept his teams of mules on the lot behind here on Mission Street. Later his son Jens, Jr. built a house on that lot. This house is part of the Beethoven House property now.

No. 422 is the Beethoven House and Beer Garden which was originally built about 1886 by Julius Piper. It was bought in 1920 by the Beethoven Männerchor and has

Onion Dome, Baja King William

since been altered and enlarged. There are wonderful German festivals here throughout the summer and during Fiesta with lots of German food and oom-pah music to polka and waltz to.

No. 430 (where Pereida, Adams, and Alamo come together), and hiding behind thick vegetation, is the 1884 house built for Benno and Mary Engleke. After he and his wife died, the property went to the niece they had raised, a local librarian by the name of Emily Netter, who lived there until she died circa 1970. The new owner still lives there as of this writing. The wild growth of trees in front gives the house a mysterious look, which is dispelled when you realize the main entrance is now around the corner on Adams Street.

15. Continue on along South Alamo Street.

1146 South Alamo was originally 105 Adam. It was designed in 1906 by Leo Dielmann for Joseph Courand, Jr. From 1951-1963 it was used by the Oblate Fathers who made extensive changes to the exterior. In 1972 it was sold to the Mission Salvation. During this period it acquired an ugly fire escape along the Alamo Street side that greatly detracted from its appearance. It has recently been restored to at least some of its original elegance. Notice the traditional blue ceiling on the porch, designed to fool wasps into thinking it is sky so they won't build their nest there.

At Wickes Street is the Alamo Street Restaurant and Theater in the former Alamo Methodist Church. The restaurant serves a buffet lunch and is noted for its great desserts. On most weekend evenings it offers dinner and a show. Its resident ghosts have never made themselves known to dining room patrons. The restaurant is a casual, friendly place.

Nos. 1210-1220 were obviously built from the same plans. They date from the 1890s.

No. 1223 across the street dates from 1902. Note the scroll work, carriage house, and playhouse in the side yard.

No. 1231 is the oldest house on this block dating from 1889.

16. Turn right on Guenther back to start.

Further down South Alamo is the Blue Star Art Space, an eclectic collection of galleries, studios, and apartments in an old warehouse complex. (See Walk 4 River Walk South.)

Entranceway, Baja King William

17 Monte Vista/Alta Vista

Features: Historic San Pedro Park, Monte Vista Historic District, and a bit of the Alta Vista neighborhood

Distance: 5.3 miles (8.5k) See Comments

Time: 2.5 hours

Night: No

Wheelchair Accessible: Yes. See Comments

Restrooms, Water, Phone: At start at library and tennis center

Restaurant: Several along San Pedro. See ☞ 10.

Getting There: **Car:** Park in the lot at San Pedro Park, corner of Myrtle and San Pedro (metered, weekdays only, 10 cents an hour, up to 10 hours—free on weekends). Also, free parking any time in lot off Ashby Place.

Bus: No. 3 or 4 San Pedro. Get off by park.

Comments:

Although in this revised edition we tried to shorten the longer walks or adapt them to be taken in shorter loops, we could not do that to our satisfaction on this walk. To tailor the walk to your needs we suggest going in two cars or stopping midway (Main and Woodlawn) for lunch and then continuing. Or, you can catch a city bus anywhere on San Pedro that will take you back to San Pedro Park.

Although most of the walk is wheelchair accessible, there are stairs at Step 5. To avoid this, at Step 4 go out to San Pedro Street and turn left, instead of cutting through the park and up the stairs.

Overview:

Mastodons and saber-toothed tigers drank from the springs in the area that is now San Pedro Park. Early inhabitants settled in this area because of its abundant water. In 1718 the first location of Mission San Antonio de Valero was established near here. In 1729 King Philip of Spain granted this area as public land, making it the second oldest municipal park in the United States. (What's the oldest one? Boston Common.)

The Canary Island settlers built the San Pedro Acequia (irrigation ditch) that brought water from the springs here to their settlement at what is now Main Plaza. The acequia served San Antonio for the next 150 years. San Pedro Creek runs from here to the San Antonio River near Mission Concepción.

In 1846, the first U.S. soldiers in Texas camped here on their arrival and again on their departure at the outbreak of the Civil War. In 1856, Jeff Davis, then U.S.

Secretary of War, camped here with his Camel Corps when he hoped that camels could replace mules. During the Civil War the Confederate army used the park as a prisoner of war camp. After the war, F. F. Duerler leased the park and created a recreation center. He built five artificial lakes along one shore of the natural lake with footpaths for strolling and offered hot air balloon rides, boats, a museum, and a zoo. San Pedro Park became the place to see and be seen on a Sunday afternoon.

Renovation of San Pedro Park is scheduled for Spring 1998 through Spring 1999. A major part of the renovation is a new swimming pool in a design reminiscent of the former lake. The grandstand at the tennis center will be removed,

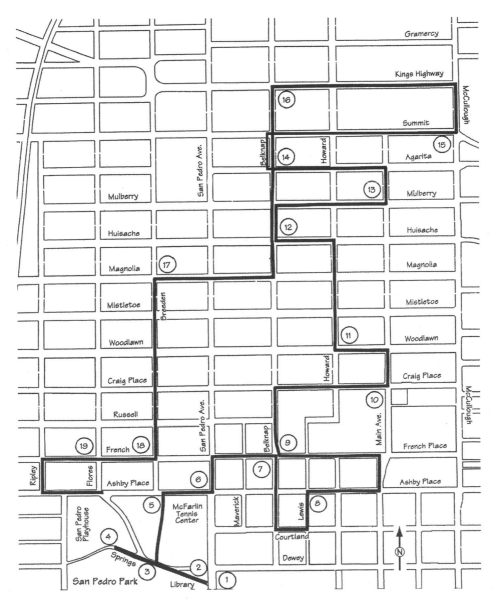

opening the visual appearance of the park. The whole will be enhanced with new landscaping and lighting.

San Pedro Park and the neighborhood to the north on this side of San Pedro Avenue are part of the Alta Vista Neighborhood whose association is very active in working to preserve the park as well as its fine old neighborhood.

Most of this walk is in the Monte Vista Historic District, the area between San Pedro and McCullough and from Ashby to Hildebrand. Originally part of a Spanish land grant to the city in the 1730s, permission for the sale of this public land was granted in 1851. Laurel Heights was the first development, followed by Summit Place which included the streets of Agarita, Summit and Kings Highway. Some of San Antonio's most prominent citizens built their homes here. Early developers' ads stressed that at 100 feet above downtown, the site offered great views and caught the sea breeze from the southeast, and that it was the "... only hill that is reached without crossing railroad tracks or passing poor houses."

1. **Start in front of the library.**

This is San Antonio's first branch library. Out on the sidewalk are two historical markers. The one on the left tells about the springs, the one on the right about an event of the Civil War.

2. **Just past the marker on the right, turn left on the sidewalk that angles across the middle of the park.**

The building behind the library is the Block House. Its origins have been obscured—it may date from 1718 as part of the Mission,—or it could date from 1862, or it could be the remains of a stockade, or maybe it was an arsenal. Nobody knows for sure. Now it's a tool shed.

The grove of trees includes mostly live oak, juniper, and persimmon. Looking through the trees you can see the fern-covered grotto built in 1884. It once had a pointed, stained-glass roof with a water fountain within. Now the water bubbles over the top. To the right of the grotto are the formal gardens. The bandstand was moved here in 1920 from Alamo Plaza. An inverted heart-shaped stone (nobody seems to know about this either), marks the entrance to the old bear pit under it.

The headwaters of San Pedro Creek are located among the live oaks to the right of the bandstand. Somewhere out there is the lost entrance to huge caves, complete with stalagmites and stalactites created by a rapidly flowing underground river. The caves were supposedly last entered in the 1890s.

3. **At the brick steps on the left, go down to the area that overlooks San Pedro Springs.**

You are on the bank of the springs, which are now dry except for times of heavy rain. The present swimming pool replaces an earlier spring-fed pool where water flowed with such volume that it flushed the pool three times every twenty-four hours. By 1940, however, the flow was too weak to keep the pool clean. That pool replaced the original natural lake.

Imagine that it's a sunny June day in 1878. You have just arrived at the park on the first streetcar to run from Alamo Plaza. The kids loved it when a snake scared the mules and caused the trolley to jump track. The conductor ran down the mules while the male passengers got the trolley back on track. The trolley had to stop at the bottom of the hill because the grade to Ashby Place was too steep for the mules. (Even today's powerful VIA buses strain to make that hill from a dead stop.) Now you are in the park, strolling among the lakes, and greeting your friends and relatives. The kids have gone off to see the animal exhibits. Later, you paddle around the lake in a canoe. When every one is hungry, you spread a cloth in the live oak grove and enjoy a picnic lunch while listening to the band concert. There are no political rallies today, but you will never forget listening as a child to the rousing speech Governor Sam Houston gave here when he was fighting against secession. Old legends say robbers hid their loot in the nearby caves and that grim specters lead searchers away from the treasure Francisco Rodriguez buried there. You shudder when you think of how they used to put a bear and a Texas longhorn steer in the bear pit and let them fight it out. After lunch and another stroll along the lake, it's time to call the kids and catch the trolley back to town.

Old light standard in San Pedro Park
(Photo by Celia Wakefield)

4. **Go up the stairs on the right by the fountain, turn right, and then left on the path alongside the tennis center.**

The McFarlin Tennis Center is considered one of the finest facilities of its kind.

Across to the left is the San Pedro Playhouse. Its facade is a reproduction of the Market House, which gave Market Street its name. The original had been saved for some future use, but by the time it had been designated for this project, the locally quarried, porous limestone had deteriorated beyond use. Architect Bartlett Cocke faithfully copied the design in a more durable stone.

5. **At the end of the path, go up the steps to Ashby and turn right.**

On the left are two homes dating from 1914 that belonged to the Frost family and are now the Kritérion Montessori School.

6. **Cross San Pedro, turn left. At French Place turn right.**

No. 1616 San Pedro, on the right at the corner of French, is a 1903 "California style" built around a central, gallery-lined patio.

No. 1717 San Pedro, across on the left, is the Woman's Club of San Antonio in the former 1904 Woodward mansion. May Bock Woodward, an artist known as the "grande dame of society," worked closely with architect Atlee B. Ayres on the design of this Classical Revival home.

French Place was the location of some of the most opulent homes in the Laurel Heights development. Several from among the finest of these have been razed, but many outstanding ones still exist. It was the destruction of these grand houses in 1975 that sparked the formation of the Monte Vista Historic District, combining Laurel Heights, Summit Place and Monte Vista into one historical district.

No. 511 West French is a 1908 Alfred Giles design.

No. 509 West is a Colonial residence built in 1907 ". . . after the fashion of the old homes in Virginia . . .."

No. 510 West is a Moorish villa that dates from 1905 and has a lush, sunken garden.

No. 501 West is an Atlee B. Ayres design from 1904.

7. **Cross Belknap, turn right, cross Ashby and walk around the Koehler block: left on Courtland, left on Lewis.**

Belknap is named for Colonel Augustus Belknap, who, among other accomplishments, replaced the old mule-driven streetcars on San Pedro with electric ones.

No. 300 French Place (corner of Belknap), is the 1910 home designed by Atlee B. Ayres for Roy Hearne. We'll come around in front of it later.

No. 306 Belknap is the original carriage house of the Hearne home. Note also the charming Victorian playhouse in the side yard.

At Ashby is Temple Beth-El, the first Jewish congregation in San Antonio, formerly located by Travis Park.

Across Belknap from the temple is a greenhouse belonging to the Koehler mansion. In the right front corner is a wheel that simultaneously opens all the windows on that side. The vents at the top are also opened by a mechanical apparatus.

No. 201 (next to the temple), is architect Atlee B. Ayres's own 1909 home in early English style that was renovated late 1996.

We felt it was worth a walk around the block to fully appreciate the grand mansion Otto Koehler built in 1900; it is still one of the showplaces of San Antonio. From the porch Koehler could watch the smokestacks at his Pearl Brewery to make sure everything was going well. The house now belongs to San Antonio College.

8. Back at Ashby, turn right, then left on Main, and left on French Place.

No. 105 East French Place (catercorner across Main) is the 1891 Queen Ann designed by J. Riely Gordon, and now part of the San Antonio Academy. A historical marker in front tells about the Monte Vista Historical District. Next to No. 105 is the early 1890s home of Eleanor Stribling.

No. 128 West French, further up on the left, is the oldest dwelling in Monte Vista, built by Nathan Gould in 1882 and called "Bella Vista." Originally even smaller, it was added on to in 1892. Gould's daughter, Emily, married Robert Onderdonk. Two of their three children, Eleanor and Julian, became famous artists. The family lived in the house for nearly a century. It has a Texas Historical Commission marker.

No. 137 West, the 1887 home of E.B. Chandler—one of the earliest and finest on French Place—was considered a Texas showplace. The house originally had a lot of Queen Anne scroll work, particularly around the roof lines above the first- and second-floor porches, which gave it a more charming appearance than it has today. It was the scene of frequent entertainment: teas, receptions, and garden parties. The Chandlers bequeathed it as the Chandler Memorial Home "for gentlewomen in needy circumstances."

At the corner of Belknap you are at the front of the beautiful Roy Hearne house.

9. Turn right on Belknap, then right on Craig.

Christ Episcopal Church began construction in 1913 on the grounds of the former Gage mansion. Atlee B. Ayres was the architect. Several other structures on the property are attributed to Ayres and his son, Robert. Note the metal sculpture by Charles Umlauf over the church entrance.

Turn right on the sidewalk to see the original Gage carriage house. It has a historical marker.

No. 505 Belknap, at the corner of Russell, is the home built for Laurel Heights developer Jay Adams. The house is attributed to J. Riely Gordon or his protégés, McAdoo and Wooley. Most notable is the metal railing beset with two griffins on the front porch. The house is now a bed and breakfast.

Craig Place is named for the Reverend William Beard Craig of the Disciples of Christ Church who purchased the land between Howard and Belknap in the early 1890s. According to an article in the *Light* in May 1902, a local resident complained to police that cattle and horses were being turned loose at night to graze, including on his lawn and shrubbery. This street presently has a nice mixture of old homes and newer town houses and no grazing horses or cattle.

No. 241 West Craig is a turn-of-the-century house that won a San Antonio Conservation Society award in 1988.

No. 238 West is an Atlee B. Ayres design dating from the early 1900s in what Ayres described as "the Colonial style," but described in the San Antonio Historic Survey as "Neo-Georgian Revival." Whichever it is, it was a favorite to photograph for articles and pamphlets describing beautiful San Antonio.

On the corner at Howard is the Castle Arms, originally a single-family home built in 1910. Additions were made as the owner's daughters married and moved in. It was converted to apartments in the 1950s.

No. 117 West Craig is the oldest home on Craig built for H. Albert Hildebrand in 1891 by the firm of Giles and Guindon. A mural in the dining room is attributed to neighbor Julian Onderdonk.

No. 107 West, on the NW corner of Main, is an Atlee B. Ayres house built in 1906 for Judge Winchester Kelso. Saved part way through an illegal demolition, its future is uncertain.

The Ike Kampmann house on Kings Highway.

10. Turn left on Main, then left on Woodlawn.

(La Fonda is a good, moderately priced Mexican restaurant. On the next block, Magnolia Gardens is also good at moderate prices.)

Ahead on Main is a commercial block that offers both delicious eating and delightful shopping and browsing in gift and antique stores.

No. 105 West Woodlawn is a beautiful example of Queen Anne architecture that dates from about 1897.

No. 117 West, dating from 1897, is reputed to be the first house built as part of the Adams's Laurel Heights development.

No. 127 West is where U.S. Congressman and Mayor of San Antonio Maury Maverick Sr. lived from the time he returned to San Antonio in 1947 until his death in 1954.

11. Turn right on Howard, left on Huisache.

No. 228 West Huisache is a modified English Tudor that has, should you care to count, sixty-six windows. Much of the original interior is intact with lovely, dark woodwork and impressive, if faded, tapestries on the dining room walls. The 1915 built-in vacuum system still works. This innovation in housekeeping was all the rage at that time and a much-touted feature in ads for homes in this area.

12. Turn right on Belknap, right on Mulberry.

Nos. 228, 224, and 222 West Mulberry were all designed by Atlee B. Ayres in 1918. Atlee Jr. lived at 224.

No. 231 West (across from 222) is the home architect Carleton Adams built as his own in 1922.

13. Turn left on Main, left on Agarita.

No. 222 West Agarita is an Italian Renaissance that dates from 1926.

No. 223 West is an Atlee B. Ayres design from 1914 built to reflect the new "open to the outdoors" trend. In front of it is one of the grandest live oaks in San Antonio.

No. 228 West is an impressive 1917 modified Italian Renaissance design by architects Reuter and Harrington.

14. Turn right on Belknap, right on Summit.

No. 240 West Summit, an elegant Italian Renaissance on the right at the corner, was designed in 1920 by Ralph Cameron. It is still considered one of the finest houses in Monte Vista.

No. 230 West is a 1925 Adams and Adams English-style design. Note the Victorian playhouse and gazebo pigeon coop in the side yard.

No. 202 West was built for one of the Frost brothers. The sycamore tree in its side yard is reputed to be one of San Antonio's largest.

No. 125 West was built for Guy S. Combs in 1913 by Adams and Adams.

No. 119 West is a distinctive home built for real estate developer Paul O'Brian in the 1920s.

No. 101 West is a "modified colonial" home designed by John Marriott. Its setting befits its lovely appearance.

No. 118 East Summit was originally built at the 101 West address, then moved here, with some modifications. It was the 1910 home of Judge J.O. Terrell. It is now apartments.

No. 129 East is a 1922 Atlee B. Ayres design described as an "Italianate farmhouse." Atlee said he got the idea for the Byzantine design on the arch over the doorways from his European travels.

No. 142 East, on the corner, is probably the oldest house on Summit, which at that time was the farthest street within the San Antonio city limits. Frank Doyle, who may or may not have been the first occupant, lived there from about 1906 and kept a dairy herd in a pasture between Summit and Kings Highway.

15.   Turn left on McCullough, then left on Kings Highway.

Across McCullough on the right is St. Anthony's Catholic Seminary.

Kings Highway became known as the Avenue of the Cattle Barons after several ranchers built their homes here; it was considered the city's most prestigious address after World War I.

No. 131 East, built for Ike Kampmann, Jr. in 1922, used materials from an earlier 1890 Kampmann home that was downtown on the site of the Scottish Rite Cathedral. The stonework on the entrance was carved by an itinerant Italian stonecutter who found his way to San Antonio. The bay windows on the east side and the gazebo in the back are from the old house.

No. 114 East, on the left, was built in the impressive Renaissance Revival style. It was designed by H. A. Reuter in 1912 for cattleman Herbert Lee Kokernot. At one time it belonged to the Right Reverend Robert E. Lucy, Archbishop of the San Antonio Catholic Archdiocese from the 1940s through the 1960s.

No. 119 East, on the right, belonged to John W. Kokernot, brother of Herbert.

There is a unique numbering system on this block, and all blocks north of here. Main Street, the east-west divider, as you saw on Summit, does not continue through. The east-west numbering does. Thus, we have 101 East and 102 East and next to them, 105 West and 108 West. Coincidentally, the two houses on East are red brick, and the two on West beige brick.

No. 101 East was built in 1929 for Mr. Hornaday, an oil and gas pioneer, by Ralph H. Cameron. It was later sold to O. Scott Pettys, who was also in oil and gas, but was a rancher as well.

No. 105 West, designed by Atlee B. Ayres in 1907, is the oldest of the Kings Highway houses.

16. Turn left on Belknap, then right on Magnolia.

Another magnificant tree is the magnolia on the southwest corner of Kings Highway and Belknap.

On the southwest corner of Mulberry is the 1921 home Atlee B. Ayres designed for oil magnate Dr. F. L. Thomson. Thomson believed in "keeping fit," and had a completely-equipped gymnasium installed.

After you cross San Pedro you are in the Alta Vista neighborhood.

17. Turn left on Breeden.

At Mistletoe, on the left, is a most unusual apartment building. It has several wonderful features. It would be nice to see it fully renovated.

Across the street on the right, the red brick building was once a Southwestern Bell switching station. It went through several transitions and is now the home of a local antique dealer.

18. Turn right on French Place.

When you get to Flores, if you are completely exhausted, San Pedro Park is one block to your left. If you have a spark of energy left, continue on for a short, but interesting excursion.

19. Continue on French, then turn left on Ripley, and finally, left on Ashby back to San Pedro Park.

When you get to Ashby, across the street is a row of small, shotgun houses. These could have been built for railroad workers, but another theory is that they were built for servants who worked in the Monte Vista area. At the time the area comprising the Monte Vista Historic District was developing (late 1800s), it was the custom that non-white servants (at that time this meant people of Mexican and African decent), had to be out of the district by a certain hour each day. These houses, as you can see, are built not only adjacent to the railroad tracks, but in a low area subject to flooding from the springs, thus making it undesirable for other development.

At the corner of Ashby and Flores are two restored commercial buildings. During the course of working on the first edition of this book we watched them change from decrepit relics to the nicely renovated buildings you see now—a good argument for restoration over demolition.

 For more information on San Pedro Park and the Monte Vista Historical District, stop in at the library. We especially recommend *Monte Vista, The Gilded Age of an Historic District, 1890-1930* by Donald E. Everett. It is full of information about the houses of Monte Vista and the people who built them.

18 Olmos Park

Features: A neighborhood of fine homes on shady, winding, slightly hilly streets

Distance: 3.0 & 1.9 miles (4.8k & 3.0k) See Comments

Time: 1 hr. 15 min. & 50 min. See Comments

Nights: No, too dark

Wheelchair Accessible: No, too hilly

Restrooms, Water, Phone: At start

Restaurants: At start

Getting There: **Car:** Park at Wildwood and McCullough.

Bus: No. 5 McCullough. Get off at Wildwood (southbound) or Hermosa (northbound). Take either to Hillside to start walk.

Comments:

The route is arranged so it can be taken in one long or two short walks.

There are no sidewalks on most of this walk, but little street traffic. Always walk on left side facing traffic.

While not exactly a "hilly" walk, it isn't flat either. There is one long, gradual grade.

Overview:

Olmos Park is one of several separate, incorporated cities surrounded by the City of San Antonio. It sits on land granted to San Antonio by the Spanish in the early 1730s. Development began in 1927 and it became incorporated as the Town of Olmos Park in 1939. There were strict building codes both for materials used and cost.

This is a particularly lovely area of mostly large homes and huge old-growth live oaks. Many large magnolias may be seen also. As with some other of the neighborhood walks, we offer it as a place to stroll and to enjoy, with little commentary.

We thank the American Institute of Architects (AIA) for permission to use descriptions of the houses from their book *A Guide to San Antonio Architecture*.

1. **Walk up Wildwood to Hillside, turn right. Turn left on Mandalay and follow it around back to Hillside.**

No. 115 Wildwood, on the left, note the carvings around the front window.

On Mandalay, on the left at the corner of Broadmore, is a house guarded by two eagles. Across Broadmore, also on the left, two dogs do guard duty. We noticed

"guards," mostly various breeds of dogs, on several houses throughout the area, more so than other neighborhoods.

No. 505 East Mandalay, on the left, actually faces on Wildwood. You will have a better view of it later.

2. **Turn right on Hillside, then right on Paseo Encinal and follow it around to El Prado.**

No. 320 Paseo Encinal has a beautiful iron fence of elaborate design.

No. 300, on the right side at Wildwood, with its many old live oak trees, is considered one of the loveliest sites in Olmos Park. This 1929 house looks even older because the stone came from an old store downtown. The property on the right also has a fine stand of oaks. In fact, the whole length of Wildwood, as you will see on the return route, is a live oak grove.

Live oak is so-called because it keeps its leaves all winter, new leaves coming out as soon as the old ones drop.

No. 111 Paseo Encinal, the yellow Mediterranean-style house with the stone gateposts and iron fence, is most impressive. Note the plaque of Mother and Child by the door.

Live oak trees

3. **Turn left on El Prado, then left on Parklane.**

   For shorter walk (3.0 miles), continue at Step 4.

   For longer walk (another 1.9 miles), go to Step 7.

4. **Turn left on Contour Drive, then left on Wildwood.**

On Contour there is a parkway on the right for walking off-street. This is beneficial because there are blind curves on the left, traffic-facing side.

Wildwood is a long grade, but fairly gradual. Now you will see what we meant about Wildwood and live oaks, while getting new views of some of the corner houses you have already passed.

Across Mandalay, on the right, is the Clements house mentioned before, designed in 1947 by Houston architect Birdsall Briscoe, who excelled in the neo-Adams and Regency styles. The AIA book notes that this house exemplifies his grand manner and ranks it as one of the area's outstanding Georgian style houses. We would describe it more simply as a "stately mansion." It is guarded by two not-so-ferocious-looking lions.

5. **At Alameda Circle walk left around circle, then turn left on Wildwood on the opposite side of No. 300 from where you came up. (Yes, both streets are East Wildwood. Crazy circle!)**

The first house to the left on the circle is No. 400. There are only five houses, numbered 100, 200, etc. No. 300, the 1929 Morgan House (between the two Wildwood street signs), is even bigger than it looks, containing over 20,000 square feet of living space.

6. **At the triangle bear left to stay on Wildwood.**

(Back at McCullough, across in The Yard, is Bakersfield, a yummy bakery that serves breakfast and lunch.)

7. **For a longer or second walk: Turn right on Contour. At Olmos, turn left, then right on Park Drive.**

We enjoy the diversity of architectural styles and details along this next section of the walk.

On Park Drive we spotted a red rooster perched on a turret and an imposing leaded glass entrance way.

8. **Turn left on Park Hill.**

Here on Park Hill are fountains, a painted tile entranceway, and some interesting stone work.

No. 214 was built for the Turner family in 1928 by Robert Hugman who designed the River Walk. The AIA book describes it as one of the best Spanish Colonial Revival houses in San Antonio. The dome-topped room on the right is

The 1929 Morgan house on Alameda Circle (Photo by Celia Wakefield).

thought to be a copy of the mission church of San Xavier del Bac near Tucson, Arizona.

Where Park Hill curves just before Olmos, on the left, is a concrete table and bench and a wonderful big tree house. After the curve, lurking on the branch of a huge live oak tree is a vulture ready to pounce.

9. Turn right on Olmos.

No. 800 East Olmos (on the corner just as you turn), was built in 1927 by the Ayres firm. It is considered one of the firm's best. The informality of the house contrasts with the formal symmetry of No. 810 next door, built by the same firm in the same year.

10. At Devine, turn left, crossing Olmos, then turn left on Park (Park is before the overpass).

Walk along the parkway on the right on Park Street to avoid blind curves on the left side of the street.

11. Turn right on Olmos, then right again on Contour. At Parklane, to continue walk, go back to Step 4.

Again, on Contour, use the parkway on the right to avoid blind curves on the left side of the street.

19 Terrell Hills

Features: A neighborhood of fine homes

Distance: 2.7 miles (4.3k)

Time: 1.0 hour

Nights: No, too dark

Wheelchair Accessible: See comments

Restrooms, Water, Phone: At start

Restaurants: At start

Getting there: **Car:**   Park at Broadway and Harrigan

                    Bus: No. 9 Broadway or No. 14 Perrin Beitel. Get off at Katherine.

Comments:

The walk starts with a long, unshaded, but very gradual uphill grade. At the top there is welcome shade and a center strip parkway with benches.

Although there are grades at either end of the walk, most of it is relatively flat. For wheelchair accessibility one could park and start at the top. There are no sidewalks, but also little traffic.

Overview:

Development of this section of Terrell Hills began in the 1910s. It was incorporated as a separate city in 1957.

A few of the original large estates have been divided into "smaller" lots, but there are restrictions on how small they can be, and the city council must approve any subdivision. Some proposals have been rejected. Not only lot size, but architectural features may be questioned by Terrell Hills residents.

1. **From Broadway walk up Harrigan. At New Braunfels, turn right, then left on Geneseo.**

Once up the hill, a center parkway adds to the ambience of this pleasant walk.

No. 305 Geneseo: According to an article in an October, 1987, issue of the *Express-News*, some local residents were aghast at the opulence of this gate and fence.

2. At Dover turn left, then left on Terrell.

In the 1930s, Terrell Road was the only paved street in the area. No. 275 Terrell, on the corner of Cross, is the gallery Alfred Warren built in 1912 to show the works of his father, Henry Warren, a British-born artist and set designer. When Alfred died in 1917, the art work was divided among his heirs, and a daughter moved into this building, converting it to a home. It remained in the family until 1965. The large, tall rooms give the outside of the house the appearance of being a two-story, but it is not.

3. At Broadway turn left back to car.

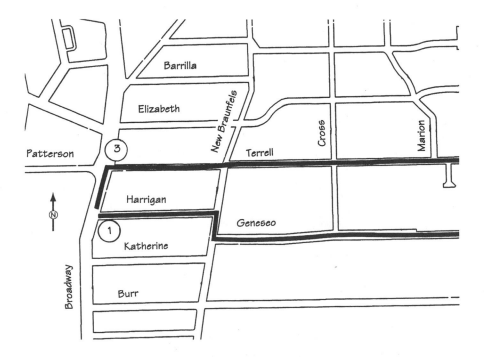

House in Terrell Hills

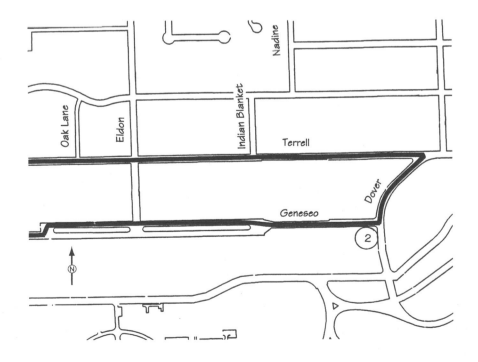

20 Westside

Features: Union Stock Yards, Produce Terminal, the murals of Cassiano Homes, "El Westside," and the Guadalupe Cultural Center

Distance: 6.7 miles (10.7 k)

Time: 3 hours

Nights: No

Wheelchair Accessible: Second part. See Comments

Restrooms, Water, Phones: Stockyards and Produce Terminal

Restaurants: At start and ☞ 2 and 3

Getting There: **Car:**   Park in front of the stockyards on San Marcos Street off Laredo Street.

                Bus: No. 54 S. Main. Get off on Furnish at San Marcos. Turn right to stockyards. To return, board across the street.

Comments:

Unfortunately, we no longer feel we can recommend the Westside for walking. Since the first edition of the book, parts of this walk have held a potential for danger, even in the daytime. Conditions have improved, but still are not good enough. Hopefully someday we will be able to take this very interesting walk again.

Meanwhile, its points of interest can be visited by car. You can drive to the stockyards (☞ 12) and the produce terminal (☞ 3) and take our tour through these facilities. You can drive past the murals at Cassiano Homes (☞ 4), and visit the Guadalupe Cultural Center (☞ 10). Also, don't overlook the Cinderella Bakery at ☞ 5 and the Segovia Mexican Candy Company at ☞ 9.

Being basically optimistic about improvements in the safety of walking on the Westside, we have left the walking instructions intact. Should you decide to walk it, just remember, daytime only, not even late afternoon. Definitely don't walk alone, and preferably walk with a small group. Don't make yourself vulnerable by wearing valuable jewelry or carrying an expensive camera.

The stockyard and produce terminal are not wheelchair accessible.

Overview:

This walk takes you to three places rarely visited by the general public.

"People don't know the Produce Terminal exists," Administrative Director Rudy Tiehes told us. Although most people know there are stockyards, few know where they are or what goes on there. And although everyone knows there's a Westside, it is not a place they think of to go walking. Juan Hernandez,

coordinator of the mural program at Cassiano Homes, says, "The local residents are proud of the murals and are used to people coming to see them."

Because these are such distinct environments, we will give an overview of each as we approach it. We begin the walk with a tour of the Produce Terminal because it should be seen early in the morning. We return to tour the stockyards at step 12.

The earlier you get to the produce terminal, the better, as activity begins to slacken after 8:00 A.M. There is still plenty to see anytime in the morning, however. The Stockyards are open 24 hours a day. Monday and Wednesday are auction days, starting at 9:00 A.M. and lasting at least until noon. That's when the action is! Other days there are mostly just empty pens to see.

1. **Facing the big longhorn steer on top of the stockyards building, turn right on San Marcos.**

A short way past the railroad tracks, in the open door of the gray metal sheds on the left, you can see workers salting down and stacking animal hides for shipment to leather processors.

2. **Turn left on Laredo.**

(Piedras Negras [Black Rocks] is a very good, inexpensive restaurant—a favorite with locals, or squeeze into the tiny J & T Cafe at 2102 Laredo for good breakfast tacos.)

Off to the left, you can see some of the old packinghouses. In the late 1800s, and until World War II, San Antonio was a major clearinghouse for livestock. Little slaughtering is done here these days.

The small houses in this area are mostly forty to fifty years old. Other, newer ones were built with federal loans in a program to upgrade housing conditions. There is a strong sense of community on the Westside. Many people, as they become more affluent, stay here and rebuild or add onto their homes rather than move away.

At San Jacinto Street, cross Laredo to the park on the right, and walk along Apache Creek.

Immediately after crossing Laredo, look across the creek and to the right. The apartment block you see is the Alazan-Apache Courts, the oldest public housing project in the United States, dating from 1942. Mayor Maury Maverick, the catalyst behind several city improvement programs, promoted it for San Antonio. The area along this creek flooded badly in 1921; houses were washed away and many people were killed. The creek bed has been widened, straightened, and cemented to control floods.

This strip park is a good place to pick up your pace and burn some calories so you can indulge later at the bakery and candy factory.

3. **Turn left on Zarzamora and turn into the parking area of the Produce Terminal.**

IMPORTANT: *Check in at the gate.* As you follow the tour, keep in mind that this is a work place. Some businesses do not mind visitors, other do. *Only go into those places we designate. Watch where you walk.* There are forklift prongs, moving trucks, and slippery floors. *Hold on to kids. Don't touch anything or disturb anyone.* Sure this sounds like a lot of rules and regulations, but we do not want to lose the privilege of being able to come in here.

Rudy Tiehes, who has been here since 1982, showed us around. He obviously loves the Produce Terminal and takes great pride in it. The market is owned by a corporation, with many of the produce houses having shares. There are twenty-five companies on the docks with eighteen more in the administration building, which houses the Terminal offices, produce and truck brokers, an office of the U. S. Department of Agriculture, and a restaurant.

The market is busiest between 5:00 and 8:30 A.M. Most produce arrives in the city by truck although some specialty items are flown in. The bulk of the produce comes from Mexico, South America, California, Arizona, and, of course, Texas. The gate is open twenty-four hours a day, with trucks coming in on an irregular basis. The busiest days are Monday (after the weekend) and Thursday (preparing for the weekend).

More and more produce houses are going into the food service business. They wash, pare, and even chop, cut, and slice vegetables for restaurant use.

Refer to map of Produce Terminal.

A. Walk up the steps at the near end of the south dock.

1. The first location is Tender Care Produce. Do not go inside the processing areas.
2. California Fruit also prefers that you do not go inside. As you walk along the dock, you can see from the labels on the boxes where the produce comes from.
3. At B. Catalani, if there is someone in the first of the glassed-in offices, ask if that person can show you the ripening boxes. If not, you can see the huge doors of the refrigerated ripening rooms through the plastic curtain. *Do not go in unescorted.* Forty thousand-pound truckloads of fruit, especially bananas, are unloaded into the coolers. Ethylene gas is poured into a catalytic generator, where it drips onto a heater to produce fumes to kill the chlorophyll in the fruit allowing it to ripen. If left on the tree, the fruit itself creates this gas to start the ripening process. After twenty-four hours, the doors are opened to let the gas escape. Bananas are then kept around 63°F for three or four days and may be kept for a week after that at 58°F. The refrigerator has an alarm system that can be set at any tolerance. If the temperature varies too much in either direction, the alarm goes off. We have been told that this process ripening does not affect the flavor of the bananas. Tomatoes, avocados, and tobacco can also be ripened this way. This part of Catalani's is all that is open to the public, and then only with an escort.

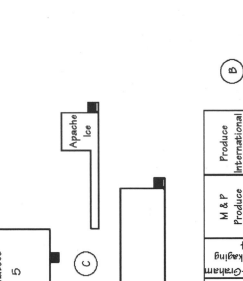

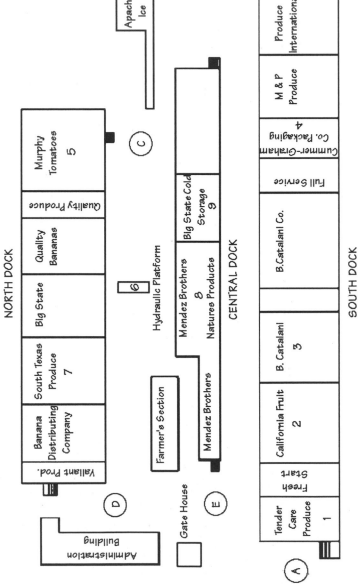

NORTH DOCK

Murphy Tomatoes
5

Quality Produce

Quality Bananas

Big State

South Texas Produce
7

Banana Distributing Company

Vaillant Prod.

Apache Ice

Hydraulic Platform

Big State Cold Storage
9

Mendez Brothers

Natures Products

Mendez Brothers

CENTRAL DOCK

Farmer's Section

Gate House

Administration Building

SOUTH DOCK

Produce International

M & P Produce

Cummer-Graham Co. Packaging
4

Full Service

B.Catalani Co.

B. Catalani
3

California Fruit
2

Fresh Start

Tender Care Produce
1

A

B

C

D

E

In the winter, you might see on the dock a strange-looking double-S-shaped rusty device made of stovepipe, with a fire in the lower part. This is a simple but effective heater invented by Aldo Bordano, a local metalworker.

4. Cummer-Graham Produce Supply sells baskets, paper bags, and other supplies to the market houses and the public. They are the only nonproduce company on the docks. A woman here makes up special occasion baskets.

B. Exit at the end of the dock, turn left, and walk toward Apache Ice. Turn left in front of it.

You might see overripe or rotten produce lying around. Hog and chicken farmers come in regularly and pick this up for feed. What is left over is picked up regularly by the Produce Terminal's two garbage trucks.

Apache Ice did a booming business until the advent of the refrigerated truck. Only a small percentage of the market houses have a need for ice now.

C. Go around the end of the ice house, and go up the steps to the north dock.

5. Murphy Tomatoes deals exclusively in tomatoes. The company has its own farms in California and Florida. From the doorway, you can see them sorting the tomatoes for ripeness.

6. From Big State Produce, look across to the left to the concrete building in the middle of the yard. Most of the time there will be a trailer tilted up on a hydraulic platform. This system unloads 40,000 pounds of potatoes in about forty minutes as opposed to the three to four hours it used to take. A conveyer belt carries the potatoes into hoppers that sort them by size. You'll see this process later.

7. At South Texas Produce, you will see open boxes, but you can buy only by the box.

D. Exit at the end of the dock. Turn back toward the main gate. Immediately on the left, you will see where the farmers set up.

Once a bustling spot, now only a few farmers and smaller produce businesses use these space.

E. To the right of the farmers section is the middle dock, built in the 1980s.

There is a lot to see on this dock, and fortunately, much of it can be seen from the dock. Absolutely do not go into any processing areas.

8. At the first open area of Mendez Brothers, you can see where the potatoes come into the three big hoppers that sort them into small, medium, and large. Rudy has seen potatoes too big to go through the large hopper, big enough to feed four people, he told us. From the hoppers, the potatoes are washed and bagged.

Mendez has open boxes where you can buy produce by the pound. They have one section of ripe produce that is ideal for the home canner.

Mural at Cassiano Homes

9. Big State Cold Storage is where fruits such as oranges, apples, grapes, peaches, and pears are held for later use.

   At the end of the dock, turn around, and walk back to the front gate.

4. **Exit the Produce Terminal, and turn right on Zarzamora, then left on Laredo, using the sidewalk on the right side of the street.**

At Elmendorf Street is the first of the Cassiano murals. In 1978, Anastacio "Tache" Torres, then a social worker, and later Executive Director of the Community Cultural Arts Organization, decided art might be a positive outlet for the group of young paint sniffers he worked with. "He showed us something else we could do with paint other than sniff it," said Juan Hernandez, one of that original group and now program coordinator, as he gave us a tour of the murals. Soon murals decorated walls formerly covered with graffiti. "There is little graffiti now," Juan told us, "because the kids involved won't let the others vandalize the murals." Although the murals reflect the Mexican-American viewpoint, 15 percent of the residents of Cassiano Homes are African-American, and 5 percent are Anglo-American. "Everything was trial and error at first," Juan said. "A lot of the paints were donated by different companies. We had oil base, acrylic, and latex, and we used them all together on a wall until we found that oil and water don't mix."

The murals are too numerous for a full description. We give you an overview.

5. Turn left on Hamilton.

Building 36: The Conquistadors watch the Aztec capital burning.
Building 42: Cortes and Montezuma.
Building 43: The Spaniards arriving off Veracruz.

(Across the street on the left at Saltillo is the Cinderella Bakery, a good place to try Mexican baked goods.)

Building 55: Our Lady of Guadalupe, the patron saint of the Mexican people. On her feast day in December, a procession goes from here to St. Timothy's Catholic Church.
Building 58: Good Friday represents hope. The city is darkness, and the Christ figure is illuminated.
Building 66: Honors Hispanic veterans from the various wars.
Building 67: Depicts the Treaty of Guadalupe Hidalgo, the signing over of a large portion of the present Southwest to the United States.
Building 70: Represents the Mexican-American War.

6. Turn right on Merida.

Building 69 (on the right): Shows the Spanish bringing Christianity to the natives.
Building 83 (on the left): Honors Scouting.
Building 81 (on the left before you turn onto Picoso): The leaders of the 1910 Mexican Revolution—Zapata, Villa, and Caranza.

7. Turn right on Picoso.

Building 65 (on the right): Shows the Flying Aztecs, a religious observance before it became a sport and a tourist attraction.
On the right, a series of murals stemming from a central figure on Building 60 represents the community. A filmstrip comes from the figure's head and goes out to the other walls, each one a frame of film representing a thought.
Building 64 represents the community working together toward something positive—building a city of gold.
Building 61: Represents war. Serpents are the symbol of life in Aztec mythology. Here the green serpent is life, and the brown serpent is death. The latter turns into barbed wire, wrapping around the city, holding it in turmoil. The little altar in the middle is like a candle that the families would light for the safe return of the young soldier. The whole scene is burning because of the problems that war brings.
Building 57: Represents education.
Building 56: Honors conjunto music with Vincent Van Gogh on guitar.

8. Turn right on Saltillo and left on Hamilton.

(At Hamilton, you have come full circle and returned to that delightful place, the Cinderella Bakery.)

The walk doubles back on itself until you cross Laredo Street. Then on the right are more murals.

Building 30: Father Hidalgo leading the 1810 Mexican Revolution and later standing in front of a firing squad.

Building 25: Honors the women who fought in the 1910 Revolution.

Building 20: The beginning of the 1810 Mexican Revolution. The central figure is Josephina Dominguez, wife of the governor of the State of Querétaro. When the revolutionary plot was discovered, she sent a rider off to warn Captain Allende and Father Hidalgo—the equivalent of our Paul Revere.

Building 17: The 1910 Revolution again. Emilio Zapata in the south was a rival to Pancho Villa in the north.

Building 16: Pancho Villa and the Americans. The blindfolded American soldier in the palm of Villa's hand represents General John J. Pershing's fruitless search for Villa in northern Mexico from 1916 to 1917.

Building 13: The National Farm Workers Union under Cesar Chavez.

Building 12: Honors Archbishop Patrick Flores of the San Antonio Archdiocese, the first American Archbishop of Hispanic decent.

Building 10: C.O.P.S. (Communities Organized for Public Service) is a grass roots citizens group that organized in 1973 to bring about needed social changes.

Building 8: Henry B. Gonzalez is a U. S. Congressman instrumental in getting federal funding for HemisFair '68. The San Antonio Convention Center is named in his honor. His district includes the poorest as well as the richest school district in the state.

Building 3: Honors Cleto Rodriguez, a Westside resident (although not in Cassiano Homes), who is a Congressional Medal of Honor winner.

9. Turn right on Guadalupe.

(Phones, and food are located at Sun Glo on the corner of Guadalupe and Hamilton.)

Guadalupe is the "Main Street" of the Westside community. The ancestors of many of today's San Antonians migrated here from Mexico during the 1910 Revolution. Many of them were poor and came up from the border on boxcars. In this neighborhood are several Christian fundamentalist churches. Several years ago Catholic Archbishop Flores held a conference in San Antonio for both lay and religious people from all of South Central Texas to discuss the problem of the Christian fundamentalist movement "stealing away" the good Catholic flock.

Past Navidad Street is Teresa's Thrift Shop, with its marvelous collection of junk—maybe even treasures. Across Cibolo Street is the Colonial Tortilla Factory, which offers barbacoa on weekends. Barbacoa is barbecued calf's head meat, a great treat.

On the corner of Sabinas is the Segovia Mexican Candy Company, whose candy can be found at the cashier stands of most Mexican restaurants in San Antonio. By now you have surely walked off enough calories to indulge in a piece (even if you stopped at the bakery too). In any event, do go inside to see the sugar-candy sculptures. One is a replica of San Fernando Cathedral, built brick by sugar-candy brick. There is also a Tower of the Americas and a charming birdhouse. The deterioration you see on the cathedral happened when they removed the airtight plexiglass cover to take some photographs and the sculpture picked up some moisture. Hopefully, it has stabilized. The cathedral took two months to build.

10. Turn left at Trinity, and right on El Paso.

Our Lady of Guadalupe Catholic Church is designated a shrine, and to many Catholics, it is the holiest church on the Westside. A beautiful and very sacred image of the Virgin of San Juan from the Shrine in San Juan de los Lagos, Mexico, is brought here from time to time. The church has an intricately carved marble altar.

11. At the church, turn right, and walk through Plaza Guadalupe, and then turn left on Guadalupe Street.

The main passage through the plaza is aligned with the church and presents a series of open air spaces for entertainment and food.

On September 13, 1987, Pope John Paul II preached here in the Plaza, in Spanish, to thousands of Westside residents.

On the northwest corner of Brazos, the old Progreso Theater has been beautifully renovated into the Guadalupe Theater. If the doors are open, go inside to see this outstanding theater designed by the firm of Reyna-Caragonne, who also designed the Plaza. There are frequently art exhibits in the gallery. The Center offers classes in literature and the arts.

On the southwest corner of Guadalupe Street are the offices of the Guadalupe Cultural Arts Center in an old, art deco drugstore. Behind it and El Parian Market is a former housing project recently renovated into town houses.

12. Turn right on Brazos, left on Laredo, and right on San Marcos and return to the stockyards.

The San Antonio Stock Yards are family owned and operated. Prior to 1886, the "stockyards" of San Antonio were on a couple of blocks of land west of the present Bexar County Courthouse. Then they moved to the proximity of the San Antonio and Aransas Pass Depot, just south of the King William Historic District on South Flores and South Alamo Street. In 1889, a group of businessmen with interest in cattle marketing began the Union Stock Yards of San Antonio at its present location, which was then on the edge of the city.

In those days, ranchers would round up their cattle, drive them to the nearest loading point on the railroad, and ship them here, where they would be sold to packers, feedlots, or other ranchers. In the 1990s, they no longer ship livestock by rail, but use trucks. No animals are slaughtered here; the meat packing industry is virtually dead in San Antonio.

On auctions days—Monday and Wednesday—the pens are bustling with activity. Depending on your outlook, you will find this tour either interesting or a good reason to be an animal rights activitist or vegetarian.

Standing in front of the stockyards, facing that big Longhorn again, look to the right to see the off-loading area for local ranchers bringing in their cattle. **Go up the metal stairway straight ahead to the catwalk.** The building to the right of the catwalk houses one of the commission companies. **Continue down to the large white building on the left. Take the first left turn, and and follow the catwalk to the steps that go down to the building entrance.** Just before the steps, looking down to your left, you can see where the livestock are herded, identified, and counted before entering the auction ring.

Go down the steps and into the building. If the auction is in progress, take a seat in the upper half of the room. Don't make any unusual movements, or you might find that you've bought yourself a steer! Just kidding. You couldn't do this even if you wanted to. The commission agents, sitting below, are the only ones who can do any buying. The telephones are always busy as the agents communicate with buyers minute by minute as to how many head they need. Two people sit alongside the auctioneer. One records essential information on a card, and the other records the selling price and buyer. Down by the entrance door sits a man controlling the cattle entrance by pushing levers.

Exit from the same door you came in. Go back up the steps to the main catwalk. Turn left. At the next turn, look down to the left and you will see the livestock being weighed. Each commission company has its own set of pens. Further ahead on the right, in the room with the window overlooking the pens, someone will be making an assignment as to which pen the last sale will go to. This is where the fastest action takes place. As the cattle are released, gates are quickly thrown open and closed to direct the cattle into their holding pens, while the yardmen nimbly leap out of the way.

Turn right to continue walking down the catwalk as far as it goes— just don't go down any steps to the ground level.

Turn around, and follow the catwalk back to the front, and exit.

(The Stockyards Cafe in the Livestock Exchange Building across the street serves good home-style cooking at very reasonable prices. Opened in 1889, they claim to be the oldest cafe in Texas in continuous use. It is open Monday-Friday. There is also a gift shop.)

A yardman prods cattle into a pen at the stockyards (Photo by Celia Wakefield).

21 Woodlawn Lake

Features: Trail around the lake with a side trip to the Catholic Chancery, Assumption Seminary, and Salvation Army Peacock Center, and another to Shrine of the Little Flower Catholic Church

Distance: 4.4 miles (7.0 k) (Lake only—1.3 miles)

Time: 2 hours

Nights: See comments

Wheelchair Accessible: Yes. See Comments

Restrooms, Water, Phone: At start, Chancery, and gym

Restaurant: See ☞ 8

Getting There: Car: Park in the lot by the Pavilion off Josephine Tobin Drive.

Bus: No. 84 Cincinnati. Get off on Cincinnati and Josephine Tobin Drive. Walk to French Place to start. To return, board across Cincinnati at Goodrich.

Comments:

The lake is popular with walkers, joggers, and families who come to stroll and visit with neighbors. As long as there are other poeple walking around, it is safe to walk here. We recommend no later than early evening.

There are few sidewalks during the first part of this walk, but traffic is light.

The terrain is a bit rough for wheelchairs, but the walk can be taken in one. There are no sidewalks in places and some curbs do not have ramps, but again, traffic is light. Sometimes it's necessary to switch from one side of the street to the other to utilize sidewalks.

Overview:

In 1888, the West End Town Company dammed Alazan Creek, turning a marshy wetland into the eighty-acre West End Lake. A trolley line put downtown fifteen minutes away. (It still takes fifteen minutes by bus—so much for modern transportation!) Two artesian wells provided water, which attracted twenty-three dairies. With a trolley, good water, and a high, healthy location, the residential area grew quickly. The lake was its social and recreational center, a favorite spot for Sunday outings.

Good trolley service also attracted schools. Of these, Peacock School for Boys became Peacock Military Academy; San Antonio Female College became Westmoreland College and later merged with Trinity University; and St. Mary's Institute downtown moved here and changed its name to St. Louis College and later became St. Mary's University.

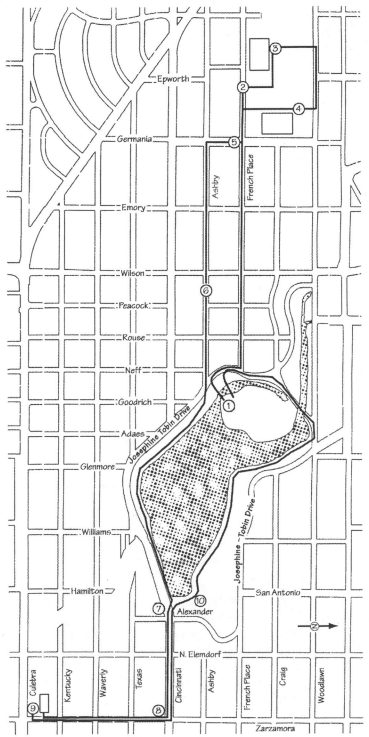

The West End Town Company eventually failed though, and, after several deed transfers, the land came to the City of San Antonio. As new suburbs developed, interest in this area declined. In an effort to create a new image, the city changed the lake's name to Woodlawn, and named the road that circled it Josephine Tobin Drive in honor of the mayor's mother.

At various times, the lake has dried up, has frozen enough to ice skate on, and has been fenced in. In more recent years, it almost became extinct through an accumulation of bottom silt.

Many political campaigns have kicked off with a rally and barbecue on the lake's shore. Texas author Katherine Ann Porter lived in the neighborhood and attended the Thomas School for Young Ladies.

Woodlawn is still a cohesive neighborhood and the lake is still its social and recreational center; it celebrated its one- hundredth anniversary in 1988.

1. **Exit the parking lot over the stone bridge. Turn right on Josephine Tobin Drive, and then left on French Place.**

At Peacock Street, 2707 French Place is nearly one hundred years old. At one time it was part of Peacock Military Academy.

Just past Germania, on the left, are the classrooms of the Mexican-American Cultural Center. On the right is the back of the Assumption Seminary and just past it, in the beige brick building that is the former Trinity University Campus, are the administrative offices and dormitories of the cultural center. The Mexican-American Cultural Center is the national center for pastoral ministry of the National Conference of Catholic Bishops. Priests, nuns, and lay persons come here from all over the world to study Hispanic culture and language.

2. **Just past the cultural center, on the right, a sidewalk runs between the building and the tennis courts. Turn right on this. Just past the courts, turn left across the field to the Chancery (☞ 3).**

Displayed in the lobby is the throne used by Pope John Paul II on his visit to San Antonio in 1987. A wall hanging behind the stairwell, done by Bexar County jail inmates, commemorates this visit. The artists used an old Mexican folk craft of laying string on a soft wax surface. You can see the detail better from upstairs. On the third floor are portraits of past bishops. The hallway has an interesting series of oil paintings of the missions, which was done in 1975 by J. Baecke.

3. **Exit the Chancery, and walk straight ahead to Woodlawn. Turn right. At the driveway to Assumption Seminary, turn right, and go up the drive. Bear left at the traffic circle in front of the administration building, and go to the sidewalk that goes off on an angle to the left. Take this over to the front of the chapel (the building with the stone and concrete wall).**

Free movie show at Woodlawn Lake (photo from North San Antonio Times, courtesy San Antonio Conservation Society Library and Archives)

The chapel was designed in 1974 by Ford, Powell, and Carson and is usually open.

4. **Exit the chapel, and turn left on the sidewalk. Follow this sidewalk, always bearing left.**

Patrick F. Flores (known as the Mariachi Bishop) is the first bishop of Mexican descent in the United States. He lives in apartments here on the Seminary grounds. Pope John Paul II stayed here on his visit. He was awakened on the day of his departure by a sixty-person mariachi band and serenaded by other groups of musicians along the six-mile route from here to his plane at Kelly Air Force Base.

5. **Turn left on French Place, right on Germania, and then left on Ashby.**

2903 W. Ashby at Wilson was the 1906 home of Edith Wing Peacock's parents. It also served as a dormitory for the Academy and as a wartime hospital.

(At Wilson, there is a Stop 'n Go one block to the right on Cincinnati.)

On the left across Wilson, at 2811 W. Ashby, is the Wesley Peacock house, one of the oldest homes in the area. Built in 1890 as a residence, it became Phelps Hall of the Peacock School for Boys in 1894. Peacock became a military training

school in 1900; it was noted for its high academic standards. In 1926, it officially
became Peacock Military Academy. While stationed at Fort Sam Houston,
Dwight D. Eisenhower was an instructor and football coach here.

All of the Academy property was deeded to the Salvation Army in 1973. A
fire in 1931 destroyed the second floor of this house so it is now considerably
smaller than it was originally. It is now a museum containing the archives and
memorabilia of the Academy and a meeting place for the Peacock Alumni Association. It is also used for Salvation Army functions. If the door is open, you
are welcome to go inside. At the present time Colonel Donald Peacock, son of
the founder, is on duty here and is most gracious in showing you around. Photographs of the original house may be seen. It is interesting to note that the colors
in the stained glass of the front windows happened to be the official colors of
the Salvation Army.

Across Wilson on the right is the Salvation Army Chapel. If it is open, you
are welcome to go inside to visit. Not many people realize that the Salvation
Army is actually a religious denomination. A dining room here serves 150 senior citizens a day. Other facilities here at the San Antonio Salvation Army Headquarters are a girls home, a community center, and senior citizen apartments.

   6. **Continue on Ashby, and go back to the lake. Turn right on the path
       around the lake.**

As you turn onto the path around the lake you are afforded a good view of Little Flower Shrine, the Tower of the Americas, and the downtown skyline.

From 1915 to 1929, the lake was leased by W. H. (Bill) Suden who made it
into a resort with boats, a dance pavilion, and various sorts of entertainment.
He built a bathhouse 125 feet long and thirty feet high that was shaped like a
steamship, complete with two large stacks. It looked so real that people asked
to buy tickets for a cruise. He put a screen on the side of the bathhouse and
showed free movies you could watch from your boat or from benches on shore.
Advertisements painted alongside the screen covered the cost of the movies.
Vaudeville acts and boxing matches took place on a stage built below the
screen. All of the island that stood in the middle of the lake, except the part the
lighthouse stands on, was lost to bulldozers when the new dam was built.

When it rains, water flows into the lake from the various creeks north of
here, spills over the dam into Alazan Creek, and from there runs into San Pedro
Creek and eventually the San Antonio River.

In recent times, so much silt accumulated in the lake that vegetation started
to proliferate, choking off oxygen and light. The water level dropped to two feet,
and old tires and junk stuck up everywhere. Finally, in 1981, after much effort
on the part of neighborhood organizations, the lake was drained and excavated
back to its original ten-foot depth. Then it was refilled and restocked with fish.
Once again, it is a pleasant place to gather, walk, boat, and fish.

7. **At the archway, leave the path, and walk straight ahead (between the stone building and the arch) on Cincinnati.**

The archway honors Josephine Tobin, mother of then Mayor John W. Tobin and wife of an early Texas Ranger.

On the corner of Elmendorf, 1000 Cincinnati is a brick and stone building that was the West End School in the early 1900s.

No. 926 with its shingles and gingerbread trim dates from the 1890s.

8. **Turn right on Zarzamora.**

(At Texas Street, Leticia's Mexican Restaurant is popular with locals.)

Across Waverly, in the backyard of the corner house on your right, are some unique and delightful pieces of rubber tire art. It is popular in Mexican-American homes to use old tires as planters, cutting them in petal shapes and painting them bright colors. This is the first time we've seen tires cut into parrots, armadillos, and other creatures.

At Kentucky Street is Our Lady of Mount Carmel and St. Theresa of the Infant Jesus Church, known more popularly as the Shrine of the Little Flower (☞ 9), built in 1931 by the Discalced Carmelite Fathers. The shorter tower is topped by a statue of St. Theresa, the Little Flower. An elaborate altar is embellished with angels and cherubs. The windows on one side depict activities of the priests, and on the other side, those of the nuns.

It is an unfortunate commentary on our times that churches can no longer be left open unattended. Little Flower is now open only for masses: 8:00 to 9:00 A.M. and 5:00 to 6:00 P.M. It is also open Saturday from 4:00 to 8:00 P.M. and all Sunday morning.

9. **Exit the shrine, and turn left on Zarzamora, retracing your steps back to the archway at Step 7. Turn right onto the path.**

The fieldstone gymnasium (where you turn back on the path), was originally a public library.

(There are restrooms inside the gym.)

10. **From the gym, continue walking around the lake back to the parking lot.**

At the upper end of the lake is a heavily vegetated point of land that is home to many varieties of birds. At the end you will cross over the creek that feeds the lake.

22 Brackenridge Park

Features: A mostly shady walk that includes River Road and crisscrosses the river through the park, plus a side trip to the Witte Museum and Texas Ranger Museum

Distance: 4.5 miles + 0.8-mile side trip (7.2 k + 1.3 k)

Time: 2 hrs. + 20-min. side trip

Nights: Early evening is okay

Wheelchair Accessible: Yes. See Comments

Restrooms, Water, Phone: At start and ☞ 9

Restaurants: Snack bar at start. Restaurants at ☞ 1 and on St. Mary's Street .

Getting There: Car: Park in the lot by miniature train station off Mulberry and North St. Mary's.

Bus: No. 8 North St. Mary's. Get off at the zoo stop. To return, board at the same place.

Comments:

This can be a two-hour walk or an all-day excursion if you include all the park attractions, especially the zoo and museums. There are picnic areas throughout, as well as restaurants at the beginning and on Broadway. The park is popular, so keep in mind that parking lots can fill up early on weekends and holidays, especially in the summer.

Paved roads and trails throughout the park are wheelchair accessibile. Where River Road crosses the river you will have to backtrack to Mulberry Street.

The park is always open, but we do not recommend walking there at night.

The Zoo is open every day. the hours from Memorial Day through Labor Day are 9:00 A.M. to 6:30 P.M. Rest of the year the hours are 9:00 A.M. to 5:00 P.M. (admission fee).

The train and the skyride, weather permitting, operate daily from 10:00 A.M. to 4:30-5:30 P.M. (admission fee).

The Sunken Garden is open 8:00 A.M. to dusk.

The Witte Museum is open Monday and Wednesday to Saturday from 10:00 A.M. to 5:00 P.M., Tuesday from 10:00 A.M. to 9:00 P.M., and Sunday from 12:00 P.M. to 5:00 P.M. (admission fee except free Tuesday from 3:00 P.M. to 9:00 P.M.

The Texas Ranger Museum is open daily from 11:00 A.M. to 4:00 P.M. September through March and 10:00 A.M. to 5:00 P.M. from April through August (admission fee).

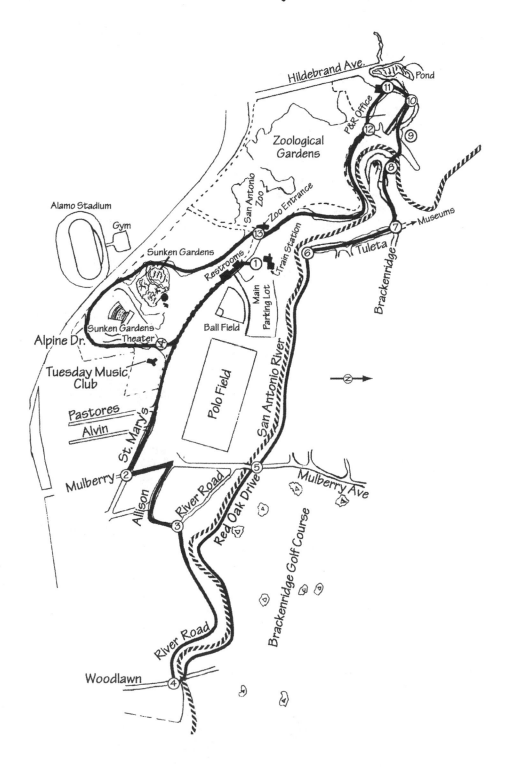

22 Brackenridge Park

1. Start in front of the train station. Walk ahead to St. Mary's, and turn left.

Trivia Quiz: Where was the last train robbery in the West? Answer: Brackenridge Park.

In July 1970, two masked men waving revolvers jumped from behind some bushes and ordered the engineer of the Brackenridge Eagle to stop the train. They relieved the passengers of five-hundred dollars in cash as well as credit cards, checkbooks, and driver's licenses, which left a lot of tourists stranded. Eventually the bandits were captured and tried and received sentences ranging from one to twenty years in the federal prison at Leavenworth.

The old Eagle was replaced in 1988, and new tracks were put down. Three trains now circle the two-mile route: the Bluebonnet, the Yellow Rose, and the Fiesta Flyer. A train ticket takes you around the park once. You can get off and back on at any of the three stops: the stables, the Witte Museum, and the Sunken Gardens.

The ball field, where both company and city league games are played, and the driving range are located on the old Polo Grounds.

(Just before St. Mary's Street are two restaurants. Buffalo Beano's is on the right, then on the left is the Bombay Bicycle Club which offers food and drink at moderate prices in a pub atmosphere. Be sure to see the mural in the back room.)

2. Cross Mulberry Street, and turn left. Turn right on Allison, the road alongside the stables.

(Across Mulberry Street in the strip mall is Joseph's Restaurant and Bakery serving good soup, salad, and sandwiches at reasonable prices.)

Extensive bridle paths meander from here through the wooded portions of the park. After you pass the stables, just before the road bends to the left, on your right is the remainder of one of the old irrigation ditches from the 1880s that ran through the Tobin Hill neighborhood near San Antonio College.

3. Turn right on River Road.

Lack of traffic and abundant shade make this area popular with joggers. The river and the golf course are on the left. Black walnut, sycamore, cypress, Texas red oak, and pecans trees grow along the river. Mustang grape vines twine around the trees.

The River Road neighborhood has always been popular with artists and writers. The building of the expressway cut off several of the entry roads, creating an island of privacy for the residents of this already isolated area. The houses date mostly from the 1920s to the 1940s. Residential gardens offer a diversity of plants. We spotted Argentina pampas grass and many magnolia trees. In the summer, crepe myrtle adds splashes of purple, pink, and white.

Low-water crossing on River Road (Photo by Celia Wakefield)

4. **At Woodlawn, turn left over the low water crossing, and then left again, following the river back to Mulberry.**

(If there is high water, don't try to cross the river, but retrace your steps back to Mulberry, turning right across the bridge. Pick up the walk again at Step 5.)

As you head back along the other side of the river, on your right is the Brackenridge Municipal Golf Course. This area is believed to have been a Native-American camping ground.

5. **Cross Mulberry. Cross the railroad tracks. Walk between the river and Red Oak Drive.**

On sunny days turtles bask on the logs and banks of the river along here. Poet Sidney Lanier described the river as "milky green." This bluish-green color is caused by the microorganisms growing there. After a heavy rain the river is brown from runoff and churned-up bottom silt. According to the diary of Francis Moore, Jr., who passed through here in 1840, there was a time when the river was "fifty yards wide and four or five feet deep . . . its waters remarkably pure and wholesome."

Except in a season of extremely heavy rains, there is no longer enough underground water to feed the springs that keep the river flowing. Most of the river flow from Brackenridge Park through downtown is water pumped from the Edwards aquifer. The quality of the water is still good as no raw sewage or other pollutants are being dumped into it.

At the bridle trail crossing, go across the road and up the incline of the slight rise on the other side. This ditch was a millrace to the river in 1877, and is now part of the bridle path. **Go back to the river and turn right.**

The opposite side of the river at this point is Koehler Park. Koehler, as head of Pearl Brewery, deeded this land to the City with the stipulation that malt liquor be sold. In contrast, most of the park was deeded to the City by George Brackenridge, who did not hold with drinking in public because it could lead to fights and other disturbances. His deed stipulates that if liquor was ever sold here, the property would revert to the University of Texas.

In earlier times, buffalo, deer, elk, and fowl were kept in the park in separate preserves. A 1908 photograph shows a deer preserve that still existed in this area.

The low water crossing to the left, just before the first intersection and behind the train station, used to be two-way. In days of less automobile traffic, people would stop here to wash their cars. When the circus was in town, the elephants were brought here for washing. There is a photograph of this at the Hertzberg Circus Museum.

6. **At the intersection of Tuleta and Red Oak, cross the street, and turn right (a sign points to the Witte Museum). Continue ahead to Brackenridge Drive.**

   Across the river on your left as you turn are Koehler Pavilion and the paddle boat dock and behind these the zoo.

7. **Cross Brackenridge Drive.**

To take the museum side trip, continue straight ahead, and turn left to the Witte Museum and Texas Ranger Museum. You might want to skip that for

The old St. Mary's Street Bridge, San Antonio's first iron bridge (Photo by Celia Wakefield).

now, though, and finish the walk, take a short rest, and then ride the train back to the museums.

(There are restaurants across Broadway from the Witte Museum.)

To skip the side trip, turn left on Brackenridge Drive and continue on the main walk.

Sometimes the river floods in the park. Mark has seen water up to the picnic tables here. The tall trees along the river on this stretch are bald cyprus, so-called because this type of pine is not evergreen but goes "bald" in the winter.

The grand old Joske Pavilion was built in 1927 with a donation from the Joske brothers (the old Joske's Department Store) in memory of their father. Mark's mother recalls coming here on school picnics. "We'd put our lunches down in a corner and go off exploring. Can you imagine doing that these days and still have your lunch?" she says.

(Across on the left is the park department's reservation office.)

8. Turn right, and follow the road across the metal bridge.

This iron bridge originally crossed the river downtown at St. Mary's Street between Commerce and Houston.

Looking down from the left side of the bridge, you can see a large green pipe spilling water pumped from the aquifer into the river. A series of steps leads up to the old pump house built in 1878 to supply the pure spring water to downtown. In the 1890s, when technology became available to drill through rock, George Brackenridge had wells sunk to pump water to the city instead of using the river water.

9. Across the bridge turn left, and then follow the street as it curves right. Walk along the ditch on the left.

At the end of the ditch is the Arbor Bridge, a fine example of the cement art of Dionicio Rodriguez, which dates from around 1929. There are examples of his work on some of our other walks (see particularly Walk 11, Alamo Heights). Go out on the bridge, which crosses the first stretch of the millrace, and look down to the right. The stream coming in from the left that joins the ditch is the outlet of the channel from the pond up ahead. Below and to the left of the road is the remainder of an earlier bridge.

10. Walk over to the pond.

The pond is fed by a well directly under Hildebrand Avenue. The actual channel of the river is east of the pond. At the end near the Arbor bridge is a stone channel that goes under the bridge as well as the road. It always contains flowing water and runs through the zoo grounds before flowing back into the river near the Koehler Pavilion. On the other side of Hildebrand on the Incar-

The railings of the Arbor Bridge are made of concrete sculpted to look like trees.

nate Word College campus is the source of the river, when it's flowing, known as the "Blue Hole."

11. **Continue along the road bearing left towards the Parks and Recreation Building and through the parking lot. The millrace will be on your left and the park building on your right.**

Park headquarters, the planning department, and other city park facilities are located in this building. To older locals, this is the Donkey Barn, so-called from the days when the park offered donkey rides.

12. **At the end of the parking lot, the street curves left. After you cross the ditch, turn right onto the brick path.**

As you turn onto the path, the cut-limestone building with the metal roof is the old pump house we talked about earlier. Across the road under the bridge, you can see a straight, smooth-sided channel leading up to it. This channel was part of a 1800s irrigation system that diverted river water down St. Mary's Street and eventually to the farm fields of the Westside. Beneath the pump house, a free-flowing well fed water through pipes to downtown.

As you walk along the brick path, the zoo is on the right. You can see and hear some of the bird exhibits.

The stone building on the left with the arches is the old bathhouse known as Fort Lambert. It has been converted into a playscape for children of all ages. Just past it, steps lead down to Lambert Beach, the swimming hole named in honor of Ray Lambert, the parks and sanitation commissioner elected in 1915. He was responsible for the greatest period of park system development in San Antonio's history. He hired Dionicio Rodriguez to design and build the Arbor Bridge and the benches, and a Japanese artist to design the Sunken Gardens. The design of the 1917 bath- house lent itself to the nickname "Fort Lambert." A suspension bridge that just cleared the water once spanned the river at the beach. The challenge was to see how long you could stay on the swaying bridge before getting dumped into the river. This was a favorite swimming hole until it closed in the 1950s during the polio scare.

Where now you see the peaked tarp roofs of one of the zoo exhibits, a grape arbor grew. It was a favorite landmark. The brick path was once a road.

The covered cement bench is another of Dionicio Rodriguez' works. Tree limbs branch off from the main trunk to support the roof.

Past the Koehler Pavilion is the outlet for the river channel that flows through the zoo.

The San Antonio Zoological Gardens and Aquarium is one of the finest in the country and is known for its outstanding breeding program, especially with gazelles, antelopes, and birds. It is a large zoo and somewhat hilly so only the most hardy should consider visiting it at this point—come back and do it at leisure another day. A descriptive pamphlet and a map are included with admission.

13. **Where the path comes out onto Tuleta at the circle, bear right. At the zoo entrance, cross the street and walk up Alpine Drive.**

As you start up the hill, you might hear barking from the building to the right, the city animal control facility.

In earlier times, instead of this road, paths through grape arbors led up and down the hill. The path to the left of the road leads into the Sunken Gardens. (Do not take this path for our tour. Stay on the road. Running alongside and overhead is the Sky Ride to the Sunken Gardens.) At the top of the road, you look down into the gardens, which were built into the rock quarry that supplied limestone for many homes and buildings in San Antonio and for the State Capitol in Austin. In 1916, Ray Lambert hired Mr. Jingu, a Japanese immigrant who sold paintings on Alamo Plaza, to design a Japanese Tea Garden. Mr. Jingu lived here with his family, running a tearoom. He died in 1938, so he never knew that due to wartime hysteria concerning people of Japanese descent, his family was told to leave. A Chinese couple moved in, and the garden's name changed to the Chinese Tea Gardens. Later, "Chinese" was dropped, and it became simply the Sunken Gardens. We have heard, but not confirmed, that this change was made in the 1950s during the McCarthy era. The original name was officially reinstated in 1985. Mr. Jingu's family returned for the occasion. These days it is known simply as the Sunken Gardens.

Continuing along the top of the hill, you can look down into the Sunken Gardens Theater, which dates from the 1920s. You might hear anything from Shakespeare to rock music performed here.

From here you get a terrific panoramic view. Following the horizon from left to right, you see the Southwestern Bell Telephone building (the old USAA headquarters), the 4001 New Braunfels condominiums, the former Brooke Army Medical Center at Fort Sam Houston, the USAA Towers, the geometric glass structures of the Botanical Center, the Fort Sam Houston Quadrangle and red tile roofs of Staff Post, the Alamodome, Tower of the Americas, and the downtown skyline.

The expressway on your right is U.S. 281, known as the McAllister Freeway. Beyond it is Alamo Stadium and Gymnasium and the carillon tower at Trinity University. Just past the theater as you descend the hill, some steps on the right lead to a historical marker that tells about the expressway. From there the hearty can cross the bridge over the expressway and connect with Walk 24, Trinity University.

At the bottom of the hill on the right, as you come to North St. Mary's Street, is the Tuesday Music Club, which supports promising young musicians of classical music. Busts of famous composers sit in niches around the building. The bronze figure, *The Genius of Music,* is a work by Pompeo Coppini and Waldine Tauch, which was funded by Harry Hertzberg in memory of his mother, Anna, one of the six founders of the club.

On the left is a bas-relief panel at the Sunken Gardens Theater entrance that honors heroes of the Texas Revolution.

14. Turn left on St. Mary's Street, and go back to the parking lot.

On the left as you turn is the entrance to the Sunken Gardens that you saw from above.

On the left also are the smokestack and kilns from the old Alamo Cement plant as described on a plaque. The small buildings were the homes of the workers. At one time, these were used by the park as a Mexican village that featured working craftsmen and a restaurant.

If it is running (only on non-windy days), the Sky Ride provides a fantastic view of the city. You can get off and back on at the top to view the gardens. A trip on the Brackenridge train takes you through the wooded sections of the park. You can get off to see the museums and then ride back here.

23 Emilie and Albert Friedrich Wilderness Park

Features: Wilderness park in typical Texas Hill Country terrain with both paved and natural trails

Distance: 4.7 miles (7.5 k)

Time: 2 hrs. 45 min.

Nights: No. See Comments

Wheelchair Accessible: Yes. See Comments

Restrooms, Water, Phones: At start

Restaurants: None

Getting There: **Car:** Take I-10 West to the Camp Bullis exit. Follow access road to the stop sign. Turn left under the expressway, then right on access road, and look for the sign for Friedrich Wilderness Park. Turn left. At the end of the road turn right to go to the park entrance.

Bus: None

Comments:

Park is closed on Monday and Tuesday. It opens at 8:00 A.M. and closes at 8:00 P.M. in the summer and 5:00 P.M. in the winter.

While our particular walk is not wheelchair accessible because we go on the unpaved nature trails, there are approximately two miles of trail paved for wheelchair accessibility. A half mile of this trail is brick-edged to make it accessible also to the visually impaired. New handicap parking places suitable for vans and a handicap-accessible restroom at the beginning of the trails help make this wonderful park available to all.

The park offers some special programs. On the first Saturday of each month, Friedrich Park interpretive guides lead natural history hikes starting at 9:00 A.M. On the second Saturday of the month, the Bexar Audubon Society and Friends of Friedrich Wilderness Park present an educational program on natural science at 9:00 A.M. Call (210) 698-1057 for schedules for these and other programs.

To help preserve the park, please observe the following rules:

No pets, bicycles, fires, smoking, or camping.
Stay on the trail. The vegetation is extremely fragile, and even one
    person straying off the path can leave a lasting impression.
Do not touch any of the plant material.

Please help keep the park clean. Carry a trash bag with you and pick up any litter that less aware persons have left behind.

Friedrick Park is patrolled by rangers on horseback who cover each trail two or three times a day, mostly in the afternoon. Be sure to sign in at the beginning of the trail when you start and sign out on your return. That way the rangers know you're here and can come looking for you if necessary. At the sign-in register, you can pick up one of the excellent park brochures that gives details on the vegetation and wildlife.

Overview:

The bulk of the park was donated in memory of Emilie and Albert Friedrich with the stipulation that the land be kept as much as possible in its natural state. It offers examples of most of the natural ecosystems that make up the Texas Hill Country. Our thanks to park naturalist Eric Lantzenheiser for an informative walk through the park.

Geology. There are three types of strata within the area. Where Interstate 10 passes is the Lower Glen Rose stratum, a fertile, deep, clay soil that supports Post and Blackjack oaks. The stratum that is actually within the park is the Upper Glen Rose, a younger, more elevated layer with less water and soil, which supports more brush and cedar. The tops of the hills comprise the third stratum, the Edwards limestone, a whitish rock that turns grey upon exposure to the weather. There are caves and faults within the park by which the Edwards Aquifer is replenished.

Vegetation. The soils formed from the limestone deposits are dark brown loam with sand, gravel, and rock, and are very alkaline. Thus, many acid-loving plants cannot survive in it. The steep hillsides have shallow, unstable soils. These soils wash down to collect in ravines and bottoms. One theory as to why the Hill Country looks as it does today is that much of it was once open grassland. Livestock grazing, suppression of fires, and denser human settlement contributed to the disappearance of the prairie grasses and other endemic plants. Erosion of soil increased until the hills became a brush forest of mostly mountain cedar—also called Mexican juniper, post cedar, or rock cedar—the scourge of over 50 percent of all San Antonians, who suffer from "cedar fever," an allergy to the pollen. At times the "smoke" of pollen is so thick that distant hills look as if they are on fire.

The culprit is the male cedar, which bears miniscule golden pine cones that release pollen when they pop open. The female tree produces a "berry," which is actually a fleshy cone. The berry is used to flavor gin. Unprocessed, they taste rather like kerosene and may be harmful to humans.

You can't necessarily tell the age of the cedar trees by their size. In bottom soil with some underground water, a huge tree could be only 80 years old, whereas on top of a hill a little runt might be 300 years old.

The species of wildflowers that are common to fields are not abundant everywhere in the Park. These wildflowers are referred to by ecologists as pioneer plants—plants that grow in disturbed areas such as roadsides, or after plowing or cutting. If an area is left alone, shrubs and trees gradually take over, shading out the wildflowers.

Late November to mid-December is the time to come for fall color, particularly the beautiful deep red of the Spanish oaks and the burnished yellow of cedar elms.

People. Prehistoric people visited the area that is now the park, coming here to quarry and rough-work the chert they used for arrows and tools. The trail crosses many of these work sites where you see chert flakes. Back at their permanent camps along Leon Creek, they would do the fine work on their stone tools and weapons.

Wildlife. Within the park are found white-tailed deer, rabbits, hares, skunks, opossums, armadillos, bobcats, ringtail cats, and foxes. Mountain lions are occasionally still seen. Javalina and bear once were present. The white-tailed deer have overpopulated due to the lack of natural predators, the control of screwworm disease, and the failure to allow hunting of enough does. The deer overeat the natural vegetation, which is endangering the blackcapped vireo, a small songbird that inhabits dense, low brush. Friedrich Park and Camp Bullis are the only known vireo habitats in Bexar County. Lack of sufficient food also drives the deer to invade gardens, thus upsetting the local residents. Because hunting in the park is prohibited, the State may start trapping deer for release elsewhere.

Bird watchers from around the world come here in spring and summer to see another endangered bird, the golden-cheeked warbler. These birds depend on the long, shaggy bark of old cedars for their nesting material. In recent decades, millions of acres of cedar have been destroyed by people who want grasslands on which to graze their cattle. Over one hundred species of birds may be seen in the park throughout the year.

Just after the park opens and before it closes are the best times for spotting wildlife.

You can identify evidence of wildlife by examining their scat. Deer leave pellets similar to those of rabbits but more flattened. Raccoon scat is larger, more like that of a small dog, but pinched on the ends and frequently with undigested seeds in it.

The Native Plant Society maintains a self-guided plant identification tour in the park near the picnic area.

1. Turn right from the parking lot on the paved trail.

Be sure to sign in and pick up a brochure.

2. Turn left to the Forest Range Trail (An easy, 30 minute walk.).

This is a paved trail, accessible to the handicapped, with three possible loops.

3. **Walk back to Main Loop Trail and turn left. At the T-intersection turn left. At the fork turn right onto the Water Trail (an easy, 20 minute walk).**

The windmill is a remnant from when the park was a ranch. Before this became the park, Camp Bullis soldiers evidently used the windmill for target practice. Shell casings dating back to the 1890s have been found.

The goldfish in the tank are not native. They were left here by a schoolteacher who moved away in 1989. The park naturalist warned that they would

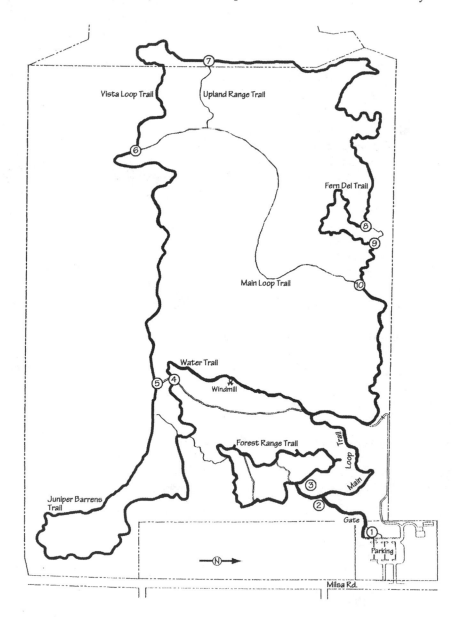

probably become dinner for a passing raccoon, but so far they have managed to evade this fate by escaping to the safety of the rocks. They live on algae and mosquito larvae. Most park wildlife don't like the tank because the water is hard to reach and deep. Even the deer prefer drinking from the puddle at the drip pipe below.

At the drip pipe, you may see animal "highways" converge like spokes on a wheel. If you sit off a ways and stay very still, you have a good chance to see some wildlife, especially around opening or closing times. The birds will come to drink any time of day. You can sit near the puddle and watch for them.

We thought this trail was so named because of the windmill and drip pipe. Then we came here after a period of heavy rain. Water, water, everywhere, gushing out of an underground spring, running in streams down the hillside. It was beautiful.

4. **Cross Main Loop Trail, and continue on Water Trail to Juniper Barrens Trail, turning left (an easy, 45 minute walk).**

At the intersection of the Juniper Barrens and the Water Trail, you might see a lot of empty snail shells. Because the shells do not deteriorate rapidly, what you see is the result of many years of accumulation. The snails are most common under the cedar trees on which they feed. They are active only during wet weather. When it turns dry, the snails seal their shells and become dormant, usually under the fine cedar duff. Because the shells are so light after the snail dies, they float to the top.

5. **Back at the Main Loop Trail, turn left.**

There is a shelter here and another one at the top of the hill from which you can look east towards I-10 and the Dominion Country Club.

6. **At the signpost, turn left onto Vista Loop Trail.**

From here you are almost level with the buzzards. Near the shelter is the start of an 1800s stone wall, which once served as a boundary marker. Originally about five feet high, it has collapsed and been partially rebuilt.

7. **At the fork, if you like rugged trails, stay left on Vista Loop Trail (difficult and steep). If not, turn right onto Upland Range Trail, then left on Main Loop Trail.**

Warning: Although the first part of Vista Loop Trail is not difficult, especially along the stone wall boundary marker, after you cross the wall the second time the trail descends steeply and roughly. It is very difficult walking. Fern Del Trail is also rugged. To avoid these take the Upland Range Trail back to Main Loop Trail.

When you reach the stone boundary marker on Vista Loop trail you are at an elevation of about 1400 feet. The highest point in the park is 1440 feet (to the right).

8. **Turn right onto Fern Del Trail. (This trail may not be marked, but it is a T-crossing. The trail is difficult and steep).**

This north-facing canyon is the coolest and wettest one in the park. It encourages the growth of ferns, which gives the trail its name.

Lacey oaks, also known as "blue oaks" because of their blue-green color, are found in the valley of this trail. This is probably one of the most southern locations of this tree. Until 1989, it was believed that the world champion Lacey oak was here, but a larger one has been found on a ranch near Spring Branch, Texas. There are some Lacey oaks planted in the parking lot.

9. **Back on Vista Loop Trail, turn right.**

10. **At the Main Loop Trail, turn left back to car.**

The metal markers with orange plastic ribbons that you may see on the trails are observation points for the National Audubon Society, which does a bird census here regularly.

Don't forget to sign out!

The windmill at the tank (Photo by Celia Wakefild)

24 Eisenhower Park

Features: Wilderness park with both paved and natural trails

Distance: 4.4 miles (7.0 k)

Time: 2 hours

Nights: Closes at dusk

Wheelchair Accessible: Only Cedar Flats Trail and Yucca Trail

Restrooms: At start and at tower

Water, Phones: At start

Restaurants: None. Picnic facilities only

Getting there: **Car:** Take I-10 West to FM 1604 East to N.W. Military Drive. Turn left to go to park entrance. The trail entrance is off the parking lot to the left of the park entrance.

                  Bus: None

Comments:

We have given directions for a walk that covers sections of five trails, part paved and part natural. Walking or hiking shoes are preferable to sneakers because of the rocky natural trails. Our walk is rugged. See map at the beginning of the trail.

Do not cross fence lines, or you will be trespassing on Camp Bullis.

The Cedar Flats Trail and the Yucca Trail are paved for wheelchair accessibility. The Yucca Trail is roped for accessibility to the visually handicapped. There are benches along the paved trails.

The park is open from 6:00 A.M. to dusk.

Overview:

Eisenhower Park offers 318 acres of Hill Country terrain with paved and natural trails. There are six primitive camping sites available by reservation. Call (210) 821-3120.

Wildlife is best seen early in the morning or at dusk. There are white-tailed deer, foxes, armadillos, raccoons, skunks, opossums, and ringtail cats.

The trees are mostly cedar (juniper), live oak, and Texas (Spanish) red oak. The latter is one of the few native trees to change color in the fall.

For a more thorough description, see the Overview of Friedrich Wilderness Park, Walk 24.

1. **Start on the path next to the sign designating "Trails."**

The Visitor Center occupies a one-hundred-year-old house that was so decrepit we wondered why they had bothered to move it from the King William Historic District. We are impressed by the powers of restoration!

2. **Turn left onto the paved path marked "All Trails." At the first intersection, take Hillview Trail P (Paved) to the right. At the fork, bear left (no sign). Turn left onto Hillview N (Natural).**

3. **At the Hillview/Shady Creek sign, turn left onto Shady Creek Trail. Cross the bridge. Turn right at the fork.**

At the bridge are benches on which to sit and enjoy this lovely spot.

4. **At the next fork, turn left, staying on Shady Creek Trail.**

5. **At the paved road (Cedar Flats Trail), turn right, and follow the road to the Tower.**

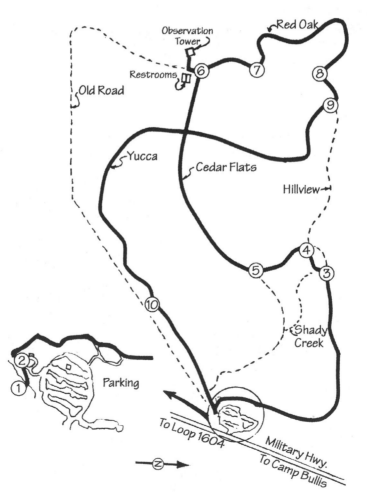

(There are restrooms but no drinking water up here.)

The paved road loops around the observation tower. From here you can see the downtown skyline, the Medical Center, Fiesta Texas theme park, Leon Creek off to the right, and up close, two rock quarries.

6. **Coming down from the Tower after you pass the restrooms, take the Hillview path to the left.**

7. **At the Red Oak/Hillview sign, turn left onto Red Oak Trail.**

This was our favorite trail—gentle grades through shady oaks. It is especially beautiful when the leaves change in late November to mid-December.

8. **Coming back onto the Hillview Trail, take the path that goes left.**

9. **At the Yucca Trail sign, turn right.**

The Yucca Trail goes through the campsites. Continue across the paved path (Cedar Flats Trail), staying on Yucca Trail.

10. **At the paved section of Yucca Trail, go left or right—it doesn't matter because it is a loop. Continue back to the parking lot.**

A section of natural trail in
Eisenhower Park

25 McAllister Park

Features: A suburban park with wooded trails, both paved and natural. Deer and other wildlife may be seen.

Distance: Cross-Country Pedestrian Trail: 5.5 miles (8.8k)
Hike/Bike Trail: 1.5 miles on each of three loops

Time: Cross-country Trail: 2.0 hr.
Hike/Bike Trail: 30 min. each of three loops

Nights: No

Wheelchair Accessible: Hike/bike trail only. Cross-country trail is too rough.

Restrooms: At start and various locations marked as small black squares on map

Water: At start and at various points along walk

Phone: At start

Restaurants: No. Picnic areas only

Getting There: **Car:** Enter the park from Jones-Maltsberger Road northeast of Starcrest (behind the airport). Watch for the park entrance just past the police substation.

Hike/Bike Trail: Once in the park, follow Buckhorn Road and park at Pavilion No. 1 (on the right where Buckhorn curves left).

Cross-Country Trail: Once in the park, follow Buckhorn Road to the left to park at Pavilion No. 2. The trail starts across Buckhorn Road from Pavilion No. 2.

Bus: None

Comments:

The park is open every day from 6:00 A.M. to 10:00 P.M.

In the first edition of this book we told how we planned to feature the Cross-Country Pedestrian Trail that ran along the perimeter of the park (installed by the Optimist Club in 1968). This unpaved trail was our favorite and less-known than the paved Hike/Bike Trail. The original trail signs had long ago deteriorated. We arranged with Boy Scout Troop 285 to put up new sign posts. No sooner was this done than the Park Department lopped off part of the trail for more soccer fields. We needed to rewalk the trail before we could include it. But this was the spring of 1992—the year that it rained ceaselessly. Much of the trail was impossible to walk. Then we heard they would be taking another section of the trail for soccer fields. We had no choice but to feature the Hike/Bike Trail and just mention the Cross-Country.

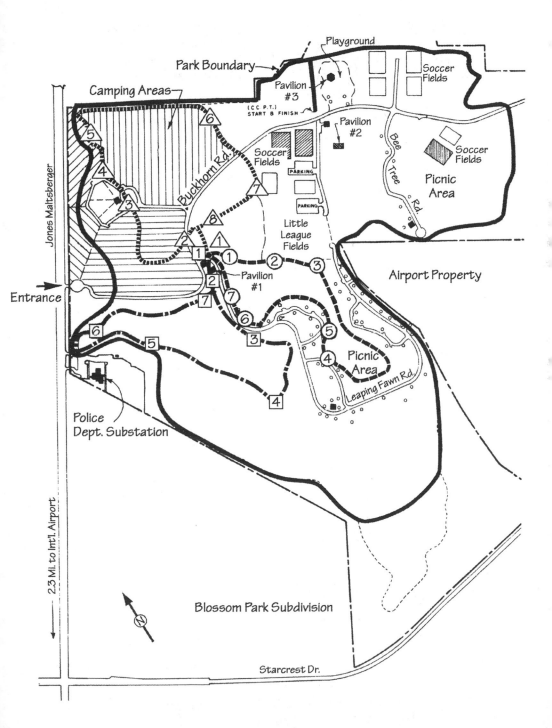

At the time of this second edition we are happy to report that no more of the Cross-Country Trail has disappeared, although a piece of it goes between a soccer field and some bleachers. Also, in 1995 Troop 285's Scout Trey McDougall, for his Eagle Scout project, rechecked the trail, replacing and repainting some of the signs. Now, as originally planned, it is our featured walk for McAllister Park.

This is a long, but easy walk on a dirt trail. If you study the map you can see places where you could cut back to Pavilion No. 2 should you care to shorten it.

We've never walked the Cross-Country without seeing some wildlife, almost always deer grazing and sometimes a snake slithering rapidly off the trail as it senses our approaching feet. This time we were privileged to see a young buck dash across the picnic area and jump the fence into the adjoining airport property.

Overview:

McAllister Park was out in the country when it opened in 1968; subdivisions now border its fence lines. Still, especially on the Cross-Country Pedestrian Trail, there are places where you can imagine yourself to be in the Hill Country. Although you are less likely to see a snake slither across the paved trail than you would on the Cross-Country Trail, you will see white-tailed deer in the wooded portions, especially late in the day, although their number is dwindling because of increased development around the park. We have also seen on the Cross Country Trail, cottontails and burrowing marks of armadillos where they have rooted for insects at night. Look also for skunk, raccoon, and opossum tracks.

Cross-Country Pedestrian Trail (Solid Line)

1. **The trail officially starts across Buckhorn Road from Pavilion No. 2. There is a signboard marking the spot.**

Walk around the signpost and up the grass road to the fence line. Turn left or right, as you please.

Signposts have been installed at various intersecting trails and service roads. *However,* they can at times be missing, broken, or turned slightly, so do consult the map when in doubt. There are enough landmarks to get you on the right trail.

It is easiest to get off the trail where it crosses Buckhorn Road by some of the soccer fields. From either direction you come out of the woods onto Buckhorn, cross it, and then turn left a short distance to get back on the trail. Even if the signs are down here, as they were when we rewalked it recently, the trail is still easy enough to spot.

There are two very short steep places on the trail, otherwise it is almost all fairly flat.

Loop 1 (Dotted Line with Triangles)

1. **From Pavilion No. 1, facing the drinking fountain, turn right. Cross the road. At the fork, go straight.**

2. **At the T-crossing, turn left. Cross the road, and continue on the trail.**

McAllister Park (Photo by Celia Wakefield)

3. **At the road the trail cuts across the campground.**

(There are restrooms in the campground.)

4. **Pick up the trail to the right across from Campsite No. 1.**

5. **The trail makes a sharp turn to the right.**

A portion of the Cross-Country Trail goes off to the left here.

6. **After a steep dip, the trail bends to the right.**

The Cross-Country Trail goes off to the left, running along the fence line of a subdivision.

7. **At the fork by the ball fields, bear right.**

8. **At the next fork, turn left, and go back to Pavilion No. 1.**

Loop 2 (Dashed Line with Circles)

1. **From Pavilion No. 1, facing the drinking fountain, turn right. Cross the road. At the fork, turn right.**

2. **At the fork stay straight ahead with the ball fields on your left.**

3. **At the fork, turn right.**

The authors relax for a moment in McAllister Park (Photo by Celia Wakefield).

4. **Turn right, away from the picnic area.**

(A drinking fountain is located here, off to the left.)

5. **At the next fork, bear right, away from the picnic area.**

(Another drinking fountain is here, off to the left.)

6. **After crossing the road, turn right at the T-crossing.**

After a rain there will be water in the usually dry wash along here.

7. **At the fork, stay straight ahead, and go back to Pavilion No. 1.**

Loop 3 (Dot-and-Dashed Line with Squares)

1. From Pavilion No. 1, facing the drinking fountain, turn left.

2. Keep straight ahead.

3. At the next fork, keep straight ahead.

4. At the T-crossing, turn right.

You are walking past an old quarry pit that has filled in. It now supports a growth of new trees and other vegetation. Ahead on the left, you can see the police substation that was built on land the City took away from the park.

5. At the fork, stay straight ahead.

A portion of the Cross-Country Pedestrian Trail goes off to the left.

6. At the fork, turn right.

The Cross-Country Pedestrian Trail goes off to the left along the subdivision fence line.

7. At the T-crossing, turn left, and go back to Pavilion No. 1.

26 Leon Creek Greenway

Features: Primitive trail along Leon Creek from Bandera Road to UTSA Boulevard

Distance: See comments

Time: See comments

Night: No

Wheelchair Accessible: See comments

Restrooms, Water, Phone: At O. P. Schnabel Park. See comments

Getting There: **Car:** Park at Schnabel Park on Bandera between Loops 410 and 1604. See comments

Bus: No

Comments:

This is a new city park that will officially open sometime in 1998. At the time of this writing, the easiest access is on the north side of the creek at Bandera. Other access points are at Old Babcock Road and at Prue. Eventually the main trailhead will be from O. P. Schnabel Park, the midpoint on the trail.

Because the creek is located in a 100-year flood plain, permanent facilities cannot be built. Additional restrooms are planned at some high points other than Schnabel Park as land becomes available.

Some portions of the greenway will be made wheelchair accessible.

The trail is not complete at this time so we cannot give exact mileage, but it will be approximately seven miles. Eventually it will extend further south and probably north to Loop 1604.

There is a high trail on one side of the creek and a low trail on the other. The trails are designated for non-motorized vehicles as well as foot traffic.

Signs will describe the degree of trail difficulty.

Because the park is linear, we have not given a specific route. It is a place to go and explore.

Overview:

The Leon Creek Greenway links neighborhoods with each other and with O. P. Schnabel Park. It has been kept in its natural state, preserving the creek bed and protecting a portion of the Edwards Aquifer Recharge Zone. The San Antonio Parks and Recreation Department worked with the Leon Creek Greenway Coalition, a group representing fifteen neighborhood associations, in planning the park. They will continue to work together on park upkeep. The park will serve as a model for other greenway projects showing how best to accomplish the

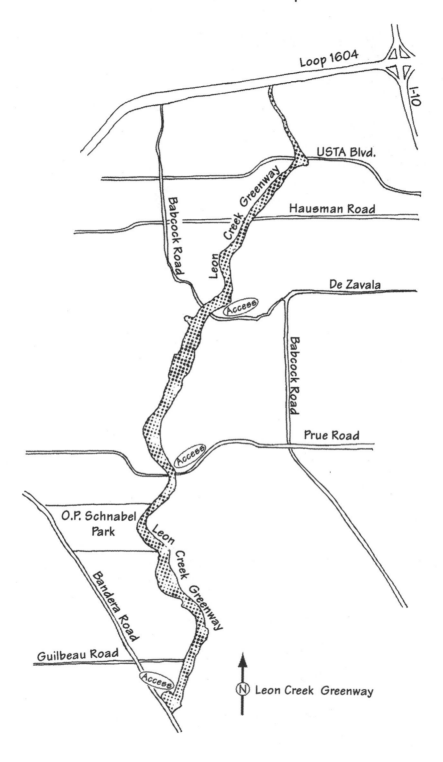

Leon Creek Greenway

The pond just north of Prue Road.

acquisition, preservation and development of recreational facilities in partnership with citizen groups. Recycled materials have been used wherever possible, including materials used to prevent soil erosion, plastic lumber, recycled aluminum for signs, and drainage pipes of recycled plastic.

Although the creek bed is dry most of the year, there is a spring-fed pond where neighborhood children like to fish, as well as numerous caves in the limestone bluffs. Native grasses, shrubs, trees, and indigenous wildlife may be seen.

Note: Signs will be posted designating sensitive areas. Please do not disturb or remove rocks and plants. Please comply with all trail etiquette signs.

27 University of the Incarnate Word

Features: The Blue Hole (beginning of the San Antonio River) and Brackenridge Villa

Distance: 2.3 miles (3.7 k)

Time: 1 hour

Nights: Yes

Wheelchair Accessible: Yes. See Comments

Restrooms, Water, Phones: Various buildings when open

Restaurants: Across Broadway from campus and the Dining Hall on campus (☞ R)

Getting There: **Car:** Park in lot along Hildebrand in front of the Science Hall (☞ A) (intersection of Broadway and Hildebrand) or in lot between Step 2 and 3.

Bus: No. 9 Broadway or No. 14 Perrin-Beitel. Get off at Hildebrand.

Comments:

The campus is accessible to the handicapped with the ramps marked on the map. There are steps to negotiate, however, to get to the path around the athletic field and the Blue Hole.

We thank University of the Incarnate Word for permission to use their campus map.

Overview:

In 1869, in answer to a call for help during a cholera epidemic, three young French nuns of the Catholic order Sisters of Charity of the Incarnate Word traveled to San Antonio by stagecoach from Galveston. Through their work they founded a hospital, now Santa Rosa Medical Center, and then later started an orphanage and a school. The last grew and eventually became Incarnate Word College and High School, and, in 1996, the University of the Incarnate Word.

Parts of the campus, including the headwaters of the river, five archaeological sites, and Brackenridge Villa have been designated a National Archaeological District.

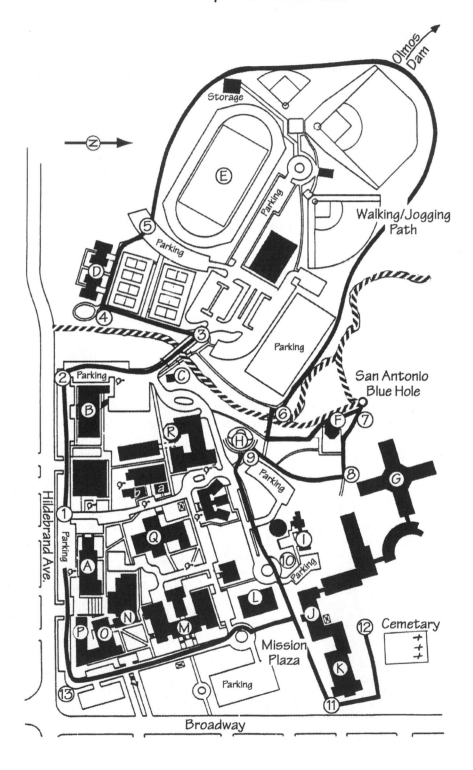

1. **Walk through the parking lot with Hildebrand on the left and the campus on the right.**

Across Hildebrand is the Southwestern Bell Telephone office for South Texas, originally USAA corporate headquarters. The building is on the site of Aureliano Urrutia's former "summer home" Mira Flores. His mansion, Quinta Urrutia, built in a Spanish/Moorish style, was about half a mile south on Broadway near Funston. Urrutia has an interesting history. He had a brilliant career in Mexico, including personal physician to President Porfirio Díaz, but like many had to flee during the revolution. Stories of dire deeds followed him here. A local legend says he gave the evil eye to an old enemy causing him to die on the spot. These tales have been refuted. On the good side is the clinic he ran for the poor down on Houston and Laredo Streets and the medical procedures he invented that are still in use. He died in 1975 at the age of 103.

Quinta Urrutia was torn down after he sold it, as was Mira Flores. However, in the sales contract for the latter he stipulated that the gardens be kept. The beautiful tile arch that first adorned the entrance to the house on Broadway, then moved here on Hildebrand to the entrance of Mira Flores, will be renovated and moved to the new Latin American wing of the San Antonio Museum of Art. True to the sales contract the gardens still exist and are part of a recreation area for Southwestern Bell employees. A tile gate remains as well as the playhouse, Quinta Maria, and reproductions of some famous statues. The Winged Victory

Fernridge and the original Sweet house(Photo by Celia Wakefield)

originally stood on the roof of Quinta Urrutia. The small entrance gate to the garden and other pieces inside are the concrete art of Dionicio Rodriguez, who, it is said, was brought to San Antonio by Urrutia.

2. **At the end of lot turn right through another parking lot. Cross the bridge coming up on the left.**

The bridge crosses the San Antonio River, which is now sometimes dry, being fed only from the natural springs.

3. **Turn left onto the path between the river and the tennis courts.**

The trees along the river are mesquite, Chinese tallow, cedar elm, and chinaberry. The latter's berries are poisonous to humans but not to birds.

4. **Turn right between the apartments (☞ D) and the tennis courts.**

After the fall of the Alamo, in the area where Olmos Creek and the San Antonio River meet, a group of Irish settlers, led by William Howth, started a city. They named it Avoca after the Vale of Avoca in Ireland, a place where two rivers meet, made famous in a poem by Thomas Moore. It had streets named Milam and Travis and a courthouse square. But it was too far from San Antonio and had no public transportation. No lots were ever sold. When the San Antonio city leaders realized that whoever owned the headwaters controlled the river, they used an old Spanish land grant to extend the San Antonio city limits to include Avoca. Workers excavating for the Olmos flood control dam in the mid-1920s found ruins of stone walls believed to be from this village.

5. **Cut straight across the parking lot to the path around the athletic field (☞ E).**

About the time Alamo Heights got started in 1890, a rock dam built across the river in this area created a lake that was a favorite boating and picnic spot for students and townspeople. The street car company that ran up River Avenue (Broadway) from San Antonio three miles away (present downtown area) even provided a band to attract riders. Until the mid-1980s, when development of the area caused it to dry up, a pond attracting migrating birds existed to the left side of the tract. There was a lot of controversy about building on this part of the campus. Many wanted to leave it in its natural state following the desires of George Brackenridge, who sold the land to the college and felt strongly that this portion should remain undeveloped. However, because the Sisters had farmed this fertile valley for decades, it was no longer in its pristine state, and the school did need to expand its facilities.

For about 10,000 years, humans have visited the headwaters of the river. Growth of the metropolitan area and of agriculture to the west of the city has lowered the level of the Edwards Aquifer beneath this region, thus drying up most of the springs (there were more than 100) except after rains such as those in 1992. At that time long-forgotten springs, not allowed for in an elaborate new "French" drainage system, kept the athletic field soggy for some time.

Scientists have documented this area as having been occupied about 8,000 B.C. by Paleoindians who hunted mastodon, giant bison, and horse. In the mid-1970s the College sponsored archeological digs here.

Before the completion of Olmos Dam, the Ponca Indians from Oklahoma came to this valley to celebrate an ancient purification rite. The valley was on the Buffalo Road or Road of the Old People. (The "Old People" were ancient people who lived here before the Poncas existed.) After the dam was completed, the Indians came no more.

The 200 Patterson condominiums loom above the north side of the field.

6. **After circling the athletic field, cross the iron bridge, and turn left. Turn left again on the unpaved path behind the swimming pool (☞ F), and walk to the end of the path.**

Inside the stone wall is the famous "Blue Hole," where, as poet Sidney Lanier wrote, "the river is forever being born." He could not have foreseen that a time would come when population growth would reduce the aquifer, and thus the springs, to such a low level that the river would not be forever born. This is a natural spring that now flows only after long periods of heavy rains such as we had in the spring of 1992. When the hole is full it is indeed blue. If it is empty, you can see the hole low in the wall that channels the spring water into the river. The gauge attached to a cedar elm measures the height of the water in the river bed.

A legend about the origin of the springs says that Don Domingo Ramón, on a quest for gold, accompanied by his Spanish cavaliers and some missionaries, stopped in a valley that offered grass but no water for their horses. Resting in the shade of a great oak tree, the good padres

Bridge over the San Antonio River near its beginning (Photo by Celia Wakefield).

prayed for water. One of them, casting his eyes heavenward, saw grapes amid the branches. These would quench their thirst. He attempted to climb the vine but slipped and fell back, his fall uprooting the vine. From the deep hole that was left burst forth a great flow of pure, cool, delicious water.

7. **Turn around and walk back toward the pool, around to the left of it, and then up the hill via the stairs.**

At the top to the left are the new retirement apartments (☞ G) for the Sisters of Charity of the Incarnate Word who run the college, Santa Rosa Hospital, and St. Rose Hospital. The facility is available not only to the nuns, but to anyone who would like to live in this lovely facility, no matter what religious persuasion, single or married, male or female.

8. **At the top of the stairs, turn right, and follow the path to the grotto (☞ H).**

A young priest designed and helped construct this replica of the Our Lady of Lourdes shrine located in France. The grotto is built of stone quarried here on campus.

9. **Go up the steps from the grotto, and walk up the driveway toward Brackenridge Villa (☞ I), keeping the red brick buildings on your right.**

In 1852, James Sweet bought this land from the City and built the one-story stone house that is the right-hand section of the Villa. George Brackenridge, founder of the San Antonio National Bank, bought it in 1869, and added a three-story Queen Anne house onto it. The new house was named Fernridge, "bracken" being the Scottish word for "fern." The variety of styles and contents in the house reflects his worldwide travels.

After his mother died, he no longer wished to live at Fernridge, and he agreed to sell the land to the City if it would buy it immediately, without debate. This the City couldn't do. Mother Madeleine Chollet, looking for some land on which to build a Motherhouse for the Sisters of Charity of the Incarnate Word, offered to buy forty acres. Brackenridge stubbornly insisted on selling "all or nothing"—280 acres, the house, and its contents—for $120,000. The Sisters agreed to buy on a twenty-five-year note. Some said Brackenridge expected them to default and thus get his property back. But they never missed a payment. After the sale, when Brackenridge returned to collect his personal library, Sister Madeleine met him at the door and politely but firmly reminded him of his "all or nothing" pledge.

Next to Brackenridge's devotion to his own mother was his devotion to Mother Nature. He donated or sold his land with the stipulation that it be kept as nature made it. For years he would drive out here frequently to make sure the sisters didn't so much as prune a branch off a tree.

The sisters renamed the house Brackenridge Villa in his honor. First, it served as the Motherhouse, and is now used as alumni offices for the college. In 1983, a fire caused extensive damage, but the sisters raised money for a full restoration. The house is open for public tours only by appointment. Call (210) 829-6012.

10. Continue along the driveway toward Broadway.

The Motherhouse (☞ J), designed in 1900 by Alfred Giles, was the first new building put up by the sisters. By 1988, it had become outdated. Because it would cost more to renovate than rebuild, they tore it down, designing a new, expanded complex with a duplication of the original facade, using some of the original stone, brick, glass, and doors. The Motherhouse is a residence for the active sisters in the order. Next to the Motherhouse is the chapel (not open to the public).

11. Bear left on the driveway, behind the chapel (☞ K), where a path goes left to the cemetery (☞ 12).

Grave markers for the founding sisters, Marie Madeleine Chollet and St. Pierre Cinquin, are in front of the cross.

12. Walk back to the front of the Motherhouse. Turn left on the path to Mission Plaza, and then continue along in front of the campus.

The plaza symbolizes the various missions of the Sisters in the United States and Mexico. The four flags represent the countries of the United States, Texas, and Mexico, and Incarnate Word College.

Walking along the Boulevard of the Nations, the first building on the right is the Incarnate Word Generalate (☞ L), the headquarters of the southwestern region of the Congregation of the Sisters of Charity of the Incarnate Word.

Next is the Administration Building (☞ M), which was the original college, built in 1922. There is a historical marker in front of it. Set back slightly is the Halligan-Ibbs Theatre and Dance Center (☞ N), named for the husband and wife team who developed the fine theater arts program at Incarnate Word. The Elizabeth Huth Maddux Theatre (☞ O) is behind it. At the end of the street is the Genevieve Tarlton Dougherty Fine Arts Center, the Interior Design Studio, the Art Gallery and a recital hall (☞ P).

Here in front of Incarnate Word College, on November 21, 1963, the day before he was assassinated, President John F. Kennedy, on the way from the airport to downtown, ordered his car to stop so he could accept a bouquet of yellow roses for his wife.

13. Turn right to go back to your car.

The library (☞ Q behind the Science Building) has an excellent Texana collection.

(There are restaurants of all types and price ranges along Broadway.)

28 Trinity University

Features: A particuarly well-designed college campus enhanced by many pieces of artwork and an adjoining portion of one of San Antonio's most prestigious early neighborhoods

Distance: 3.8 miles (6.1k)

Time: 1 hr. 45 min.

Nights: Yes

Wheelchair Accessible: Yes

Restrooms, Water, Phones: Library, Coates University Center (A)

Restaurants: Coates University Center (A)

Getting There: **Car:** Use parking Lot B off Stadium Drive, behind Laurie Auditorium

Bus: No. 8 N. St. Mary's. Get off at the first Trinity stop. Reboard at same place.

Comments:

Individuals are welcome to walk through public areas of the campus, but access to the residence halls is restricted because these are private. If organizations wish to arrange group walks, they are asked to please contact the Public Relations Office at (210) 736-8406 for approval.

We thank Trinity University for permission to use their campus map.

Overview:

Trinity University was established in 1869 in Tehuacana, Texas, as a Presbyterian college. It moved to San Antonio in 1942 from Waxachachie. In 1969 it became independent from the church, although it still maintains a covenant relationship. Trinity offers undergraduate degrees in liberal arts and sciences, as well as masters programs, and is known for its high academic standards. It is considered a cultural center for the community, by virtue of its lectures, concerts, and theater.

The University is built on an old limestone quarry. The buildings fit so well into their surroundings that the campus is considered one of the most attractive in the country. The architecture is attributed to the firms of Ford, Powell, and Carson; O'Neil Ford and Associates; and Bartlett Cocke and Associates. Works of art abound throughout the campus.

The administrative and academic buildings are set among live oak trees and mountain laurel shrubs on the higher ground above the quarry pits in which the dormitories and athletic fields are located.

1. From the parking lot, facing Laurie Auditorium, turn right on the driveway that runs along the back of Laurie.

Laurie Auditorium is named for James Laurie, president of the University from 1951 to 1970. The lower levels are for parking. Above this is the 3,000 seat auditorium.

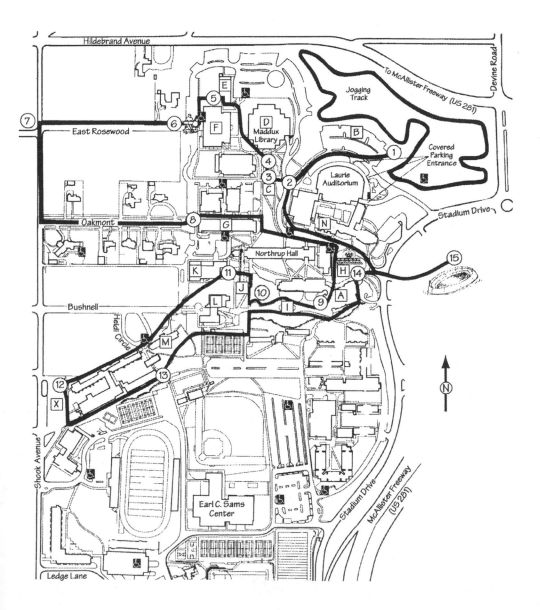

2. **Where the road splits, cross it, leaving the road, and go straight ahead to the sculpture (C).**

This abstract of bronze and stone by Barbara Hepworth is titled *Conversation Between Magical Stones.*

3. **Turn right, walk to the library and enter (D).**

The four-story Elizabeth Coates Maddux Library is set in a hollow below the surrounding buildings and is entered on the third floor. Its serrated profile provides reading nooks with a view. Inside, an imposing mural by James Sicner entitled *Man's Evolving Images* wraps around the staircase.

4. **Exit the library where you entered, turn right, and then immediately right again, keeping right to the Ewing Halsell Center (E), the last building on the left.**

Inside is a large oil painting by Peter Hurd, but we brought you in to see the mesquite-block floor. Mesquite wood is exceptionally durable. Blocks like these were used for street paving during the late 1800s. We spotted some in an alley downtown where the tarmac had worn away, and during a street renovation downtown the workmen found many pieces.

5. **Exit the building by the same door, follow the sidewalk to the street, and turn left to the Chapman Memorial Building (F).**

The interior architecture of the building is interesting because of the open feeling imparted by the large, glassed-in, central patio. In the patio, note the tile stream and waterfall.

Students chat in front of the Eugenia Miller Fountain.

Exit by the same door and cross to the Chapman-Cowles Fountain.

There is an inscription quoting Emerson on this fountain designed by Waldine Tauch, "The scholar is the student of the world." The seated figure turns from studying the Book of Knowledge to gaze at a globe of the world above which he holds the Torch of Enlightenment.

6. Leaving the campus, continue straight ahead down Rosewood.

No. 438 Rosewood is a 1928 modified Italian design by Robert Kelly.

No. 411 is one of the most photographed houses of its time. It was designed in 1930 by Beverly Spillman and his son and described as ". . . a type of architecture found in the Spanish cities of Segovia and Toledo . . ."

410 (left-hand corner) was designed by Harvey Smith in 1928 in a "rambling Spanish style," and described as "One of the most charming of the finer homes of San Antonio . . . ."

No. 401 (right-hand corner) is a very English style considered at the time of its completion as ". . . one of the finest homes in San Antonio," a comment which Donald Everett in an article on Monte Vista said had ". . . become somewhat hackneyed" for describing residences in this area. This only serves to illustrate that we have many fine homes in San Antonio.

7. Turn left on Shook, then left on Oakmont.

Half a block down Shook from Oakmont is the entrance to the Hannah Landa Memorial Library. Harry Landa willed his house—a 1929 Italian style designed by Robert B. Kelly—to the city for a library. There is extensive use of marble and tile floors as well as tile trim and wrought iron imported from Italy. It included an art gallery to display the Landa's fine collection of European art. It has recently undergone a complete renovation. This lovely library is well worth a visit.

Across from the library on Bushnell are the Bushnell Apartments, also by Robert Kelly and dating from 1925. There was much controversy at the time over building a high-rise in this neighborhood. Each of its seven floors has four apartments. Besides many fine features, its grandest innovation was two high-speed automatic elevators so the residents ". . . will not have to worry about whether the elevator boy is asleep or off talking to his girl . . . ."

Many of the residences on Oakmont have been acquired by Trinity University for its senior administrators.

No. 106 Oakmont is also considered among the most imposing. It is an Italian-style villa designed in 1926 by the Kelwood Company.

No. 139 is a newer house designed in 1950 by O'Neil Ford for Mayor Sam Steves.

No. 151 is a 1926 house described as having "the atmosphere of a real English country home."

No. 150 is a Spanish style built on a grand scale in the late 1920s. It is used as the home of the University President.

The Thomas Franklin Murchison Memorial garden

8. **Back on campus, walk straight up the steps between the buildings, with McLean Science Center (G) on your right. At the end of that building, turn right, and then left at the fork. After turning left, the Ruth Taylor Fine Arts Center is on your left. Proceed to the Eugenia Miller Fountain (H). From the fountain enter the Coates University Center (A).**

To the right of the fountain is the Coates University Center (A) with restrooms, telephones, dining room, bookstore, and a post office. From the back patio you can enjoy a magnificent view of the downtown skyline beyond the limestone quarry that extended from Brackenridge Park to here. Below, in the old quarry pit, are the residence halls and sports complex.

9. **From the back patio of the Coats Center, turn right along the Coates Esplanade, past the sculpture (I), and along the cliff.**

The Henry Moore piece, entitled *Interior Form,* presents his use of the hole, which he says ". . . can possess as much form significance as a piece of mass. The air can become the object of the sculptor . . . ."

Past the sculpture, down the cliff to the left is the Thomas Franklin Murchison memorial, a lovely landscaped area on the slope of the cliff. Murchison, an alumnus, was a dreamer of dreams. We think this spot, which is certainly conducive to quiet meditation, is appropriate to his memory.

10. **Turn right to the Murchison Memorial Tower (J) and the Margarite B. Parker Chapel (K).**

The Murchison Tower carillon can be heard over the entire campus as it chimes the quarter hour.

The chapel was designed in 1966 in the "medieval modern" style by O'Neil Ford. The *Christ of the Open Arms* bronze is by Charles Umlauf, whose work can also be found on the Witte Museum grounds. Although Umlauf's work includes a range of subjects, two themes are dominant: events in the life of Christ with Christ always depicted as a figure of compassion, and the family unit as the fundamental element of society. Works of art inside the chapel include a series of tapestries by Martha Mood, leaded-glass windows alongside an enclosed patio, and the sacristy collection of religious artifacts.

11. **Exit the chapel, and immediately turn right down the steps, then go along the path that angles between the chapel and the George Storch Education Center (L). Cross the street, and continue on the sidewalk in front of the Elizabeth Rhea Health Services Building and the Susanna Wesley Hall (M), keeping the circular drive on your right. Continue on this path to the parking lot (X).**

(Giving directions on a campus is sure complicated! Our thanks again to Trinity University for permission to use its excellent map.)

12. **Turn left, walking alongside the parking lot and keeping the ends of the residence halls on your left. Turn left onto the walkway (before the last residence hall) that follows the cliff, keeping residence halls on your left.**

The view from the cliff is spectacular, day or night. The white church steeple above the trees to the right is Trinity Baptist Church.

13. **At the end of the buildings, continue on the sidewalk, crossing the open space at an angle, to the Storch Education Center (L). Continue along the cliff above the tennis courts, turning left at the end of the courts, turning right on the esplanade returning to Coates Center (A). Pass between it and the bookstore.**

Also nestled in the old quarry pits are the campus tennis courts and swimming pool.

14. **From the fountain (H) turn right and cross Stadium Drive to Alamo Stadium (15).**

Alamo Stadium serves the San Antonio Independent School District. The tile murals at its entrance were commissioned by the Work Projects Administration (WPA) in 1940.

The first panel, Military Plaza, shows the back of the old San Fernando Church, as if you were standing with your back to the Spanish Governor's Palace looking across the plaza watching an archery contest and a rooster race.

The second panel, Alamo Plaza, with the Menger Hotel to the right, depicts a cock fight and a Mexican hat dance in progress.

The third panel shows the 1900 San Antonio Fair and Rodeo where a roping contest and bulldogging are portrayed. The location of this fair was on what is now the Riverside Golf Course on South St. Mary's Street. The Crystal Palace was the main pavilion of the 1892 World Exposition. You can see one of Teddy Roosevelt's Rough Riders off to the right of the panel. Perhaps the artist who created this panel was the little boy or girl watching the scene.

The last panel depicts the inside of Alamo Stadium circa 1941.

15. **Cross back to the campus, walking to the right of the fountain along the driveway. Walk around the Ruth Taylor complex and Laurie Auditorium back to Parking Lot B.**

The Ruth Taylor Fine Arts Center (N) is on the right. Working with theatrical director Paul Baer, architects O'Neil Ford and Arthur Roberts designed this building to house three distinct theater spaces. Baker wanted flexible, readily adaptable performance and work spaces and asked for a "masterpiece of space," not just a bland container. Philip John Evett, a fellow professor at Trinity, created the welded aluminum sculpture in front of the Center.

Entrance to the Landay Library

29 Off-Street Fitness Walks

These walks feature paved and measured routes that are safe, off-street places to walk. Some are designed especially for fitness and include exercise stations. We give the location and distance and list special features of each one separately.

UNIVERSITY OF TEXAS HEALTH SCIENCE CENTER (UTHSC) FITNESS WALK

Location: Babcock Road and Merton Minter Boulevard

Distance: 0.5 miles (0.8k) (Slight grades)

Nights: Yes. Very popular. Safe alone.

Restrooms, Water, Phones: Next to track

Special Features: Self-explanatory exercise stations at various locations around the track. Adjacent to track are a children's play area, picnic area, ball fields, and tennis courts.

FORT SAM HOUSTON WORLD TRAIL

Location: Fort Sam Houston, off Stanley Drive. (See map, Walk 9, for location). Park in the circular lot in front of the former Brooke Army Medical Center. Trail is to the right and behind the hospital.

Distance: 0.5 mile (0.8k) (Slight grades)

Nights: No. Not lighted.

Restrooms, Water, Phone: Lobby of the building if open, or Roadrunner Community Center at Stanley and Schofield

Special Features: Self-explanatory exercise stations at various locations around the trail. A unique setting in a wooded park.

TRINITY UNIVERSITY FITNESS WALK

Location: Park in Lot B behind Laurie Auditorium (off Stadium Drive). Trail next to parking lot. (See map, Walk 28, for location.)

Distance: 0.75 mile (1.2k) (Slight grades)

Nights: Yes. Okay alone early evening. Better with a partner.

Restrooms, Water, Phone: On campus

Special Features: Landscaped, gravel path

TRINITY UNIVERSITY SOUTH CAMPUS RECREATION AREA FITNESS TRAIL

Location: Corner of Mulberry and Stadium Drive

Distance: 1.0 mile

Nights: Yes

Restrooms, Water, Phone: At the shelter

Special Features: An outstanding characteristic of this trail is its padded surface, which makes walking a pleasure. Please note, however, that no wheeled vehicles or shoes with cleats are allowed on this trail. A fitness station offers instructions for a series of exercises of progressive difficulty, including heart-healthy exercises.

30 The Malls

Given the climate of South Texas, if you want to walk regularly, every day of the year, malls come in handy. Malls offer a safe, climate-controlled place to walk, making them especially popular with older folks.

The popularity of shopping-mall walking has spawned walk groups. Most of these meet once or twice a month and are sponsored by the community outreach programs of various hospitals. Their meetings offer health screenings as well as speakers on various health-related subjects. One such group, the dynamic A Walk In The Park at Central Park Mall, is part of the Northeast Independent School District's community education program. It meets weekly and offers speakers on a variety of topics. All groups serve refreshments. Meeting times and dates may change. Not all malls have walk groups at the present time. We suggest calling the mall office for updated information.

The mall has, in a way, replaced the town square. Here you can meet friends, sit at an "outdoor" cafe, and chat or people-watch. All the malls open their doors early to accommodate walkers. One or more food concessions usually open early as well.

Here, then, is an alphabetical list of the malls, an overview of their walking programs, and other relevant information about their walking facilities.

CENTRAL PARK MALL

Doors Open: 6:00 A.M.

Distance: 3/8 mile (0.6k) each on two levels

Walking Surface: Carpeted

Program: A Walk in the Park. Meets every Thursday, 8:15 A.M., at Luby's Cafeteria. Meetings have speakers on a variety of topics. Members receive a T-shirt after walking 150 miles.

Sponsored by: Northeast Independent School District Family Resource Center, (210) 377-1513.

This group is by far the most active of mall groups. Attendance on Thursday runs from 100-150 people. Some are the regular Central Park walkers, others come from North Star Mall across the street, and still others come just to enjoy the program. Members rotate chairing the weekly meetings.

Some of the members also work as volunteers in the school district's tutorial program. The group plans occasional walking tours, both in the city and out of town.

30 The Malls

CROSSROADS MALL

Doors Open: 7:30 A.M. (10:30 Sunday)

Distance: Lower level, 2 laps = 1 mile (1.6k). Upper level, 2.5 laps = 1 mile (1.6k)

Walking Surface: Tile

Program: Crossroad Cruisers. Meets every third Tuesday, 8:00 A.M., at the Burger King. Meetings have speakers on health-related topics. Blood-pressure tests at 7:30 A.M. on day of meeting.

INGRAM PARK MALL

Doors Open: 7:00 A.M. (Sunday, 10:00 A.M.)

Distance: Upper and lower levels combined = 1 mile plus (1.6k)

Walking Surface: Tile

Program: None

McCRELESS MALL

Doors Open: 7:00 A.M.

Distance: 2 laps = 1 mile (1.6k)

Walking Surface: Carpet and tile

Program: Morning Miles. Meets second Tuesday, 8:00 A.M., at Chick-Fil-A. Speakers on health-related subjects. Blood pressure testing on day of meeting. Mileage incentives.

NORTH STAR MALL

Doors Open: 7:00 A.M. at two entrances: Saks Fifth Avenue garage, 3rd level bridge and Rector Street near HairCrafters. (Sunday 10:00 A.M.)

Distance: 1.5 miles (2.4k)

Walking Surface: Tile

Program: None

RIVERCENTER

RiverCenter is more of a shopping/dining/entertainment center than the usual mall. Its horseshoe shape does not lend itself to exercise walking as well as the circular malls. However, for those staying downtown and wanting to walk indoors, we give the following information.

Doors Open: 7:00 A.M. (Sunday, 8:00 A.M.)

Distance: Each "horseshoe" = 0.3 mile (0.5k)

Walking Surface: Tile

Program: None

ROLLING OAKS MALL

Doors Open: 6:30 A.M. (Sunday, 9:00 A.M.)

Distance: 2.5 laps = 1 mile (1.6k)

Walking Surface: Tile

Program: Tread Setters. Meets third Friday at 7:30 A.M. at the food court. Blood pressure tests are given at 7:00 A.M. on day of meeting. T-shirt awards for attaining mileage goals.

SOUTH PARK MALL

Doors Open: 6:30 A.M.

Distance: 0.5 mile (0.8k)

Walking Surface: Tile

Program: South Park Pacers. Meets first Thursday, 8:00 A.M., at the food court. Speakers on health-related subjects. Blood pressure screening at 7:00 A.M. on day of meeting. T-shirt awards for attaining mileage goals.

WINDSOR PARK MALL

Doors Open: 7:00 A.M. (Sunday 10:00 A.M.)

Distance: 0.5 mile (0.8k) each of two levels

Walking Surface: Marble

Program: None

Appendix A

Points of Interest

Place	Walk No.	Walk
Alamo	Downtown I	1
Alamodome	Downtown II	2
Arneson River Theatre	River Walk South	4
Big Bend	River Walk South	4
Blue Star Art Space	River Walk South	4
Botanical Gardens	Fort Sam Parade Ground	9
Brackenridge Park	Brackenridge Park	22
Buckhorn Museum	Mission Trail North See Downtown I	6
Cassiano Homes murals	Westside	20
Cemeteries	Eastside	12
Chapel of Miracles	Downtown I	1
Convention Center	Downtown, River Walk	2, 4
Dignowity Hill Historic District	Eastside	12
Espada Dam and Acequia	Mission Trail South	7
Fort Sam Houston	Fort Sam Houston	8, 9, 10
Governor's Palace	Downtown I	1
Our Lady of Guadalupe Church	Westside	20
Guenther House	River Walk, King William	4, 16
HemisFair Park	Downtown II	2
Hertzberg Circus Museum	Downtown II	2
Institute of Texan Cultures	Downtown II	2
Japanese Sunken Gardens (Japanese Tea Gardens)	Brackenridge Park	22
Jefferson High School	Jefferson/Monticello	15
King William Historic District	River Walk, King William	4, 16
La Villita	Downtown II	2
McNay Art Museum	Alamo Heights	11
Market Square	Downtown I	1
Mexican Cultural Institute	Downtown II	2
Mission Concepción	Mission Trail North	6
Mission San José	Mission Trail South	7
Mission San Juan Capistrano	Mission Trial South	7
Mission Trail	Mission Trails	6, 7
Monte Vista Historic District	Monte Vista/Alta Vista	17
Monticello Historic District	Jefferson/Monticello	15
Navarro Historic Site	Downtown I	1
Olmos Dam	Alamo Heights	11
Paseo del Rio	River Walks	3, 4

Appendix A

Pioneer Flour Mill	Downtown II,	
	River Walk South	2, 4
Pioneer Museum	Brackenridge Park	22
Produce Terminal	Westside	20
Quadrangle, The	Fort Sam Houston	8
RiverCenter	Downtown II, River Walk	2, 4
River Walk	River Walks, Bridges	3, 4, 5
San Antonio Botanical Gardens	Fort Sam Houston	9
San Antonio Conservation Society	King William	16
San Antonio Museum of Art	River Walk North	3
San Antonio Stockyards	Westside	20
San Antonio Zoo	Brackenridge Park	22
San Fernando Cathedral	Downtown I	1
San Juan Woodlands Trail	Mission Trail South	7
San Pedro Park	Monte Vista / Alta Vista	17
Southern Pacific Depot	Downtown II	2
Southwest Craft Center	Downtown I	1
Spanish Governor's Palace	Downtown I	1
Steves Homestead	King William	16
St. Paul's Square	Downtown II	2
Sunken Gardens	Brackenridge Park	22
Texas Ranger Museum	Brackenridge Park	22
Tower of the Americas	Downtown II	2
Tower Life Building	Downtown II	2
Union Stockyards	Westside	20
Ursuline Academy (original)	Downtown I, Riverwalk	1, 3
Witte Museum	Brackenridge Park	22
Wulff House	King William	16
Yturri-Edmunds Historic Site	Mission Trail North	6

Appendix B

Night Walks

Mostly we do not recommend walking alone at night. There are exceptions.

We believe that as long as there are other pedestrians on the street it is safe to walk alone at night in that area. This would include the parts of downtown and the River Walk that have activity, but not those parts with little or no foot traffic.

Most of the neighborhoods in this book are safe to walk with a partner or in a small group. Do what you feel most comfortable with.

The chart below gives our recommendations. If a walk is not listed it is because we deemed it unsafe at night, even in a group.

Walk

No.	Name	Comments
1	Downtown I	Alamo Plaza, alone. Plaza to Market Square, with partner
2	Downtown II	As noted in Comments
3	River Walk North	Big Bend only
4	River Walk South	Big Bend only
8	Fort Sam Quadrangle	With partner. Quadrangle itself is closed.
9	Fort Sam Parade Ground	Probably okay alone
10	Fort Sam Training	With partner. No acitivity at night
11	Alamo Heights	With partner. McNay closed
13	Hill Country Village	With partner, but too dark to see anything
14	Inspiration Hills	With partner. Great views at night
15	Jefferson/Monticello	With partner
16	King William	With partner
17	Monte Vista/Alta Vista	With partner, perhaps better in small group
18	Olmos Park	With partner, but too dark to see anything
19	Terrell Hills	With partner, but too dark to see anything
21	Woodlawn Lake	Lake only. Okay alone as long as others there. Rest of walk safe in small group, but points of interest closed.
22	Brackenridge Park	Small group, but most of our walk too dark
27	Univ. of the Incarnate Word	Okay alone except around track and to Blue Hole which is too dark anyway
28	Trinity University	Alone on campus, with partner off-campus neighborhood portion
29	Fitness Walks	UTHSC and Trinity South Campus okay alone. Other Trinity walk, okay alone early evening. Ft. Sam trail not lighted for night walking

Appendix C

Review of Walk Conditions

+ after Time means add time for side trip
– after Night means not all of the trip can be taken at night
C means see Comments for that walk

Walk No.	Name	Distance in Miles	Time in Hours	Nights	Wheel-chair
1	Downtown I	3.3+2+1.4	2.1+	Yes-	Yes
2	Downtown II	3.1	2.0	Yes-	Yes
3	River Walk North	2.5+1.8	1.0+	Yes-	Yes,C
4	River Walk South	4.5+0.7	2.0+	Yes-	Yes,C
5	Bridges	3.7	1.5	No	Yes,C
6	Mission Trail North	6.0+2.0,C	3.5+,C	No	Yes
7	Mission Trail South	9.7,C	5.0,C	No	Yes
8	Fort Sam Quadrangle	3.5	2.0	Yes	Yes
9	Fort Sam Parade Ground	4.6+3.4	1.5+	Yes-	Yes
10	Fort Sam Training	2.1	1.0	No	Yes,C
11	Alamo Heights	4.5+1.7	2.0+	Yes-	No
12	Eastside	4.3+1.5	3.7+	No	Yes,C
13	Hill Country Village	5.1,C	1.8	No	Yes,C
14	Inspiration Hills	2.7	1.0	Yes	No
15	Jefferson/Monticello	2.6 & 2.7	1.0&1.0	Yes	Yes,C
16	King William	2.4 & 2.5	1.5&1.5	Yes	Yes,C
17	Monte Vista/Alta Vista	5.3	2.5	Yes	Yes,C
18	Olmos Park	3.0 & 1.9	1.3&0.9	No	No
19	Terrell Hills	2.7	1.0	No	Yes,C
20	Westside	6.7,C	C	No	Yes,C
21	Woodlawn Lake	4.4	2.0	Yes-	Yes,C
22	Brakenridge Park	4.5+0.8	2.0+	Yes,C	Yes,C
23	Friedrich Park	Varies,C	Varies,C	No	Yes,C
24	Eisenhower Park	Varies,C	Varies,C	No,C	Yes,C
25	McAllister Park	1.5-5.5,C	0.5-2.0,C	No	Yes,C
26	Leon Creek Greenway	Varies,C	Varies,C	No	Yes,C
27	Univ. of Incarnate Word	2.3	1.0	Yes-	Yes,C
28	Trinity University	3.8	1.6	Yes	Yes

APPENDIX D

Walk Groups

The following groups sponsor walks in San Antonio and the surrounding area.

Sierra Club, Alamo Group

Meets third Tuesday of the month at 7:30 P.M. at First Unitarian Church at the intersection of I-10 and I-410 across from Crossroads Mall. Call (210) 222-8195 for information on meetings, current walk schedule, and newsletter.

American Volksport Association

Call the direct line, (210) 659-2112, 9:00 A.M.-5:00 P.M., Monday-Friday, for information. At other times call the Hot Line: from San Antonio call (210) 231-5738 or from other areas call 1-800-830-9255.

Bexar Audubon Society

Meets the third Thursday of the month at 7:00 P.M. at the Ruble Center, 419 East Magnolia. Call (210) 822-4503 for additional information.

On the second Saturday of the month at 9:00 A.M. Bexar Audubon and Friends of Friedrich Wilderness Park present an educational program at Friedrich Park. (See **Comments**, Walk 23.)

San Antonio Audubon Society

Meets first Thursday of the month at 7:30 P.M. at the Ruble Center, 419 East Magnolia. Call (210) 733-8306 for meeting and special event information as well as recent bird sightings.

A regularly scheduled Beginners Bird Walk meets the second Saturday of the month at 8:00 A.M. at the Jack Judson Nature Trail on Viesca Avenue in Alamo Heights (off Devine and Alamo Heights Boulevard near swimming pool).

Appendix E

For More Information

For further reading, we suggest browsing local libraries, both public and university, and bookstores. There are usually special sections for regional books.

A standard reference book for San Antonio is *San Antonio, A Historical and Pictorial Guide* by Charles Ramsdell. University of Texas Press, Austin, 1985.

For general reading and history:

Voices from the San Antonio Missions by Luis Torres. Texas Tech University Press, Lubbock, 1997.

San Antonio, The Enchanted City by Frank Jennings. *Express-News*, San Antonio, Spring 1997.

Saving San Antonio, The Precarious Preservation of a Heritage by Lewis F. Fisher. Texas Tech University Press, Lubbock, 1996.

San Antonio Uncovered by Mark Louis Rybczyk. Wordware Publishing, Plano, 1992.

San Antonio Legacy by Donald E. Everett. Texas University Press, San Antonio, 1979. (Look for other titles by this author.)

City of Flaming Adventure by Boyce House. Naylor, San Antonio, 1968.

Fabulous San Antonio by Albert Curtis. Naylor, San Antonio, 1957.

San Antonio, City in the Sun by Green Payton Wertenbaker. McGraw, New York, 1946.

Books by Mary Ann Noonan Guerra.

Books by David Bowser.

For more information on the King William Historic District:

The King William Area, A History and Guide to the Houses by Mary V. Burkholder. The King William Association, San Antonio, 1973.

Down the Acequia Madre, In the King William Historic District by Mary V. Burkholder. Privately printed, San Antonio, 1976.

For more information on the Monte Vista Historic District:

Monte Vista, *The Gilded Age of an Historic District, 1890-1930* by Donald E. Everett. North San Antonio Times Supplement, January 28, 1988. Available at the Central Library in the Texana Department.

For more information on the river:

A Dream Come True: Robert Hugman and San Antonio's River Walk by Vernon G. Zunker. V. G. Zunker, San Antonio, 1983.

Crown Jewel of Texas, The Story of San Antonio's River by Lewis F. Fisher. Maverick Publishing Co., 1997.

Appendix E

For more information on architecture:

> *A Guide to San Antonio Architecture*, San Antonio chapter of the
> American Institute of Architects (AIA), San Antonio, 1986.
> *The Texas Star Trail*, San Antonio Conservation Society pamphlet (for
> buildings in the downtown area). San Antonio Conservation
> Society, 1986. Available at the Wulf House, King William Walk 16.